"Doctrines seem to wax and wane in their popularity and the attention scholars give them. The ascension of Christ has been hidden out of sight in modern theological accounts of salvation, with a few significant exceptions, but of late this trend has been reversed, and Ross Hastings's work is the latest offering on the topic. We find in this work what we have come to expect from Hastings, a work attentive to Scripture, theologically rich, and pastorally thoughtful. Doctrine sings, and in Hastings's hands, the ascension of Christ strikes a rich and compelling note. If the rich expanse of a soteriology that includes Christ's ascension becomes more popular among our pastors and preachers, it will be in no small part due to the influence of this impressive work."

Myk Habets, head of theology and senior lecturer in theology at Laidlaw College

"Christian theology is characterized by interrelationships, balance, and proportion, as doctrines shape and support each other. In his account of Christ's ascension, Ross Hastings helps restore some of that proportion to a Protestant theology by means of what amounts to a small systematic theology of the ascension, shot through with biblical and historical theology. To read this book is to dwell richly on why the Apostle's Creed includes the vital fact that 'he ascended into heaven.'"

Adam Johnson, professor of theology at Torrey Honors College at Biola University

"*The Glory of the Ascension* is a different kind of Christology from above that takes its bearings not from Christ's pre-existence (i.e., the eternal Logos) but, rather, from Christ's post-existence (i.e., resurrection, ascension, heavenly session). In retrieving this undeservedly neglected episode, Ross Hastings convincingly shows how the ascension is central to Jesus' identity and work, to the whole of salvation history, and ultimately to the glorious end for which the world was created in the first place."

Kevin J. Vanhoozer, research professor of systematic theology at Trinity Evangelical Divinity School

"In this insightful work, Ross Hastings attends to the ascension, that most overlooked event in the history of Jesus Christ, and presents a luminous account seeking to retrieve its significance and highlight its wonder. Hastings offers an account that is—characteristically—deeply informed by Scripture and tradition, encouraging us to consider the doctrinal landscape from the refreshing perspective of the ascension. But this account also cares deeply about the Christian life and about the church and its mission in the present. Perhaps above all, this is an uplifting book, drawing our vision upward toward the glory of God, the beauty of the ascended Christ, and the assurance of heaven, offering hope in uncertain times. It comes warmly recommended."

Paul T. Nimmo, King's Chair of Systematic Theology at the University of Aberdeen

"Ross Hastings is unfailingly a theologian for the life of the church. Following his works on the atonement and the resurrection, he now focuses our eyes on the glory of God veiled in flesh and made manifest in the ascension of Christ. Seated at the right hand of the Father, Christ takes our humanity into God's presence that we might share in his glory. Drawing together exegetical, historical, and systematic insights, Hastings invites us into a deeper comprehension of the ancient Christian confession that Jesus is Lord."

Austin Stevenson, assistant professor of theology at Palm Beach Atlantic University

"This is a lively and informed exposition and interpretation of the doctrine of the ascension. Although a key doctrine at the heart of the gospel, the ascension is too little discussed. Ross Hastings's thought-provoking and insightful exploration addresses the significance of the ascension for the priesthood of Christ and the atonement in ways that challenge and correct conventional perspectives. This book invites readers into a bold and distinctive viewpoint. Whether or not you agree with all Hastings's conclusions, this book will stimulate serious reflection on a theologically foundational affirmation."

Alan J. Torrance, emeritus professor of systematic theology at the University of St Andrews

THE GLORY OF THE ASCENSION

CELEBRATING A DOCTRINE FOR THE LIFE OF THE CHURCH

W. ROSS HASTINGS

An imprint of InterVarsity Press
Downers Grove, Illinois

InterVarsity Press
P.O. Box 1400 | Downers Grove, IL 60515-1426
ivpress.com | email@ivpress.com

©2025 by William Ross Hastings

All rights reserved. No part of this book may be reproduced in any form without written permission from InterVarsity Press.

InterVarsity Press® is the publishing division of InterVarsity Christian Fellowship/USA®. For more information, visit intervarsity.org.

All Scripture quotations, unless otherwise indicated, are taken from The Holy Bible, New International Version®, NIV®. Copyright © 1973, 1978, 1984, 2011 by Biblica, Inc.™ Used by permission of Zondervan. All rights reserved worldwide. www.zondervan.com. The "NIV" and "New International Version" are trademarks registered in the United States Patent and Trademark Office by Biblica, Inc.™

The publisher cannot verify the accuracy or functionality of website URLs used in this book beyond the date of publication.

Cover design: Faceout Studio
Interior design: Jeanna Wiggins

ISBN 978-1-5140-1061-7 (print) | ISBN 978-1-5140-1062-4 (digital)

Printed in the United States of America ∞

Library of Congress Cataloging-in-Publication Data
A catalog record for this book is available from the Library of Congress.

31 30 29 28 27 26 25 | 12 11 10 9 8 7 6 5 4 3 2 1

THIS BOOK IS DEDICATED

to Reverend Michael Wimmer, rector of St. Michael of All Angels Church, Chemainus, British Columbia, whose eucharistic, liturgical, and sermonic practices have mentored and inspired me.

CONTENTS

Introduction	1
Abbreviations	3
1 Why the Ascension Matters for Everybody and Everything	5
2 Methodology: The Biblical-Christological Unveiling of the Ascension	33
3 The Glory of His Deity: Ascension by the God of Iridescent Glory	46
4 Glory Concealed, Glory Revealed	65
5 The Glory of His Threefold Office as Prophet, Priest, and King	80
6 The Glory of a Completed Atonement, the Glory of an Eternal Salvation: Atonement Accomplished in the Session, Atonement Applied in the Intercession of Christ	102
7 The Glory of God in the Ascended Human: Implications for All of Human Life	130
8 The Glory of a Finished Objective Atonement	151
9 The Glory of the Heavenly Application of the Atonement	170
10 Glory in the Church	193
11 The Glory of the Kingdom Come, His Coming Again in Glory: Inaugurated and Future Eschatology	205
12 The Shared Glory of the Cosmic Christ	213
13 The Glory of Heaven	227
Conclusion	255

Acknowledgments	257
Bibliography	259
General Index	271
Scripture Index	275

INTRODUCTION

In one sense, this treatment of the ascension of the Lord Jesus Christ is the last piece in a trilogy in my written work. I refer to my previous works *Total Atonement* and *The Resurrection of Jesus Christ*. This work is a capstone to the atonement as the history of the person of Jesus, and though distinct from the resurrection, it is inseparable from it. The resurrection is the completion of the atonement, and the ascension is the celebration of its completeness at the right hand of the Father, where Jesus sat after he ascended in glory. The primary theme of this exposition will be the glory of the ascension, that is, the glory of the ascended Son. This glory is expressed in his coronation, in the acclamation of the Father and the heavenly hosts. This glory is expressed in the offices he assumes, that is, his priestly, kingly, and prophetic ministry in heaven. It is expressed in his reigning over the cosmos at the right hand of the Father; in his recapitulation as the last Adam to form a new humanity; in his application of the atonement to the church and its people; in his sending of the Spirit to incorporate the church in Christ and empower it for its mission to the world, advancing his kingdom and the revelation of his glory throughout the world, anticipating the full expression of the kingdom and glory of Christ at his coming again; in his leading of his church in worship and prayer; in his bringing comfort to suffering humanity.

All that the ascension accomplishes is a huge source of encouragement for the faithful people of God in the troubled times in which we live, just as it was for the persecution-fatigued people to whom the writer of Hebrews wrote. My prayer is that it will be a tonic for people struggling with their prayer lives, for people who have suffered loss or are enduring pain, for people whose faith may be shaken by the state of the world and the state of the church, for people who need assurance that the Son with whom they are in union ever lives and has a permanent priesthood: "He's there from now to eternity to save everyone who comes to God through him, always on the job to speak up for them" (Heb 7:24-25 MSG).

ABBREVIATIONS

ANF   *The Ante-Nicene Fathers.* Edited by Alexander Roberts and James Donaldson. 1885–1887. 10 vols. Repr., Peabody, MA: Hendrickson, 1994

JTI   *Journal for Theological Interpretation*

LNTS   Library of New Testament Studies

NPNF   *A Select Library of Nicene and Post-Nicene Fathers of the Christian Church.* Edited by Philip Schaff and Henry Wace. 28 vols. in 2 series. 1886–1889. Repr., Peabody, MA: Hendrickson, 1994

SJT   *Scottish Journal of Theology*

WJE   *The Works of Jonathan Edwards.* 26 vols. New Haven, CT: Yale University Press, 1977–2009

1

WHY THE ASCENSION MATTERS FOR EVERYBODY AND EVERYTHING

Thou art the King of Glory, O Christ.
Thou art the everlasting Son of the Father.
When Thou tookest upon Thee to deliver [humanity],
Thou didst not abhor the Virgin's womb.
When Thou hadst overcome the sharpness of death,
Thou didst open the kingdom of heaven to all believers.
Thou sittest, at the right hand of God, in the glory of the Father.

"Te Deum Laudamus," Book of Common Prayer

IN THIS INTRODUCTORY CHAPTER, I will set the context for this study of the ascension first by creating the need for the study, given the relative infrequence of reference to ascension in the academy and the pulpit, and then by introducing the significance of the doctrine by indicating the major themes of this study, but especially by emphasizing the constructive nature of the study around the primary theme of the glory of the ascension.

RECOVERING FROM THE ECLIPSE

What could motivate a theologian to write about the ascension of the Lord Jesus Christ? One could be energized by the paucity of writing on this theme in the theological academy and the infrequency of sermons preached on it in the church, to the impoverishment of both. Compared to the atonement or the resurrection of Jesus, the ascension is a much-neglected topic in the church's life. One aspect of this is that the contemporary Christian may be unable to articulate why the ascension matters to their devotional life.

By contrast, when the writer of Hebrews begins an epistle that has as one of its primary themes the believer's access into the presence of God, he does so with a summary (Heb 1:1-3) of the great themes of the gospel of Christ that includes a phrase about the ascension. That phrase is, "he sat down at the right hand of the Majesty in heaven" (Heb 1:3). There is no mention of the resurrection, though it is implied, whereas this ascension phrase is one of the main clauses, indeed, the climactic clause. The writer wants to stress the ascension in this up-front, cryptic, yet majestic summary of the being and actions of the Son-Priest that are the subject of this epistle. This is fitting, for it is not an exaggeration to say that the ascension is central to that subject matter, central to an understanding of the identity and saving work of Jesus.

This great passage conveys the multifaceted glory of the Son who is the ultimate *Prophet*, the revelation of who God is ("In the past God spoke to our ancestors through the prophets . . . but in these last days he has spoken to us *in Son*," Heb 1:2 NIV, adapted to reflect literal translation); the *King* of the cosmos ("heir of all things," Heb 1:2; "sat down at the right hand of the Majesty in heaven," Heb 1:3); and—crucially for our access to God and communion with him—the great High *Priest* ("After he had provided purification for sins, he sat down," Heb 1:3). In my reflection on these verses, I have always thought that these introductory sentences have a chiastic (a-b-c-c-b-a) structure (see chapter five). Crucially, the first statement, which concerns the intended reign of Christ over the whole creation ("heir of all things"), is answered in the final clause by "when he had by himself purged our sins, *he sat down at the right hand of the Majesty on high*" (KJV). This writer alludes to the resurrection only obliquely (see Heb 7:16, "the power of an indestructible life"). Christ's once-for-all sacrificial and victorious atonement is a central and vital theme in the mission of the King-Priest in Hebrews. But here and in many other passages in the epistle, the ascension is depicted as central and crucial in the salvation history of Jesus. In this text, the ascension is both the sign that his atoning work is finished and the sign that something is *not finished* and has only just begun.

In Hebrews 10, the Father tells the ascended Son to sit on his throne *until* his enemies are made his footstool (Heb 10:13). His kingship is a present reality in heaven, but it is being effected gradually on earth by the Spirit and through his church on mission. It will be revealed, climactically, when he returns at the parousia (second coming). Similarly, throughout the epistle it becomes clear that in addition to his finished atoning work, there is an unfinished work of priesthood that Jesus fulfills, interceding in heaven for his church and its members on earth. Jesus uniquely combines the office of king and priest under an order that Melchizedek prefigures in the Old Testament (Gen 14:18; see Heb 5:10; 6:20; 7:1-17). As king and priest, he does ongoing salvific work as he guides the cosmos and shepherds his people.

Why is the ascension important? We may say that Christ's *atonement* was completed on earth by his death and resurrection but that it was accepted and celebrated by the Father *when he ascended.* He presented his humanity, his offering of himself, and his work on behalf of humanity when he ascended on high. The words "sat down" signal completion. There were no seats in the Hebrew tabernacle or temple simply because the atonement achieved by animal sacrifices was never complete. Those sacrifices only prefigured the work of the Lamb that was to come.[1] The seat in the heavenly sanctuary is a throne, and his sitting on that throne is a signal of coronation and

---

[1] See, e.g., C. H. Spurgeon, "The Only Atoning Priest" (sermon, February 4, 1872), www.spurgeon.org/resource-library/sermons/the-only-atoning-priest/#flipbook/.

completion, resulting from a victory won over sin, Satan, and death (Heb 2:14-15).

However, although the *atonement* was completed when Jesus sat down, the church's *salvation* was not yet completed and will not be until the consummation of all things. The writer reflects this when he states, "Because Jesus lives forever, he has a permanent priesthood. Therefore he is able to save completely [right on to the end] those who come to God through him, because he always lives to intercede for them" (Heb 7:24-25). That is, in Pauline terms, the church that Christ purchased once and for all ("Christ loved the church and gave himself up for her," Eph 5:25) is still in need of perseverance and of purification ("to make her holy, cleansing her by the washing with water through the word," Eph 5:26), again and again, until Jesus comes.

Another way to say this is that the enacting of atonement, *objectively* speaking, was finished when he ascended and sat down. However, *subjectively* speaking, the application of the atonement would constantly be needed throughout the church's corporate life and all through the personal life of each believer. In this vein, Calvin speaks of Christ's death as an intercession and insists that his heavenly intercession is not a repetition of the atonement but a reflection and representation of his death.[2] The significance of the ascension, therefore, was that it signaled the beginning of Christ's intercessory work in heaven, enabling us to worship and pray. His priesthood is how we, his people, are priests (Heb 8:1; see Heb 9:14). His offering and ongoing priestly intercession also enable us to be holy and become holy (Heb 10:10, 14). He gives longevity and resilience to every true believer, bringing them all the way to glorification.

In a nutshell, the believer's devotional life is possible only because Christ ascended for us after having lived and died for us. That is how important the ascension is. Through it, we now have access as priests to God (Heb 9:14) in the one great High Priest (Heb 8:1-3) through

---

[2]See John Calvin, *Institutes* 2.16.2.

the blood he shed and the body he offered up to the Father (Heb 10:19). We have access because when he ascended, he offered up his humanity for us, a humanity he had freely taken up in his incarnation. By the hypostatic union, he who was one with God (*homoousion*—a Nicene conviction) became one with humanity (*homoousion*—a Chalcedonian reality). Thus, he acted representatively for humanity in his life, death, resurrection, and *ascension*. However, having access into God's presence through the finished work of atonement is not the same as accessing that access. That requires his ongoing, unfinished work as our Priest.

One great theme of the ascension is that, in Christ, we are already seated in the heavenlies (Eph 2:6). Hebrews, which will be a primary source for our consideration of the doctrine of the ascension, provides insight into what that means, as already noted. It does so more than the rest of the New Testament put together. It does so by describing the intercessory priesthood of Christ that engraces and enables our access and communion with God. It does so by describing his communication of comfort and strength to his people (Heb 4:14, "Jesus," who is also "the Son of God"). It clarifies that we can pray only because he intercedes in his ongoing work as the High Priest for us.

One of the key exhortational (i.e., hortatory) hinge passages in Hebrews (Heb 10:19-23) makes it clear that we have confident access into the heavenly presence of God, a confidence grounded in the blood and body of Jesus, what he did, and facilitated by who he is in his high priesthood there. The grounding of our access is clear, but the exhortations motivated by the completed work of Christ and his ongoing representative presence in the heavenly tabernacle are nevertheless emphatic and reveal what his unfinished work is. The hortatory phrase is in italics:

> Therefore, brothers and sisters, since we have confidence to enter the Most Holy Place by the blood of Jesus, by a new and living way opened for us through the curtain, that is, his body, and since we have a great

priest over the house of God, *let us draw near to God* with a sincere heart and with the full assurance that faith brings, having our hearts sprinkled to cleanse us from a guilty conscience and having our bodies washed with pure water. (Heb 10:19-22)

Here we see the distinction between the finished and unfinished work of the Priest. A way into the heavenly sanctuary ("through the curtain") has been opened as a fait accompli. On the other hand, however, we note the grace-enabled responses that are exhorted. The first is the invitation to "draw near," which presumably means "come into the presence of God through prayer." Paul might say it this way: since you are seated in the heavenlies in Christ (Eph 2:6), then live there, live the life of prayer (Eph 3:14-21). Access your access. The writer of Hebrews says it similarly but distinctively, with specific instructions on how we are to pray. Our prayers are facilitated by Christ, by divine grace, but we are active in this praying, not passive. We pray in participation with his praying, but we pray nevertheless.

And two stipulations guide us in how we pray: first, we pray on our part with "a sincere heart and with the full assurance that faith brings," and second, because we can never measure up fully to that first stipulation, we pray always in a way that includes confession: "having our hearts sprinkled to cleanse us from a guilty conscience and having our bodies washed with pure water." This infers the ongoing work of the ascended Christ *applying* the accomplished atonement—not for our justification, which is a fait accompli for humanity in Christ—but for daily cleansing from the defilement of sin; for relational restoration to the Father, not forensic acquittal, which the Son has once for all enacted. Hebrews 10:12 makes this abundantly clear: "But when this priest had offered *for all time one sacrifice for sins*, he sat down at the right hand of God."

So we may say that God's yes over humanity in Christ and creation has been declared due to his life, death, and resurrection for us. That yes might be considered to have been given visible expression in the ascension. However, as justified people, we are not yet holy in ourselves, and our sins must be forgiven and our lives continually cleansed. Upon our confession, Christ sprinkles our fallen, wayward, and broken hearts, cleanses our consciences, and washes our whole beings, making our hearts fit for his presence. This aligns with what John says in 1 John 1:9. Confessing Christians (is there another kind?) are not just forgiven of specific confessed sins but are also being cleansed, in general, from "all unrighteousness."

This speaks to the lack of emphasis in our churches and our preaching on occupying heaven (Col 3:1-2) in order to bring heaven to earth in our embodied experience. Being heavenly minded in order to be useful on earth is the ideal to which we are called. For the writer of Hebrews, that is where we are meant to reside. Paul is no different. In Colossians 3:1-2, Paul exhorts, "Set your hearts on things above, where Christ is, seated at the right hand of God. Set your minds on things above, not on earthly things." Why does the ascension matter? Because it invites us to focus on heaven. Because that is where Christ is, and Paul adds, "For you died, and your life is now hidden with Christ in God" (Col 3:3). This is our deepest reality as the people of God. Our identity and our place, our home, if you like, is in Christ, in the triune God. Whereas earthiness is a big theme in contemporary theology, heavenly orientation *in* our earthiness is good in Paul's mind. This is our spiritual privilege as the people who are in Christ, hidden in him: to be in his presence in heaven by prayer, through the Eucharist, and in every waking moment. Of course, this may sound like the Gnosticism that Irenaeus, the great church father, countered at great cost. But it is not Gnosticism. Living a life of prayer and practicing the presence of Christ is intended to facilitate living on earth in earthly ways that define what it means to be human. It is also not Gnosticism, or even Platonism, to argue that our spiritual access and exercise in the heavenlies now anticipates the second coming, when as resurrected believers we will ascend as whole human persons to be permanently in God's presence in heaven, with a view to a return to earth as fully human persons defined as fully human by the one human who is the prototypical and perfect human for all humanity, the last Adam, who recapitulates the first Adam.

Paul anticipates this in the next verse of Colossians 3: "When Christ, who is your life, appears, then you also will appear with him in *glory*" (Col 3:4). Note that the glory of the people of God will be a reflection of the iridescent radiance of the Son. They will have experienced the beatific vision. They will have seen his face and become like him (1 Jn 3:2). They will be displayed in the derived glory of the intrinsically glorious Son. Their glorification will then be completed. And they will be complete with body, soul, and spirit intact as heavenly humans on earth. This is what the ascension anticipates, for it is an ascension of a man, *the* man, into heaven for humanity. The correspondence between the ascension and the second coming is communicated clearly at his ascension when the angels say, "This same Jesus, who has been taken from you into heaven, will come back in the same way you have seen him go into heaven" (Acts 1:11). As he has ascended into heaven as a fully human and fully divine person, he will return as a fully human and fully divine person. As further revelation unfolded, it became clear that his people, with whom he entered into union by the incarnation and who appropriate that union by the work of the Spirit in regeneration and incorporation, would also be with him forever in the full possession of their humanity. Theosis, properly understood, is the transformation of humans to become like Christ. It does not have as its aim our dehumanization or our being "Godded with God." Instead, it teaches that we become fully human, glorified humans, and appear "with him in glory" (Col 3:4).

The notion that heaven is not our final destination, popularized by some by overemphasizing the kingdom's horizontal nature, seems to need some correction. We occupy heaven in our prayers now. We will ascend to heaven one day in a manner that corresponds to and is anticipated in Jesus' ascension. Of course, I agree that heaven will come to earth (Rev 21:2), and I believe in an earthly new creation. However, to eliminate heaven is unfortunate. Heaven on earth will be heaven still. The truth is that one day, in a manner anticipated by Hebrews and even by the fact that there is already a true Man in heaven, heaven and earth will give way to the end of dualism, and heaven and earth will be one. And as such, it will be heaven where the Lamb is the center and the light. This is already anticipated in the ascension of a man into heaven. All will be sacred space then because it is already that for Jesus. There is a new cosmology to be discovered in the ascension of Jesus.

Even Hebrews 1:3, in its cryptic way of expressing the death and ascension of Jesus, seems to anticipate this: "When he had by himself purged our sins . . ." (KJV). *Where did that happen?* On earth? At the cross, as Jesus offered himself without spot to God, shed his blood, and accomplished our purgation and reconciliation? Yes, but the very next phrase says, "he sat down at the right hand of the Majesty in heaven." *Where did that happen?* Certainly, this phrase is meant to be cryptic. It omits any reference to the resurrection and the forty days. But it seems that the writer wants us to see that as Jesus is purging our sins, he is doing so in the presence of God in heaven, even while he is on earth. Or, putting it another way, since he is himself God, it is within his own being that he is accomplishing our atonement, and therefore, though on earth he is hanging on a tree, he is necessarily also in the presence of God in heaven as he does so. That is why he can purge our sin on a hill outside Jerusalem and then sit down on a throne in heaven—he has not left heaven even as he is on the cross for us. When he said that he was perpetually in the Father and the Father in him in John 10:38, that did not cease to be true on the cross.

WHY THE ASCENSION MATTERS FOR THEOLOGY: CONSTRUCTIVE RETRIEVAL

On the academic side, there has also been an eclipse of the ascension, which merits an emphasis in our time. It has been neglected especially since the era of the church fathers, though it is somewhat sparsely spoken of even in their writings. Although there are sections devoted to the ascension in more recent systematic theologies, few significant works dedicated to this theme have been written in the last century.[3] Two authors have written works that I would consider seminal studies. The first is J. G. Davies in a book arising from his 1958 Bampton Lectures at Oxford University, *He Ascended into Heaven: A Study in the History of Doctrine*.[4] It is an exemplary model for how the discipline of the history of doctrine should be carried out in that it begins with the biblical account and canonical assertions of both the Old and New Testaments and then moves to consideration of the tradition as it is expressed in the ante-Nicene fathers—in particular those active in the writing of the conciliar creeds—and on to the Greek and Latin writers.

Two books written by Douglas Farrow of McGill University are also seminal: *Ascension and Ecclesia: On the Significance of the Doctrine of the Ascension for Ecclesiology and Christian Cosmology*, which traces the doctrine from the Scriptures, the Fathers, the eucharistic liturgy, the Reformers, and on into modern theology; and *Ascension Theology*, which again begins with locating the doctrine in its biblical context, then moves on to consider the implications of the ascension of Christ in the flesh as expounded especially in the work of Irenaeus and the

---

[3]See sections for example in Karl Barth, *Church Dogmatics*, ed. G. W. Bromiley and Thomas F. Torrance, trans. G. W. Bromiley (London: T&T Clark, 2009), IV/1-4; Thomas F. Torrance, *Royal Priesthood* (Edinburgh: Oliver & Boyd, 1955); Torrance, *Theology in Reconstruction* (Grand Rapids, MI: Eerdmans, 1965), Torrance, *Space, Time, and Resurrection* (Grand Rapids, MI: Eerdmans, 1976); Torrance, "The Ascension of Jesus Christ," in *Atonement: The Person and Work of Christ* (Downers Grove, IL: IVP Academic, 2009).

[4]John G. Davies, *He Ascended into Heaven: A Study in the History of Doctrine*, Bampton Lectures (London: Lutterworth, 1958).

later tradition.[5] Farrow focuses on what he considers to be the two key theological issues of the ascension: the identity of the risen Christ and the church. Within his ecclesiology, the sacrament of the Eucharist is a major focus, mirroring the presence-absence tension of the ascended Christ, who is absent from us and yet present to us by the Spirit. He also engages the topic of atonement, especially as relates to its ongoing application to the cleansing of heavenly things and what this means for the earthly worship of the church.

In a further chapter in a book that expounds the Nicene Creed (which curiously does not devote a chapter dedicated to the ascension clause of the creed), Farrow highlights the neglect of this doctrine.[6] He refers to "a long history of assault" on the particulars of the four christological clauses in the creed that follow the resurrection clause, the first of which is "He ascended into heaven." The ascension as a distinct event in the story of Jesus, "we are frequently told," is a "Lukan invention" (as in Davies's thought) and best considered to be merely "an aspect of the resurrection," says Farrow.[7] Poignantly, he asks

> whether the first of the four clauses now before us is not, in fact, the very point in the creed at which we are confronted not with a theological revolution such as that connected to *ex nihilo* or to the *homoousion* or to the doctrine of the resurrection, but rather with a failure of the revolutionary spirit of Christian theology; that is, with a lapse back into a speculative, fanciful cosmology, and so into mythological godtalk.[8]

---

[5] Douglas Farrow, *Ascension and Ecclesia: On the Significance of the Doctrine of the Ascension for Ecclesiology and Christian Cosmology* (Grand Rapids, MI: Eerdmans, 1999); Farrow, *Ascension Theology* (London: T&T Clark, 2011).

[6] Douglas Farrow, "Confessing Christ Coming," in *Nicene Christianity: The Future for a New Ecumenism*, ed. Christopher R. Seitz (Grand Rapids, MI: Brazos, 2001), 133-48.

[7] Farrow, "Confessing Christ Coming," 135. Davies suggests that Luke did not write his account of the ascension in Acts 1 with strictly historical intent but rather with a view to fitting the story with the Old Testament forty-day typology associated with Elijah's ascent, for example. Davies insists that Jesus ascended on the first Sunday evening after he rose again and that all the rest of the appearances were visitations of the ascended Christ from heaven. See Davies, *He Ascended into Heaven*, 17, 18, 56-58.

[8] Farrow, "Confessing Christ Coming," 135-36.

Farrow convincingly demonstrates the surprising influence that the doctrine of the ascension has had within Christian and Western thought. He also addresses difficult questions regarding it that others have shied away from. His systematic treatments of the ascension are seminal, and though this treatment will show a significant commonality of interest, my emphases may be slightly different on some key points. Further shorter monographs and some significant journal articles have been written to bring the ascension into greater spotlight in the academy.[9] Davies and Farrow are exceptional for their systematic, constructive retrieval of the writings of the Fathers, the Scholastics, and the Reformers.

The doctrine of the ascension has been a minor one in modern theology due to several factors. Cambridge theologian David Fergusson outlines three of these, and all three have to do with cosmology. The first was "the assimilation of earlier accounts of the ascension to a Ptolemaic worldview," which "led to some skepticism in a post-Copernican age." The second explicitly relates to how we think about heaven: "The heaven of Scripture could no longer be understood as spatially related to this world by virtue of its position at the outer reaches of the cosmos." Third, this "generated a problem for any notion of the body of Jesus going somewhere along a spatial trajectory at a time subsequent to the resurrection."[10] These challenges exacerbated a tendency of historical criticism to conflate resurrection,

---

[9]Peter Atkins, *Ascension Now: Implications of Christ's Ascension for Today's Church* (Collegeville, MN: Liturgical Press, 2001); Gerald O'Collins, *Jesus Our Priest: A Christian Approach to the Priesthood of Christ* (New York: Oxford University Press, 2010); Johanna Kramer, *Between Earth and Heaven: Liminality and the Ascension of Christ in Anglo-Saxon Literature*, Manchester Medieval Literature and Culture (Manchester: Manchester University Press, 2014); Patrick Schreiner, *The Ascension of Christ: Recovering a Neglected Doctrine* (Bellingham, WA: Lexham, 2020). The work of T. F. Torrance in *Royal Priesthood* and *Atonement* has been a significant influence in most recent work on the ascension.

[10]David Fergusson, "The Ascension of Christ: Its Significance in the Theology of T. F. Torrance," *Participatio* 3 (2012): 92. See also Fergusson, "He Ascended into Heaven: The Ascension and Agency of Christ in the Theology of T. F. Torrance," in *What Is Jesus Doing? God's Activity in the Life and Work of the Church* (Downers Grove, IL: IVP Academic, 2020), 27-46.

ascension, and exaltation, except in the case of Luke–Acts, "with its more stylised forty-day interval between the two events."[11]

In response to these challenges and in agreement with Fergusson, rather than assigning the doctrine to the Bultmannian category of myth, I adopt a constructive approach here as the appropriate way forward. This has already been championed by Karl Barth, Robert Jenson, and Douglas Farrow. I resonate fully with Fergusson's assertion that even though in the study of the ascension we are "at the very limits of human speech and knowledge," that "substantive claims about the identity of the risen Christ in relation to God and the church are at stake in the creedal affirmation that 'he ascended into heaven and sitteth on the right hand of God the Father Almighty.'" That there is a declaration of the ascension in the creed says something about its importance, to be sure. But Fergusson asserts further that the ascension "is vital to the shape of Christian faith and the role of Christ as an active subject in the life of the church and the world."[12]

Any attempt to dismiss either the *distinctiveness* or the unique significance of the ascension of Jesus needs to take into account, for one thing, that the most-quoted Old Testament verse in the New Testament is Psalm 110:1, "The LORD says to my Lord: Sit at my right hand until I make your enemies a footstool for your feet." It is quoted twenty-three times.[13] Why is this verse, which speaks distinctively of the session of Jesus at his ascension, so important for New Testament theology? Contrary to the opinion that the resurrection and the ascension of Jesus to the right hand of God are conflated, this verse highlights precisely the important distinction to be made between these two events. Though associated, they are not one event but two. A strong vindication of the distinct importance of the ascension lies

---

[11] Fergusson, "Ascension of Christ," 92-93.
[12] Fergusson, "Ascension of Christ," 93.
[13] David M. Hay, *Glory at the Right Hand: Psalm 110 in Early Christianity* (Nashville: Abingdon, 1973), 44.

in the fact that by it the Son of David, who is also the Son of God, was enthroned as King.

The importance of the ascension in the biblical story is further emphasized by the fact that Psalm 110:4 ("The LORD has sworn and will not change his mind: 'You are a priest forever, in the order of Melchizedek'") is a, if not *the*, key Old Testament text that is expounded to explain the priesthood of Jesus in the epistle to the Hebrews, especially in its ongoing, eternal aspect, and especially as that priestly office is united to his kingship. This psalm reveals that the ascended King (Ps 110:1), David's son who is David's "Lord" (see Mt 22:41-45), is also a "priest" (Ps 110:4). This combination of offices was a possibility only because Jesus operates within the order of "Melchizedek," who was "king of Salem" and yet "priest of God Most High" (Gen 14:18-20). Jesus is not just priest, in the estimation of the writer of Hebrews; he is the *great* High Priest (Heb 4:14), the Priest of all priests. Though his priestly work, as expounded in Hebrews, included his sacrificial work while he was on earth (see, e.g., Heb 8:3; 9:11-14, 26; 10:10-14, 19-20), the primary intent of Psalm 110:4 ("a priest forever, in the order of Melchizedek"), taken alongside Psalm 110:1, is to portray it as a *kingly* priesthood. This is evident in the hinge passages of Hebrews.

For example, in Hebrews 8:1, the writer says, "We do have such a high priest, *who sat down at the right hand of the throne of the Majesty in heaven.*" Moreover, in Hebrews 10:21, after referencing the body and blood of Christ, by which he accomplished atonement, the writer says, "And since we have a great priest *over* the house of God . . ." These references to the priesthood of Christ emphasize his ascension into heaven and his ongoing work there as a *Priest* who is King. They major on his ongoing intercessory work, the atoning work having been completed on earth. His session at the Father's right hand rewards and honors the atoning work. But his humiliation, death, and resurrection appearances were over. There had been a decisive transition from the Son of God who had been "crucified in weakness" (2 Cor 13:4) to the

Son of God "in power" (Rom 1:4). His installation and enthronement as King-Priest happened by way of the ascension.

The apostle Paul also expresses the clear distinction between the resurrection and ascension, and the glorious universal exaltation of the Son as a consequence of the death and resurrection events, in Ephesians 1:19-21: "That power is the same as the mighty strength he exerted when he *raised Christ from the dead* and *seated him at his right hand* in the heavenly realms, far above all rule and authority, power and dominion, and every name that is invoked, not only in the present age but also in the one to come."

Theologian Stephen Seamands eloquently puts it this way: "Proclaiming the ascension is therefore crucial in fully and properly exalting Christ. For Jesus is *not only risen but reigning*. Not only alive but sovereign, not only central but supreme." Summing up the extensive work of Doug Farrow on the ascension, Seamands adds: "Whenever we fail to proclaim the ascended Christ, enthroned and exalted, something else—our personal agendas, the world's agendas, the church's agendas—moves in to fill the vacuum. Mark it down: when we fail to exalt and enthrone Jesus, something or someone else inevitably assumes the throne."[14] Categorically, then, the ascension is not an appendage to the resurrection, as if they were one event. In one of the most significant treatments of the ascension in the twentieth century, that of T. F. Torrance, the resurrection and the ascension are treated in this way, as closely related yet distinct events.[15] On the one hand, Torrance describes them as inseparable: "the fusion of resurrection with the ascension in one indivisible exaltation."[16] On the other hand, he emphasizes their distinctness within that inseparability,

---

[14]Stephen A. Seamands, *Give Them Christ: Preaching His Incarnation, Crucifixion, Resurrection, Ascension, and Return* (Downers Grove, IL: InterVarsity Press, 2012), 141, emphasis added.

[15]David Fergusson pays tribute to T. F. Torrance's theology of the ascension as "one of the richest treatments of the subject in modern theology" ("Ascension of Christ," 94). Torrance's treatment is found in Torrance, *Atonement*, chap. 9, and in Torrance, *Space, Time, and Resurrection*, chaps. 5-6.

[16]Fergusson, "Ascension of Christ," 94.

citing Karl Barth: "The resurrection and ascension of Jesus Christ are two distinct, but inseparable moments in one and the same event. The resurrection is to be understood, as the *terminus a quo*, its beginning, and the ascension as its *terminus ad quem*, its end."[17]

The ascension is therefore crucial for understanding the whole history of Jesus Christ, and in particular its relation to the incarnation is important. It must not be taken out of the context of the history of Jesus Christ—the whole movement of the incarnation onward, with all of its saving significance. In light of the flow of the epistle to the Hebrews, T. F. Torrance notes, "The ascension must be understood in a correlation with the incarnation, as the *anabasis* (ascent) of the Son of God corresponding to his *katabasis* (descent)."[18] This, he notes, was also Irenaeus's favorite theme.

The distinction between the resurrection and the ascension of Jesus is also seen in Paul's description of the effects of each event in the believer's life. In participation with Christ risen, yes, we are "made alive," but in Christ ascended, we are also "raised up" and "seated" in the heavenly realms (Eph 2:6). Furthermore, a resurrection without the ascension would mean that there is, on God's part, no acceptance and celebration of the atonement, no enthronement of King Jesus, no outpouring of the Spirit, and on Christ's part, no entry into high priesthood for us, no mediation of our prayers in his prayers, no empathy in our sufferings, no presence in the Eucharist (however one may understand that), and no second coming that corresponds to how he ascended (Acts 1:11).

Above all, there would be no revelation of the glory of Christ in heaven (1 Tim 3:16, he "was taken up in glory"), or when he returns (Mk 13:26, "people will see the Son of Man coming in clouds with

---

[17]Barth, *Church Dogmatics* IV/2, 150. Torrance's account has much in common with the treatment of Karl Barth, but it differs significantly with respect to Barth's view of the church, the sacraments, and ministry, "all of which are crucially related to his account of the ascension" (Fergusson, "Ascension of Christ," 94).

[18]Torrance, *Space, Time, and Resurrection*, 123.

great power and glory"), no glory in the church in union with him (Eph 3:21, "to him be glory in the church"), and no being caught up in glory in union with him in the Eucharist (1 Cor 10:16-17). Glory is the key concept of the ascension.

THE GLORY THEME OF THE ASCENSION: OVERCOMING THE ECLIPSE

Making a further contribution to the recovery of this doctrine, especially in constructive patristic retrieval, and engaging in the minor points of disagreement with the authors above is appealing, to be sure. However, I am not drawn primarily by this need but rather by the wonder of the subject material. The primary motivating purpose of this study is to describe the sheer glory of the ascension and of the ascended Lord so that readers may be wooed into worship and find themselves entering into their life in the ascended Son. My aim is to be evangelical and not legal in approach. To scold the church for its lack of emphasis and knowledge of the ascension is legal and ultimately unproductive. To paint a picture in words of the Son of God in his glory, and in light of the added glory of his salvific accomplishments, so that the people of God may contemplate and fall afresh in adoring love with him—this is my goal. This is, in other words, an invitation to adopt the posture of gazing at glory as the disciples did when they were transfixed as they saw him go up (Acts 1:10). It is in keeping with Paul's cryptic, precreedal summation of the ascension in 1 Timothy 3:16: he "was taken up in glory." Of course, in adopting this contemplative approach, we will find another way of saying how crucial the doctrine of the ascension is for all doctrines.

One theologian known for his theology of beauty, Jonathan Edwards (1703–1758), once commented that the relations of an object define its beauty, that is, by its being in relation. This was part of his attempt at a philosophical proof of the triune being of God. God could not be beautiful if he were merely one, he argued. Using an aesthetical argument, he stated, "One alone cannot be beautiful."[19] For Edwards, beauty, as defined by the Trinity, was a product of the consent within the three persons of the one God, of the interpenetrative relation of the persons to one another, each being in the other without loss of the identity of each, each interanimating the other in perfect harmony. Robert Jenson sums up his study of Edwards in *America's Theologian* in this manner: "As we have had occasion to note in almost every chapter, the very template of his vision is that God as Triunity is 'the supreme Harmony of all.'... Indeed, he did not merely maintain trinitarianism; he renewed it."[20]

Whether one is convinced of Edwards's philosophical argument as proof of the Trinity or not (it is, after all, an a priori argument, as opposed to the more convincing a posteriori evidence for the Trinity gained from the historical revelation of the Father, in the Son, by the Spirit), the essential reality that beauty is defined by the relations of an object to other objects is a fair one. What does this have to do with the ascension? I want to argue throughout this book that the act of the ascension and the person of the Lord who ascended, and all the consequences of that ascension, are beautiful and worthy of the study of the church and its theologians *precisely because of its relations.*

The ascension is beautiful because by it Jesus reveals his glory. As he ascends, he displays the body of glory—glimpsed on the Mount of Transfiguration and in resurrection appearances—which Davies calls a "heavenly body, of shining ethereal substance," fitting for the divine,

---

[19]Edwards states, "But in a being that is absolutely without any plurality, there cannot be excellence, for there can be no such thing as consent or agreement" (*WJE* 6:363). He also writes, "One alone without any reference to any more cannot be excellent; for, in such case, there can be no manner of relation no way, and therefore no such thing as consent." See Edwards, *The Philosophy of Jonathan Edwards from His Private Notebooks* (Eugene: University of Oregon Press, 1955), 26; cf. "Miscellany 117" (*WJE* 13:283).

[20]Robert W. Jenson, *America's Theologian: A Recommendation of Jonathan Edwards* (New York: Oxford University Press, 1988), 91.

heavenly realm.[21] This sight will be replicated on the great resurrection day when bodies "sown in dishonor" will be "raised in glory" (1 Cor 15:43). In a similar vein, Laura Cerbus in a recent article argues that beauty has been neglected in the pursuit of the good in modernity. She presents a compelling argument that despite the Copernican challenges of the ascension, the beauty of the ascended Christ is the antidote for this. She states, "The abuse of beauty can be resisted not by spiritualising beauty, but by ordering physical beauty to its eschatological end. This end is most clearly seen in the ascended Christ, with his beautiful body that is human, wounded and hidden."[22]

The ascension is beautiful because of its relation to the incarnation. That is, there is a symmetry of glory hidden and then glory revealed in the history of Jesus Christ. His glory was veiled at the incarnation, but there is an answering epiphanic restoration of glory as he ascends to the Father. In the words of Torrance, "The ascension is the obverse of the incarnation and marks its fulfilment."[23] The ascension is beautiful mostly because it forever established the *identity* of the one who, as anticipated in Psalm 24, is the "King of glory," before whom the gates of heaven must lift their heads and the ancient doors welcome him in. This is but one example of how the ascension is prefigured in the Old Testament and fulfilled in the New, giving evidence of harmonious relations between the two Testaments in Holy Scripture.

The ascension is beautiful also in that it is the climactic, celebrated outcome of an atonement that was fully accomplished and yet the beginning of the application of the atonement forever to the people of God in union with Christ. It is beautiful because of the symmetry of a humanity created and fallen in the first Adam with a humanity

---

[21] Davies, *He Ascended into Heaven*, 59, here referencing G. H. Boobyer, *St. Mark and the Transfiguration Story* (Edinburgh: T&T Clark, 1942), 23.
[22] Laura Cerbus, "The Beauty of the Body and the Ascension: A Reclamation and Subversion of Physical Beauty," *SJT* 77 (2024): 1.
[23] Torrance, *Atonement*, x.

recapitulated, recreated, and glorified in the ascension of the last Adam. The ascension reflects a relation between the Son and his people, with whom he became one in the incarnation—his people who have died and risen with him and, more than that, are now seated with him in his ascended place in the heavenlies (Eph 2:6). Inherent in the ascension, therefore, are the great realities of the gospel that the Son became one with humanity in order that humanity in Christ might become one with him by the Spirit's work of regeneration, adoption, and embodiment into the church so that they might be justified, sanctified, and glorified—that is, deified—in Christ.

The ascension is beautiful in that it causes us to understand that the whole redemptive story of humanity is contained in the *person* of the Son of God, Jesus Christ. Thus, the ascension signals a soteriology in proper relation to ontology. In other words, it tells us that the work of Jesus Christ cannot be separated from his person—they are in proper relation. Underlying this is perhaps the greatest mystery of the ascension, carried over from the incarnation—the presence of a man in the Godhead. Here two great realities of relation come together: first, the relations in the Godhead itself between the persons of the Father, the Son, and the Holy Spirit, described by the term *homoousion*, and, second, the relations within the Second Person of the Trinity, also expressed in the word *homoousion*, indicating the union of the two natures of Christ, that is, his deity and his humanity. Even though all through his life here on earth the Son, as a divine-human person, already and always lived in perfect communion with—indeed, *in*—his Father (Jn 5:16-19; 10:38), there is something distinct, something beautiful yet almost jarring, about his presence as a man in the Godhead in heaven, in the harmony that always characterizes the relations of the Trinity, a harmony unthreatened, even enhanced, by the presence within it of a man. Humanity in God—indeed, the humanity of God—is a remarkable relation. As in the incarnation and onward to the ascension, it is an unconfused union, as the Chalcedonic definition expresses it. God and humanity cannot be mixed, but they are in union, in relation. This is gospel, good news, for sure.

Given that the flesh the Son took on at his incarnation entails his coming into union not just with humanity but with creation, that incarnation (and its perpetual extension into his ascension and post-ascension being) signals a very significant relation between God and his creation. This has repercussions for the relationship between the disciplines that describe God and creation in the human pursuit of knowledge: theology and science. Instead of a conflict model, a coinherent model of theology and science is possible.[24] The ascension of the Man, the last Adam, who represents and recapitulates humanity as the head of creation, is a paradigm for the intended relation between humanity and creation, one intended to be respectful and harmonious. The beauty of humanity in and with creation, in harmony, is indeed idyllic and attractive.

The identity of that glorious ascended person is also expressed in the interrelatedness of his three main offices: prophet, priest, and king. The union of his priesthood and kingship lies in an order created by a mysterious figure of the Old Testament, Melchizedek, a king-priest. The ascension is beautiful also in that it anticipates the day Christ will descend, reflecting a certain other symmetry, that is, at the parousia. As Farrow indicates, Gregory Nazianzen long ago understood that "the logic of the ascension, must respond to the logic of the *parousia*."[25] And as already noted, the church "will appear with him in glory" (Col 3:4). This relation will be further developed in due course.

Between these cataclysmic events, the parousia has been put on hold. The ascension has created "a pause in the *parousia*, creating time for the gospel before the final coming of Jesus."[26] As the missional

---

[24] As I have contended in W. Ross Hastings, *Echoes of Coinherence: Trinitarian Theology and Science Together* (Eugene, OR: Cascade, 2017).
[25] Farrow, "Confessing Christ Coming," 137.
[26] Torrance, *Atonement*, x.

people of God continue to live and witness here on earth, there is a heaven-to-earth relation between them and their great High Priest in heaven. He intercedes and prays for them, imparting his sympathy, strength, and security until they finish their course. The ascension signals a relation between two realities related to the kingdom of God: the accession of a King who is exalted over all and seated at the right hand of God in heaven, and, on the other hand, an eschatological reserve on earth such that the King's enemies are only gradually being subdued. The kingdom on earth that has come but is not yet fully come influences the "already but not yet" attitude of the people of God, which causes them to avoid triumphalism on the one hand and defeatism on the other.

In sum, with this doxological focus in mind, I hope to emphasize the importance of the ascension and celebrate it in light of what it reveals

- about the *person* and exalted *glory* of the ascended Christ himself and his offices;
- about the nature of *humanity* and its glory in light of his glorified and perpetual humanity—"the glory of God" that "is the living man" envisaged by Irenaeus;
- about the celebrated glory of the finished *atonement* (Heb 1:3; 8:1; 9:26, 28; 10:12; 12:2) and its unfinished application (Heb 7:11-28; 9:24) in the person of Jesus;
- about the glory of the *church*, its sacraments, its preaching, and its mission;
- about its importance for the *Christian life* (Heb 10:19-25) as a participation in his glory (Eph 2:6), and the engraced nature of the prayers of the people of God in the intercession of their great High Priest, and their comfort in suffering (Heb 2:17-18; 4:14-16);
- about its significance for *the* kingdom of God in the present age (*eschatological* reserve), in which the Spirit is at work on earth

in union with the Son, and for its future glorious manifestation (*eschatological* fulfillment) when he comes again in glory ("the earth will be filled with the knowledge of the *glory* of the LORD as the waters cover the sea," Hab 2:14); and

- about its *cosmological* significance, spelling the death of all dualisms, urging integration of theology and science and the arts, challenging the rampant neo-gnosticism that governs the ethics of our time.[27]

THE GLORY THEME OF THE ASCENSION: ITS VARIOUS FACETS

This book builds on the hard exegetical and theological work that has been done on the ascension and the epistle to the Hebrews. However, after perusing what has been written, I have concluded that *glory* is the appropriate window through which to view the ascension. This book's essence is the doxological contemplation of the *doxa* of Christ, a glory that is intrinsic, accrued, and shared with humanity and creation, leading to practicing an ascension lifestyle and many pastoral applications.

Although this book is unapologetically scholarly, I sincerely hope that its contents will filter down from pastor-scholars and academics into the life of the church and the lives of its people. I have one major intent in this book: to focus on and exalt the glory of our Lord Jesus Christ in his ascension, and therefore that of the triune God. I want to exalt Christ's intrinsic or *essential* glory as God of very God, to exalt his essential glory as the Son of God who is also man and has taken our humanity into the Godhead, and to exalt the ascended Christ also for his *accrued* glory, the glory he acquired by virtue of what he has accomplished by his incarnation, vicarious life, death, and resurrection. If the notion that glory may be added to an already fully glorious God seems strange, we must not forget that the meaning of glory is the

---

[27]Irenaeus, *Against Heresies* 4.10.7 (ANF 1:490).

revelatory luminosity of inward excellence, the iridescence that shines out from all that God does in his acts. It is the reverberation of the totality of his communicable attributes, the loveliness of all his virtues in perfect harmony, as seen and praised by humans and angels. God cannot but reveal his glory in all he does.

As he approached the whole paschal event, which includes the ascension, Jesus prayed that glory would emanate from it and that he and his Father would receive glory. In John 12:23, Jesus states, "The hour has come for the Son of Man to be glorified," and in John 12:28, in response to his prayer, "Father, glorify your name!" John records that "a voice came from heaven, 'I have glorified it, and will glorify it again.'" This provides some evidence that glory can be accrued to God.

Indeed, the ultimate end for which God created and redeemed the cosmos is the revelation of his glory. This Johannine text would seem to suggest that Jesus and the Father were glorified at the cross, and this is absolutely true. In the act by which Jesus atoned for the sin of humanity and cleansed it (*Christus vicarius*), the act by which he won the victory over Satan (*Christus Victor*), God's love, justice, and righteousness were revealed unprecedentedly. However, the full and climactic manifestation of God's glory in the whole history of Jesus is surely expressed in the ascension. This is why the ascension is vital. At his ascension, the glory he had with the Father before his incarnation was restored (Jn 17:3). By this event, the Son as *human* was "taken up" into the Father's presence, but the Son who is also fully God ascended in his own right. Christ's accomplished atonement, enacted in his humanity, is celebrated at the right hand of God, where he offers up that humanity to the Father. In the Father's presence, the atonement as accomplished in Christ's person is celebrated, and its completion is expressed by the session of the Son at the Father's right hand, as I have already affirmed. In the Father's presence, the Son is crowned King, the Son of Man (Dan 7), and Messiah. In the Father's presence, Jesus takes up the glory of priesthood and kingship in accordance with the order of Melchizedek. In a nutshell, glory does not add new attributes to God. It is simply the revelation of those attributes to creatures such as humans and angels.

In addition to his essential and accrued glory, our purpose is to exult in the *shared* glory of the ascended Christ for humanity. In union with the ascended Christ, the church finds itself becoming the expression of his glory. There we may find his corporate glory "in the church" that Paul refers to in Ephesians 3:21 ("to him be glory in the church and in Christ Jesus throughout all generations"). This is a consequence of the ascension because by it Jesus brought humanity into the presence of God so that the church now shares in the glory of Christ through its relational union in Christ with God. Its glory is a derived one. It is imparted to us by Christ. But this is also true for each person in the church. In contemplating the Lord's glory, each of us is being changed from "one degree of glory to another" (2 Cor 3:18 ESV). This transformation in glory is a consequence of the two hands of the Trinity, as Irenaeus called the Son and the Spirit.[28] We contemplate the Son who has ascended in glory, and as we do so, we are the subject of the internal work of the "Lord who is the Spirit" (2 Cor 3:18), the one who came down because the Son went up.

There are two aspects to this shared glory with respect to timing, one present and one future. Already in the now, we enter into the glory of being seated in the heavenly places with Christ and are able to pray as priests in the Priest, in unhindered fashion, engraced and enabled in our prayers by the Spirit's intercession on earth and the Son's intercession in heaven. Christ has brought "many sons and daughters to glory," as the writer of Hebrews says (Heb 2:10). When the Son ascended, the church ascended in him, spiritually speaking. However, if that was all, we would be guilty of the Gnosticism that church fathers such as Irenaeus sought to counter. At the fullness of the eschaton, we must enter heaven at the consummation in the

---

[28]Irenaeus, *Against Heresies* 5.6.1 (*ANF* 1:530).

totality of our human personhood. Platonic dualism does not prevail but Judeo-Christian holism. This full realization of our glorification awaits the parousia, that further symmetry in the history of Jesus—he ascended and he will descend—he "will come back in the same way you have seen him go into heaven" (Acts 1:11) in order that we might ascend. Then, the called and justified will also, as Paul anticipates, be "glorified" with and in Christ (Rom 8:30). How this will happen is the beatifying vision, as John indicates in 1 John 3:2—"we shall be like him, for we shall see him as he is."

After a discussion of methodology in chapter two, in chapters three through seven the focus will be on what the ascension says about *the glory of the person and work of Christ*: the glory of his essential deity in chapter three, and in chapter four, the glory associated with the bookends of Christ's ministry on earth, that which was concealed at the incarnation and then revealed in heaven at his ascension. In chapter five, I will also consider the glory of his threefold office as prophet, priest, and king. In this chapter I will focus especially on the grace and glory of his kingly priesthood, with an emphasis first on his punctiliar session, by which his kingly coronation is enacted and his sacrifice as Priest accepted. Second, I will emphasize his continuing *intercession* for his church.

There is an aspect of the glory of the ascension that transcends our full understanding, matters relating to Christology of the incarnation and ascension of Jesus, which cannot be covered in detail here. This includes issues such as how the divine-human person of the Son in the incarnation—and the continuance of that divine-human person in his ascension and session—relates to his eternal, unchanging being as the eternal Son, that is, the unchanging nature of God.[29] What the

---

[29]For a nuanced discussion of this issue, see the work of Bruce L. McCormack, "The Ontological Presuppositions of Barth's Doctrine of Atonement," in *The Glory of the Atonement: Biblical, Theological and Practical Perspectives*, ed. Charles E. Hill and Frank A. James (Downers Grove, IL: InterVarsity Press, 2004), 346-66; also Maximus, *On Difficulties in the Church Fathers: The Ambigua*, ed. and trans. Nicholas Constas, Dumbarton Oaks Medieval Library 28 (Cambridge, MA: Harvard University Press, 2014), 7.22; Jordan D. Wood, *The*

ascension means for the personhood of Christ within the Trinity, and for divine and human personhood, is also a matter for further development. Personhood in the divine being is not univocal with human personhood, but the presence of the divine-human person of the Son eternally in the Godhead suggests a bridge between divine and human personhood.[30]

Discussion of the relation between the Son's divine and human natures, and to what extent they communicate with each other (*communicatio idiomatum*), will be deferred until chapter ten, when I give consideration to the significance of this relation for the nature and the glory dynamics of the Eucharist. I will consider his glory expressed in the sending of the Holy Spirit and the coinherent work of the Son and the Spirit in the sanctification of his people in chapter nine, "The Glory of the Heavenly Application of the Atonement." His glory in the kingdom and the church, and his glory revealed on earth and the whole cosmos at his parousia, will be considered in later chapters on inaugurated eschatology (which will include a section on pneumatology), on ecclesiology (which will also contain a section on pneumatology), and on future eschatology (chapters ten and eleven). The glory of the one who participated in humanity as the incarnate one and who now represents that humanity as the ascended one—the glory he shares with humanity in general, and the glory he shares in his union with redeemed humanity in the church and every believer, as a result of our participation with Christ, or union with Christ, by the Spirit—will the focus in corresponding chapters on anthropology (chapter seven), soteriology (chapters eight and nine), and ecclesiology

---

Whole Mystery of Christ: Creation as Incarnation in Maximus Confessor (Notre Dame, IN: University of Notre Dame Press, 2022).

[30]It should be noted that a Christian trinitarian metaphysics affirms the *person* as fundamental and *real*. Together, these discoveries give human persons real, foundational existence, as well as imbue said persons with a real power of (in some sense) self-determination, since their hypostases are grounded in the personal hypostases of trinitarian ultimate reality. See Catherine Pickstock, "Duns Scotus: His Historical and Contemporary Significance," in *The Radical Orthodoxy Reader*, ed. Simon Oliver and John Milbank (London: Routledge, 2009), 132, for an explanation of why human freedom is preserved in classical metaphysics.

(chapter ten). The nature of the humanity of Christ, its continuities and discontinuities before and after the resurrection, and therefore in the ascension and session of Jesus, and what this means for our redeemed humanity at the parousia will be discussed in chapter eleven. Matters of cosmology relating to the shared glory of the ascended, cosmic Christ and the glory of heaven will bring the book to a close in chapters twelve and thirteen.

2

METHODOLOGY

The Biblical-Christological Unveiling of the Ascension

IN THIS CHAPTER I discuss the basis for our knowledge of the ascension—that is, epistemology. It includes a discussion of what we can and can't know. It indicates the sources of knowledge in the Holy Scriptures, the creeds, and the tradition. It discusses also biblical interpretation, including theological and christological interpretation. It then indicates the various areas of theology the ascension addresses and illumines. It concludes by expressing the central glory orientation of this treatment of the ascension.

In approaching what we can know and cannot know about the ascension or the ascended one—how it happened, what he became, how he functions in heaven—we are dependent on divine revelation. There is no denying the *cataphatic* nature of Christology as revealed in the Word of God. However, an element of mystery will always remain—the *apophatic* element in theology. The mysterious element of the ascension may account for the relative scarceness of treatments of the doctrine in the ancient and recent traditions.

In his candidating lecture at Regent College, my colleague Jonathan Anderson offered incisive comments about artistic depictions of the ascension in history, specifically about Giotto's work *L'Ascencione* in Scravengi Chapel, Padua, Italy (AD 1305).

> There is something consistently disappointing about most images of the ascension—especially in the West, from about the late Middle Ages

to today. Even in Giotto's incredible paintings in the Arena Chapel in Padua, there is a remarkable sense of indecision built into his image of this subject. The ascension passages at the end of Luke and beginning of Acts provide the reader with some key elements: there is a gathering of disciples, Jesus is "taken up," a cloud hides him from their vision, and "two men in white clothing" appear (Acts 1:9-10). Giotto includes all this, but he doesn't seem to know what to do with Jesus once he puts everything in the scene into a single spatial framework (which is one of the primary innovations of the Renaissance that Giotto helped to spark). Amidst this indecision, Giotto places the ascending Christ up against the end of the pictorial frame and allows his hands (but not his halo!) barely to break it. *This is very interesting to the extent that it achieves a kind of apophatic modesty.* For Giotto, *where* is Christ?—out of our visual frame, and that's about all we can say about it.[1]

Apophatic modesty is, of course, absolutely appropriate in a study of the ascended Christ. The event and the reality it entails have all kinds of questions of a transcendent nature that may not be completely decipherable. We cannot fathom all its details, though we can explore and adore the depths—or, better, the heights. The exploration must, of course, be guided by what has been revealed. Thus, the theological approach in this book is responsive to divine revelation as it has been given, especially as this is communicated by the relation between the Old and New Testaments, as these are especially united around the living Word, the person of Jesus Christ.

One issue arising from Anderson's helpful comment on Giotto's painting is the reference to the fact that Luke describes the ascension in the passive voice. There are two sets of passages in the New Testament account, some of which state that the ascension *was enacted by the Father* who exalted him: "until the day he was taken up into heaven" (Acts 1:2; see Acts 1:9; Lk 24:51; and see Acts 2:33, where Peter says, "Exalted to the right hand of God, he has received from the

---

[1]Jonathan Anderson, lecture, Regent College, March 1, 2023.

Father the promised Holy Spirit"), whereas other passages assert the agency of the Son himself. It seems that Jesus attained exalted status in his own right by virtue of his finished atonement, his victory over sin and Satan, and his priestly kingship (Eph 4:8; Heb 1:4; 4:14; 8:1, citing Ps 68:18). Whichever rich facet one focuses on, the outcome is doxological of the Father, who expresses his estimate of the Son and his atoning work, and of the Son, who ascends by virtue of his being God and the conquering Son of Man.

Matters of the timing and manner in which Jesus ascended are important and will be considered, but our primary concern is this: What does the ascension mean, and where shall we go for information to arrive at some conclusions about its meaning?[2] "To the Holy Scriptures" must be any serious Christian theologian's first and ultimate answer. If there is no obvious relation between the clear assertions of the Word of God and our theology of ascension, this will be cacophonous rather than harmonious to our theological sensibilities.

But what about the great *tradition* of scholarship throughout the ages, crystallized in the creeds of the church—the writings of church fathers such as Irenaeus and Athanasius and Augustine, all the way through to the Scholastics, such as Thomas Aquinas and Anselm and Peter Lombard, and to Reformers such as Martin Luther and John Calvin, and post-Reformation theologians such as John Owen and Baxter and Jonathan Edwards, down to modern theologians such as Karl Barth and Dietrich Bonhoeffer and Jürgen Moltmann and Wolfhart Pannenberg, and so on? What about geographically wide and historically deep scholarship, that is, the perspectives of African and Asian and liberation theologians in South America? And what about the perspectives of female scholars? It is the task of a serious theologian to seek harmony between the deep and wide tradition and the Scriptures on any subject, including that of the ascension, a task to which I will seek to be faithful.

---

[2] This mirrors the approach taken with regard to the resurrection of Jesus in W. Ross Hastings, *The Resurrection of Jesus Christ: Exploring Its Theological Significance and Ongoing Relevance* (Grand Rapids, MI: Baker Academic, 2022).

I come to this matter from a broadly "always reforming" or reenvisioning Reformed perspective, and my answer is that the Holy Scriptures are the *norma normans*, the norming norm of my theology. They are, as carefully interpreted, the *ultimate* authority in all matters of faith and practice. By *carefully*, I mean interpretation that is properly grammatical, historical, rhetorical, and genre aware; an interpretation guided by the immediate context; and an intratextual interpretation. That is, given the infallibility of all Scripture, interpretation operates on the basis that the interpretive context of any text is the entire Scripture, a hermeneutical principle of the Reformation called the analogy of faith.

However, if the study of the Scriptures must be our primary source and ultimate authority, it would be naive to assume we could study the Scriptures as mere individuals, apart from the tradition. The concept of *sola Scriptura* in the Reformers was not individualistic; it was not *nuda Scriptura*. Though not uncritically, they valued the insights of the Fathers and the Scholastics in their scholarship, seeking harmony between the major chord of Scripture and these minor chords of tradition. Similarly, in our day, we seek the harmony of the Scriptures as our norming norm (*norma normans*), taking seriously the normed norm (*norma normata*) of the writings of the doctors, scholars, and preachers of the church from the time of the apostles until now in the task of interpreting the Scriptures to affirm doctrines. We must pay attention to the hard work of the scholars of the church as they expressed divine truth at the ecumenical councils of the church—the Nicene Creed (AD 325), the Niceno-Constantinopolitan Creed (AD 381), the Apostles' Creed (mid-fifth century AD), the Athanasian Creed (late fifth or early sixth century AD), the Chalcedon Definition (AD 451), and so on. We can term all of these influences for our communal or ecclesial consultation *norma normata* (the normed norm). They are all subject to revision under the final authority of the Word of God; they are normed by Scripture.

Nevertheless, they are to be considered seriously and as weighty—the creeds especially hold an authority related to the fact that they were written and agreed on by church scholars at ecumenical councils as being reflective of Scripture. Could a creedal statement such as the one that governs my meditation in this book, "He ascended into heaven and is seated at the right hand of the Father," be changed if somehow a biblical text or texts were discovered to contradict it? The answer is a very low probability yes. However, the creeds and councils of the church and the writings of the doctors of the church are vital for our harmonious formulations of doctrine, and they will inform this study of the ascension, along with the Word of God.

BIBLICAL INTERPRETATION

This brings us to consideration specifically of the Scriptures concerning the ascension and their interpretation. Many texts in the New Testament refer to the ascension, and close scrutiny of these texts is a central concern for us. A critical exercise in interpreting these texts will be comparing the accounts of the various authors of the New Testament. That we should do so follows the conviction that all Scripture is God-breathed and that harmonizing the accounts of the ascension and the expressions of its meaning must be possible. Indeed, it is more than possible. It is fruitful.

What may come as a surprise is that the ascension of Christ is prefigured in several Old Testament passages. But this should not shock us, given that Christ, the living Word, is the integrative center of the written Word. The written revelation bears witness to God's personal revelation in Christ in both Testaments. Jesus bears witness to this in his sermon to the two on the road to Emmaus: "'Did not the Messiah have to suffer these things and then enter his glory?' And beginning with Moses and all the Prophets, he explained to them what was said in all the Scriptures concerning himself" (Lk 24:26-27). Christological interpretation does not mean we can ignore a text's original context and meaning. Typological, as opposed to allegorical, reading of the Old Testament values the grammatical-historical or historical-critical exegesis of a text and the authorial intent of the writer. Davies expresses this clearly when discussing Old Testament prefigurements. He acknowledges "that only those passages may be deemed relevant where the literal and historical sense, as far as it can be discovered, corresponds with and is not contradictory of the typological."[3] Typological reading is most safely validated by direct reference in the New Testament to the type as such, though the criterion that it honors the theological assertions of the New Testament may also be considered.

The prefiguring of the ascension in the Old Testament ought not to shock us for the further reason that one of the most important principles of biblical interpretation is the harmonious unity of the Old and New Testaments, a notion reaffirmed and referred to by some theologians as consistent with *intratextuality*. Postliberal theologian George Lindbeck coined this term to describe the interrelationality of the Scriptures.[4] He also coined the terms "biblical story" and "story-shaped church," which are used so frequently in evangelical theology in our time. Lindbeck draws on the cultural-linguistic assumption that cultural-linguistic systems always shape our interpretations of external reality. He affirms the place of Scripture as Christianity's "lexical core," thus making theology intratextual in the sense that it is ultimately Scripture that offers the normative account of reality in postliberal theology. Lindbeck's Yale colleague Hans Frei provided the key dynamic for understanding this intratextuality. While refusing the allegorism sometimes present in the Fathers as a means to unite the Testaments, Frei nevertheless validated typology, or "figuration," as the classical means of unifying the canon.[5] This was the accepted

---

[3] John G. Davies, *He Ascended into Heaven: A Study in the History of Doctrine*, Bampton Lectures (London: Lutterworth, 1958), 15-16.
[4] George A. Lindbeck, *The Nature of Doctrine: Religion and Theology in a Postliberal Age* (Philadelphia: Westminster, 1984), 136 and passim.
[5] Hans W. Frei, *The Eclipse of Biblical Narrative: A Study in Eighteenth and Nineteenth Century Hermeneutics* (New Haven, CT: Yale University Press, 1974), 2. The difference between

practice of the church in the precritical era before the eclipse of the biblical narrative in modernity. Postliberalism, by contrast, defined itself by refusing this reversal of precritical interpretive direction. Following suit, it is safe to say that the New Testament account and teaching concerning the ascension are illuminated by and must be in relation with the prefigurings of the Old Testament.

A principle governing the direction of interpretation in precritical hermeneutics was that present life should be incorporated into and understood in light of the biblical story, not vice versa. According to Frei, this was a feature of both the text as a realistic narrative and the concept of figuration. Since the unified narrative sequence depicted by Scripture belonged to the same temporal sequence as the present day, it was possible for the interpreter, and indeed was the interpreter's duty, "to fit himself into that world in which he was in any case a member." The means of doing this was precisely figuration: earlier biblical stories were seen as types or figures of later events without losing their own literal sense. The precritical interpreter, Frei insists, "was to see his disposition, his actions, and passions, the shape of his own life, as well as that of his era's events as figures of that storied world."[6] Crucial and central to the types and figures these theologians defended, and their whole theological movement, was the person and work of Jesus Christ.[7] Robert Barron, in applying postliberalism to Catholicism in a way that transcends the liberal/conservative and Protestant/Catholic divides, makes it clear that a focus on Christ creates such a possibility.[8]

---

allegorical interpretation and typology is not always clear. For a useful summary of the issues see Brent E. Parker, "The Differences Between Typology and Allegory," *Christ over All* (blog), September 7, 2023, https://christoverall.com/article/concise/the-differences-between-typology-and-allegory/. See also Richard M. Davidson, "The Eschatological Hermeneutic of Biblical Typology," *TheoRhēma* 6, no. 2 (2011): 5-48.

[6]Frei, *Eclipse of Biblical Narrative*, 3, 6.

[7]The influence of Barth's Christocentrism stays with these theologians, including Lindbeck, Frei, and Stanley Hauerwas.

[8]Robert Barron, *The Priority of Christ: Toward a Postliberal Catholicism* (Grand Rapids, MI: Baker, 2010).

In his book on the ascension of Jesus, Davies reflects a hermeneutical approach that predates but is similar to postliberal intratextuality and figuration, which he treats as synonymous with typology. Davies believes that the ascension is most definitely *prefigured* (rather than *predicted*) in the Old Testament. He affirms that "Christianity divorced from its roots in the Old Testament would cease to be Christianity" and that the "thought forms" of the New Testament cannot be penetrated apart from those of the Old Testament. In contrast to the allegorical approach of Augustine, however, Davies upholds a typological approach in which the literal and historical senses of Old Testament passages are preserved in their integrity, acknowledging that the text "corresponds with and is not contradictory of the typological."[9] In the first chapter of his book, Davies provides several examples of how the Old Testament prefigured this great event. We will refer to his work in both the Old Testament and the New Testament from time to time.

THEOLOGICAL INTERPRETATION

In addition to being biblical, the hermeneutical approach to this topic of the ascension will, as has already become apparent, also be theological. Authors such as R. W. L. Moberley, Francis Watson, Daniel Treier, Richard Hays, Joel Green, and Kevin Vanhoozer have recently offered expositions seeking to retrieve what theological interpretation means.[10] In his review of *The Dictionary for Theological Interpretation*

---

[9]Davies, *He Ascended into Heaven*, 13, 15-16.
[10]R. W. L. Moberly, "What Is Theological Interpretation of Scripture?," *JTI* 3, no. 2 (2009): 161-78; Francis Watson, "Theological Hermeneutics," in *Text, Church, and World: Biblical Interpretation in Theological Perspective*, ed. Francis Watson (Edinburgh: T&T Clark, 1994), 223-40; Daniel J. Treier, "Biblical Theology and/or Theological Interpretation of Scripture?," *SJT* 61, no. 1 (March 2008): 16-31; Richard B. Hays, "Reading the Bible with Eyes of Faith: The Practice of Theological Exegesis," *JTI* 1, no. 1 (2007): 5-21; Ellen F. Davis and Richard B. Hays, eds., *The Art of Reading Scripture* (Grand Rapids, MI: Eerdmans, 2003); Joel B. Green, "The (Re-)Turn to Theology," *JTI* 1, no. 1 (2007): 1-3; Kevin J. Vanhoozer, "What Is Theological Interpretation of the Bible?," in *Dictionary for Theological Interpretation of the Bible*, ed. Kevin J. Vanhoozer (Grand Rapids, MI: Baker Academic, 2005), 19-25.

of the Bible, Michael Gorman sums up the essence of this impulse by stating that the book, along with the *Journal of Theological Interpretation*, "gives voice to a growing sentiment among biblical scholars and theologians alike: a desire to explore and articulate ways of biblical interpretation that attend primarily to the biblical text as theological text, as a vehicle of divine revelation and address."[11]

This movement is rooted in and a retrieval of the ancient church's practice of using the rule of faith (also called the "rule of the truth") in interpreting Scripture. Indeed, prior to the completion of the canon of Scripture, a rule of faith (truth), referenced even as early as Irenaeus, not only guides interpretation but also becomes the basis on which books in their theological content are adjudged to be canonical.[12] Proponents of theological interpretation contended that biblical exegesis does not operate in a theological vacuum. Theology of a core, creedal kind is always at play as exegetes carry out their work. There need be no nervousness on the part of biblical scholars who may worry that core theological commitments threaten grammatical-historical interpretation, especially christological commitments, as if the latter might exercise hegemony over the former. In articulating the basic truths found in Christ and the apostles, Irenaeus employed Scripture extensively, including that from both Testaments.[13] The core of the matter is that grammatical-historical interpretation is surely not likely to overthrow the creed, and indeed, it plays a vital role that I would describe as iterative. Biblical scholarship that affirms Scripture as theologically revelatory and christologically centered, and the *consensus fidelium* (doctrines of the apostolic faith affirmed by the

---

[11] Michael J. Gorman, "A 'Seamless Garment' Approach to Biblical Interpretation?," *JTI* 1, no. 1 (2007): 117-28.

[12] Irenaeus, *The Demonstration of the Apostolic Preaching*, trans. J. Armitage Robinson and Iain M. MacKenzie (Burlington, VT: Ashgate, 2002), 3; Irenaeus, *Against Heresies* 1.10.4, 1.10.1 (*ANF* 1:330, 344). This was a succinct body of truth believed to have been handed down from the apostles. It was the core of trinitarian faith.

[13] See Thomas C. K. Ferguson, "The Rule of Truth and Irenaean Rhetoric in Book 1 of *Against Heresies*," *Vigiliae Christianae* 55, no. 4 (2001): 356-75.

historic church), must be in constant dynamic conversation. I hope this dynamic will be in evidence as we consider the doctrine of the ascension throughout this book.

As a subset of theological interpretation, and indeed its core, is the question of christological interpretation. To suggest that Christ is the center and fulcrum of biblical revelation and the source of Old Testament and New Testament harmony should go uncontested. There is ample evidence of this understanding in the tradition going back to the early church father Ignatius, the bishop of Antioch (d. ca. AD 140). When a Judaizing party challenged Ignatius's teaching concerning Jesus because it was not found in the Old Testament, Ignatius's counter was to argue that the only proper way of understanding the Jewish Scripture was to do so in light of Christ: "But to me Jesus Christ is in the place of all that is ancient: His cross, and death, and resurrection, and the faith which is by Him, are undefiled monuments of antiquity; by which I desire, through your prayers, to be justified."[14] Similar sentiments are expressed by Irenaeus of Lyons (AD 130–200/203) in his *Adversus Haereses*:

> If anyone, therefore, reads the Scriptures with attention, he will find in them an account of Christ and a foreshadowing of the new calling [*vocationis*]. For Christ is the treasure which was hid in the field, (Matthew 13:44) that is, in this world (for the field is the world Matthew 13:38); but the treasure hid in the Scriptures is Christ, since He was pointed out by means of types and parables.[15]

There are, however, forms of christological exegesis in the patristic tradition and in some contemporary church circles that verge on the fanciful and thereby give christological exegesis a bad name. Thus, authorized by Jesus' own hermeneutic in Luke 24, as mentioned above, and inspired by the theologians of the New Testament (especially the author of Hebrews) and the first generation of theologians after the

---

[14]Ignatius, "The Epistle of Ignatius to the Philadelphians" (*ANF* 1:84).
[15]Irenaeus, *Against Heresies* 4.26.1 (*ANF* 1:496).

apostles, it seems prudent to stand on a qualified version of christological interpretation that will enrich this study of the ascension. Historical-critical interpretation without the christological dynamic can lead to spiritual sterility; christological exegesis without the grounding of historical-critical interpretation and the corroboration of New Testament principles and precedent can lead to flights of fancy.

With a qualified theological, christological hermeneutic that is also respectful of historical-critical interpretation as the modus for this theological study of the ascension, *six* main areas of theological interest emerge surrounding the glorious event and person of the ascension. These are suggested by the biblical material and its interpretations in the tradition. They are as follows:

Christology, what the ascension reveals about the *person* of Jesus Christ. Who he is as the ascended Christ, that is, matters concerning his *being* (ontology), are of first-order concern in and of themselves but also for how they govern our thinking about atonement and salvation (soteriology). Here we will consider his essential glory as God, his glory veiled in the incarnation and unveiled in his ascension to glory.

Anthropology, what Jesus' ascension confirms and reveals about the nature of humanity and what it means to be human. For example, what does the presence of the divine-human person in the triune being of God have to say about the analogy or correspondence between divine and human personhood? Here we will also discuss the recapitulation of humanity in the last Adam and humanity in him, as he is exalted in kingly and priestly glory over all creation, fulfilling God's original purpose for humanity in its caring lordship over creation.

Soteriology, what the ascension reveals about the *work* of the ascended Christ, the atonement that he accomplished in his person (soteriology cannot be separated from ontology) and that is celebrated in his ascension, the salvation that he accomplished for his people whom he represents—the salvation that, in another sense, is ongoing and reliant on his functioning as a Priest at the right hand of God interceding for his people in "the power of an indestructible life" (Heb 7:16). This entails considering his functioning conjointly as prophet, priest, and king, sometimes called the *munus triplex*. It also invokes *pneumatology*, for it includes consideration of the coinherent work of the Holy Spirit, who descends once the Son ascends, in response to the ascension. The pastoral implications of this are considerable.

Ecclesiology, the question of the church's identity. Questions regarding what union with the ascended Christ means, and what the present status of the human-divine Christ in heaven means for the church's understanding of the Eucharist as real-presence-by-the Spirit during his real absence, flow out of consideration of the identity of Christ as revealed by the ascension.

Eschatology, what the ascension meant for the church and the coming of the kingdom of God. Issues that deserve attention include the eschatological reserve imposed by the ascension, the inaugurated and the future aspects of eschatology—the eschatological inbreaking flowing from the reign of Christ, manifested by the outpouring of the Spirit (pneumatology once again arises) and expressed in the mission of the church; and the anticipation of the second coming (parousia) of Christ contained in the ascension event.

Cosmology, as a study of Christ's ascension cannot ignore what the ascension means for our understanding of heaven and earth as well as heaven on earth—how the atonement of the Priest, his ascension, and his ongoing priesthood seem to assume that all is sacred space and anticipate redemption of the cosmos as God's temple.

The chapters of the book reflect these theological areas. In each case, biblical assertions will be the primary consideration, alongside theological reflections from the tradition past and present, all with an eye toward the glory of the ascension.

The glory theme of the book will develop along the following lines. First, the *essential glory* of the ascended Son as deity is celebrated. His visible, *regal glory*, relinquished at his incarnation, again becomes visible in his ascension. Second, the *salvific glory* accrued by Christ—through the saving work he accomplished in his person (soteriology cannot be separated from ontology), which is consummated and celebrated in his ascension and session—is celebrated. This salvation involves the glory of the atonement accomplished by his death and resurrection, and the atonement applied in Christ's ongoing priesthood. Although its aim is filial, the forensic aspects of the atonement are necessary, for he has, on behalf of the church, made a multifaceted sacrifice once for all (Heb 1:3; 9:14, 26; 10:10-14), bringing glory to God, his righteousness and justice. The once-for-all dimension of the atonement is coupled with the ongoing aspect of salvation, which is reliant on Christ's continued functioning as a priest at the right hand of God (Heb 9:24, "now to appear for us in God's presence") interceding for his people in "the power of an indestructible life" (Heb 7:16). This involves their justification, sanctification, ongoing confession and absolution, worship, comfort, prayers, and mission.

Third, we celebrate the *shared glory* imparted by the perpetually human Son to the church, the new humanity. This is filial, involving his bringing of sons and daughters to glory, which includes the reaffirmation of their co-dominion over creation (Heb 2). All creation will thus also share in his glory at the consummation. This leads to consideration of theological anthropology, the glory of the human; ecclesiology, the glory of the church; eschatology, the glory of the end; and cosmology, the glory of heaven come to earth, with all its mystery.

3

THE GLORY OF HIS DEITY

Ascension by the God of Iridescent Glory

THIS CHAPTER FOCUSES ON the distinctive yet much-neglected event of Christ's ascension and its significance for his *identity*. By looking at various biblical passages, it will address *ontological* matters related to the *being* of the person of the incarnate, resurrected, and ascended Christ, his deity and intrinsic glory in particular. Who does the ascension say he is?

Before embarking on discussion of this Christology of glory in the ascension, one final introductory matter must be considered in order to provide the context for this discussion. This has to do with the timing of the ascension.

THE TIMING OF THE ASCENSION

Some controversy has existed as to the timing of the ascension of Jesus. In Luke's account in Acts 1, which appears to be historical and literal, Jesus ascends forty days after the resurrection. His ascent physically in a human body into heaven is of critical theological importance. The historical, theological, and contemporary significance of the ascension is summed up eloquently by theologian-pastor John Stott in his commentary on Acts: "According to the New Testament gospel, however, he is historical (he really lived, died, rose and ascended in the arena of history), theological (his life, death, resurrection and ascension all have saving significance) and contemporary (he lives and reigns to bestow salvation on those who respond to him)."¹ A medical doctor is telling the story in Acts, conveyed with simplicity and without extravagance. Even liberal scholar Ernst Haenchen admits, "The story is unsentimental, almost uncannily austere."²

However, following the perceived Johannine order, J. G. Davies thinks that the ascension took place on the evening of resurrection Sunday, when Jesus told Martha, "I am ascending to my Father and your Father, to my God and your God" (Jn 20:17). All the postresurrection events where he was present after this were, on Davies's view, appearances of the already ascended Christ, who came back down from heaven for each postresurrection encounter.³ This would include the appearance to the ten (Jn 20:19-23), to Thomas (Jn 20:26-27), and to Peter and the disciples (Jn 21). Davies thinks that the forty-day period spoken of in Acts 1 is Luke's attempt to fit the story into the forty-day typology associated with the ascension of Elijah (and other forty-day events in the Old Testament and the life of Jesus). Luke's account, according to Davies, is therefore meant to be mythological or nonliteral.⁴

In my opinion, the opposite seems much more credible. If any of the Gospel writers is cryptic and metaphorical, is it not John? He says nothing of the institution of the Lord's Supper and instead gives us an inkling of it in Jesus' feeding of the five thousand with the most graphic description of the Eucharist in the New Testament following it. He says nothing of the church but gives us a vivid picture of it in John 20:19-23 when Jesus comes to stand amid his disciples to constitute and impart its missional nature. John's record of the statement by Jesus on resurrection morning to Mary, "I am ascending," is not

---

¹John R. W. Stott, *Acts: Seeing the Spirit at Work* (Downers Grove, IL: InterVarsity Press, 2008), 19.
²Ernst Haenchen, *The Acts of the Apostles: A Commentary*, trans. Bernard Noble, Gerald H. Shinn, and Robert M. Wilson (Louisville, KY: Westminster John Knox, 1971), 151.
³John G. Davies, *He Ascended into Heaven: A Study in the History of Doctrine*, Bampton Lectures (London: Lutterworth, 1958), 52-54.
⁴Davies, *He Ascended into Heaven*, 52-54.

intended by Jesus to be taken literally from a temporal perspective, I think. "I am ascending" could mean "I am on the way to ascending" or "my next move is ascension" without undue violation of the text. The admonition to Mary not to hold on to Jesus would be applicable throughout the whole time between the resurrection and the ascension. The nature of his risen body, already capable of transcending the physical realm, implies that holding him is inappropriate to that state and that phase of his ministry. Thomas may be permitted to touch his wounds but not hold him down.

In favor of the Lukan account, Paul in Acts 13:31 confirms that Jesus "for many days . . . was seen" by the disciples between the resurrection and the ascension. Contrary to Davies's opinion that these appearances referred to by Paul after resurrection Sunday were appearances of Christ from heaven, to which he had already ascended, it seems better to say he did not ascend until forty days after he rose.[5] The ascension event the disciples saw was the sign that there would be no more resurrection appearances.

Luke's plain account involves two main details of the ascension: that Jesus was "taken up" and that a cloud accompanied him in his ascension. First, the ascension is described in the passive, "taken up," signifying an action by the Father in heaven—his pleasure in the Son and all he has accomplished by his atoning life, death, and resurrection. Passages that reflect the active nature of the ascension on the part of Jesus suggest that he ascended as God of very God, in his own right, but the passive indicate that he was taken up as man, for humanity, by the Father.

Second, the presence of a cloud accompanying Jesus has great significance, both answering profound typological events before it, such as the Shekinah cloud hovering over the tabernacle, and anticipating the second coming after it. Davies comments that "the

---

[5]Davies, *He Ascended into Heaven*, 54. Haenchen actually proposes there were two ascensions, one on resurrection morning and one after forty days (*Acts of the Apostles*, 151).

cloud is not primarily a cloud of our atmosphere at all, but the cloud of the divine presence," which had rested on the tabernacle, the temple, and the transfiguration. Perhaps it was both a literal cloud and the sign of the divine presence and pleasure, but Davies is right when he ventures that "St. Luke, in fact, is affirming by the use of this imagery that the ascension was no more and no less than the entrance of Christ *into the divine glory*."[6]

After laying this brief historical groundwork and having expressed support for the historicity of the Lukan account and its compatibility with the Johannine intent, we may now contemplate what the ascension accounts of the Scriptures teach us about his being.

THE GLORY OF THE DEITY OF CHRIST: IRIDESCENT GLORY

This section explores the intrinsic, iridescent glory of the deity of the ascended Christ. I now apply the theological, christological, and typological interpretive principles outlined in the previous chapter to the Old and New Testament passages concerned with the ascension. The aim is to elucidate first what they say about the *identity* of the ascended one—his being (ontology is our focus). I will not do this in strict biblical sequence, from Old Testament to New Testament, but rather by gathering passages that relate to each aspect of his identity, with an eye toward the glory of the ascended one.

Several anticipatory Old Testament and descriptive New Testament passages teach us that the person who ascended is *God*. The Old Testament prefigures this in the case of two people who ascended—Enoch and Elijah—each described as having a close intimacy with God (Enoch "walked faithfully with God," Gen 5:22, 24; Elijah is called a "man of God," 2 Kings 1:11-13, and is a close confidant of God in his life and prophetic ministry) and consequent moral uprightness. They escape Sheol and ascend into the direct presence of God ("raised

---

[6]Davies, *He Ascended into Heaven*, 57, emphasis added.

to the society of God") as a result.[7] Davies believes they are "prefigurative of the lot of the truly righteous individual" and are a "*legitimate type of Him who knew no sin.*"[8] The word in Hebrew for "took" in Genesis 5:24 is *laqah*. This word is repeated in the case of Elijah in 2 Kings 2:11. Davies suggests that Enoch's ascent is in mind in Psalms 49:15; 73:24, both of which generalize the primal ascent of Enoch for the psalmist and the godly. Psalm 49:15 states, "But God will redeem me from the realm of the dead; he will surely *take* me to himself." Psalm 73:24 states, "You guide me with your counsel, and afterward you will *take* me into glory." Interestingly, New Testament or patristic authors never use these two psalms to refer to the ascension. The ascensions of Enoch, Elijah, and those anticipated by these psalms can therefore only at best be considered to be suggestive of the ascension of Jesus (and the people of his church). That the majority of the texts in the New Testament use the analogous word in Greek, in the passive voice, to describe how Jesus in his ascension was "taken up" does provide some evidence of Jesus as the antetype, as well as that he merited the ascension by his impeccable life in the closest intimacy possible between himself and his Father, an impeccability and intimacy possible only for a person who is God.

However, the writings of the tradition frequently cite four psalms as referring to the ascension of Jesus, and all strongly ascribe deity to the one ascending. These psalms, in the order in which we shall consider them, are Psalms 47; 24; 68; 110. Although their content far transcends this, all four have been associated with an Israelite New Year Festival based on the narrative of the return of the ark of the covenant to Jerusalem by David, as described in 2 Samuel 6. The festival contained four movements:

> A procession which ascended the hill of Zion and escorted both the ark of Yahweh and the Davidic king into the temple precincts. Second,

---

[7]Davies, *He Ascended into Heaven*, 17.
[8]Davies, *He Ascended into Heaven*, 18, emphasis added.

a ritual combat which re-enacted the triumph of Yahweh and his anointed representative over the forces of death and chaos. Next, the re-enthronement of Yahweh as King and of the contemporary ruler and, finally, the sacred marriage.[9]

In the first of these psalms, the divine identity of the ascending one is unequivocal:

Psalm 47:5-9.
God has ascended amid shouts of joy,
    the LORD amid the sounding of trumpets.
Sing praises to God, sing praises;
    sing praises to our King, sing praises.
For *God is the King* of all the earth;
    sing to him a psalm of praise.
God reigns over the nations;
    God is seated on his holy throne.
The nobles of the nations assemble
    as the people of the God of Abraham,
for the kings of the earth belong to God;
    he is greatly exalted.

This psalm anticipates the one who is the antetype of the ark, the one who is also David's son and the fulfiller of the Davidic covenant. However, to fulfill the sentiments of this psalm, it must be God himself who ascends. The only one who qualifies for this ascension is the one who does not merely fulfill the messianic kingly sonship (Ps 2:7) but is the eternal Son of the Father, Yahweh (along with the Father and the Spirit). This psalm anticipates that when the Son ascends, it is God who is ascending, for he is nothing short of full deity. Old Testament scholars have for centuries spoken of this psalm as an ascension psalm. For example, Old Testament scholars C. F. Keil and Franz Delitzsch confirm the association of this psalm with the ascension when they state, "The ascent of God presupposes a previous

---
[9]Davies, *He Ascended into Heaven*, 19-20.

descent."[10] Delitzsch is referring to the Pauline reference to the ascension of Christ: "What does 'he ascended' mean except that he also descended" (Eph 4:9). We may conclude that the eternal glory of the Son was not visible when he became incarnate, but when he ascended, this visibility was restored in heaven. He never lost his deity, but his glory was veiled on earth until that glorious moment when he ascended on high.

> *Psalm 24:3-4, 7-10.*
> Who may ascend the mountain of the LORD?
>   Who may stand in his holy place?
> The one who has clean hands and a pure heart,
>   who does not trust in an idol
>   or swear by a false god. . . .
> Lift up your heads, you gates;
>   be lifted up, you ancient doors,
>   that the King of glory may come in.
> Who is this *King of glory*?
>   *The* LORD *strong and mighty,*
>   *the* LORD *mighty in battle.*
> Lift up your heads, you gates;
>   lift them up, you ancient doors,
>   that the King of glory may come in.
> Who is he, this King of *glory*?
>   The LORD Almighty—
>   he is the King of glory.

This psalm has been associated with the ascension for centuries and most famously found its way into Handel's remarkable musical expression of the saving history of Jesus in *The Messiah*. There is good reason for this association.[11] The already-mentioned theme about

---

[10]C. F. Keil and Franz Delitzsch, *Commentary on the Old Testament: Psalms* (Grand Rapids, MI: Eerdmans, 1971), 341. See also Derek Kidner, *Psalms*, Tyndale Old Testament Commentaries 15 (Downers Grove, IL: InterVarsity Press, 2014), 195-96.

[11]See Kidner, *Psalms*, 130-31.

someone meriting the ascension by his holiness recurs here in Psalm 24. We may observe three primary themes in this psalm that find their fulfillment in the ascended Christ of the New Testament. The first is the vicarious *human* holiness of the one who ascends (Ps 24:3-4). So, the one ascending is fully human. The only human person with clean hands and a pure heart was Jesus, and we may, based on the vicarious nature of the humanity of Jesus, assume that he was holy *for us*. The second theme is the *deity* of the one who ascends. He is "the LORD strong and mighty . . . the LORD Almighty" (Ps 24:8, 10). The one ascending is none other than Yahweh. And third, notice the triumphant (Ps 24:5, 7) and glorious *kingship* (Ps 24:7-12) of the one who ascends. This psalm emphasizes the kingly nature of the ascended one, which may have influenced T. F. Torrance to declare that, in the *triplex munus,* the designation *King* takes priority.[12] It also gives further evidence of the centrality of the theme of glory in the ascension. He is the King of glory.

The sentiments of this psalm evoke our worship, and one verse of Charles Wesley's hymn "Hail the Day That Sees Him Rise" gives an apt expression of this:

> There for him, high triumph waits; alleluia!
> *Lift your heads*, eternal gates; alleluia!
> He hath conquered death and sin; alleluia!
> *Take the King of glory in.* Alleluia![13]

Psalm 68:15-18.
Mount Bashan, majestic mountain,
    Mount Bashan, rugged mountain,
Why gaze in envy, you rugged mountain,
    At the mountain where God chooses to reign,
    Where the LORD himself will dwell forever?

---

[12] T. F. Torrance, *Space, Time, and Resurrection* (Grand Rapids, MI: Eerdmans, 1976), 106.
[13] Charles Wesley, "Hail the Day That Sees Him Rise," Hymnary.org, accessed June 21, 2024, https://hymnary.org/hymn/CP1998/247.

> The chariots of God are tens of thousands
> and thousands of thousands;
> the LORD has come from Sinai into his sanctuary.
> When you ascended on high,
> you took many captives;
> you received gifts from people,
> even from the rebellious—
> that you, LORD God, might dwell there.

Paul applies Psalm 65:18 to the ascension in Ephesians 4:7-10.

> But to each one of us grace has been given as Christ apportioned it. This is why it says:
>
> "When he ascended on high,
> he took many captives
> and gave gifts to his people."
>
> (What does "he ascended" mean except that he also descended to the lower, earthly regions? He who descended is the very one who ascended higher than all the heavens, in order to fill the whole universe.)

The most obvious conclusion we may ascertain from Paul's freedom to use what was a reference to the ascension of God the Lord (Ps 68:16-18) for the ascension of Jesus is that he considered Jesus to be God. We may well ask what gives Paul the authority to change "received gifts" (passive) in Psalm 68:18 to "gave gifts" (active) in Ephesians 4:8. The answer is that the word in Hebrew for "receive" (*laqah*) has a semantic range that includes both receiving and giving.[14] The meaning could even be "to receive in order to give." In other words, we might say Christ received the spoils from the battle of his atoning work and now dispenses these to his people from heaven.

Psalm 2:1-8.

> Why do the nations conspire
> and the peoples plot in vain?

---

[14]Davies, *He Ascended into Heaven*, 62-63, 108.

> The kings of the earth rise up
>> and the rulers band together
>> against the LORD and against his anointed, saying,
> "Let us break their chains
>> and throw off their shackles."
> The One enthroned in heaven laughs;
>> the Lord scoffs at them.
> He rebukes them in his anger
>> and terrifies them in his wrath, saying,
> "I have installed my king
>> on Zion, my holy mountain."
> I will proclaim the LORD's decree:
> He said to me, "You are my son;
>> today I have become your father.
> Ask me,
>> and I will make the nations your inheritance,
>> the ends of the earth your possession."

This psalm embodies the hope of Israel that one day an extraordinary person of destiny would, by the grace of God, fully redeem God's promises to David (2 Sam 7; Ps 89). What was not altogether clear to Israel then was that the Son depicted in this psalm would be not just the son of David but the Son of God in a profoundly ontological sense. This becomes clear in the context in which Psalm 2:7 is quoted by the writer of Hebrews (Heb 1:5) in a chapter devoted to demonstrating the deity of the Son. In an antecedent verse (Heb 1:3), he speaks of the "Son" in that passage as the same person who is "the radiance of God's glory and the exact representation of his being, sustaining all things by his powerful word," ascriptions that can legitimately be made only to a person who is God. And in the succeeding context, the writer urges all of God's angels to worship him, an act reserved for God alone (Heb 1:6). In Hebrews 2, the writer will tell us that Jesus was, in his humanity, made lower than the angels for the salvation and comfort of humanity. However, in Hebrews 1, the key emphasis is that he was and is eternally God and that his ascension demonstrated that he was much higher than the angels. As R. C. Chapman writes, "Christ twice passed the angels by. He sank far below them in His humiliation; He rose far above them in His exaltation."[15] Then, removing all doubt about who the Son of Psalm 2:7 is, in Hebrews 1:8 the writer quotes Psalm 45:6-7, applying it directly to Jesus: "But about the Son, he says, 'Your throne, *O God*, will last for ever and ever.'" In the flow of thought of Hebrews 1, the entry of Jesus, who is God, into the office of the king, as pronounced in Hebrews 1:8, is actually on the occasion of his ascension, as Hebrews 1:3 indicates: "After he had provided purification for sins, he *sat down* at the right hand of the Majesty in heaven." He ascended as God of very God.

Daniel 7:9, 13-14. Moving from the Psalms to the writings of a prophet, we find Daniel 7:9, 13-14 describing a vision of God, the "Ancient of Days," in which coming world powers threaten to eliminate the covenantal people of God. These powers must bow to the sovereign majesty of the Ancient of Days and his Son, described here as "one like a son of man, coming with the clouds of heaven."

> As I looked,
>
> thrones were set in place,
>   and the *Ancient of Days* took his seat.
> His clothing was as white as snow;
>   the hair of his head was white like wool.
> His throne was flaming with fire,
>   and its wheels were all ablaze. . . .
>
> In my vision at night I looked, and there before me was one *like a son of man, coming with the clouds of heaven*. He approached the Ancient of Days and was *led into his presence*. He was given authority, glory and sovereign power; all nations and peoples of every language worshiped

---

[15]Frank Holmes, "A Selection of 'Choice Sayings' of Robert Cleaver Chapman," Plymouth Brethren Writings, accessed June 21, 2024, https://plymouthbrethren.org/article/6376.

him. His dominion is an everlasting dominion that will not pass away, and his kingdom is one that will never be destroyed.

A few observations from this magnificent vision, as seen in the light of other related passages in the New Testament, point inevitably to the deity of the "one like a son of man," who comes "with the clouds of heaven," and who "approached the Ancient of Days and was led into his presence." What draws us to this conclusion is first that the description of God in Daniel 7:9 bears a striking resemblance to another description of the Son of God, in Revelation 1:13-14: "And among the lampstands was someone like a son of man, dressed in a robe reaching down to his feet and with a golden sash around his chest. The hair on his head was white like wool, as white as snow, and his eyes were like blazing fire" (see also Rev 4:3, 9-11; 19:12).

Second, the phrase "the coming with the clouds of heaven" is quoted almost verbatim in Mark 14:62, when Jesus is speaking of his own ascended state. "'I am,' said Jesus. 'And you will see the Son of Man sitting at the right hand of the Mighty One and coming on the clouds of heaven.'" These words of Jesus certainly echo those of Daniel 7, and the meaning of the title "Son of Man" here in Mark 14 is interpreted by the high priest as a claim to deity, for he tore his clothes having heard what he believed to be blasphemy in light of the undifferentiated monotheism of his Jewish faith (Deut 6:4).

Revelation 1:6, a text of effulgent praise for the "glory and power" of the one "who loves us and has freed us from our sins by his blood, and has made us to be a kingdom and priests to serve his God and Father," uses the "coming with clouds" language again, this time about the second coming. It alludes directly to Daniel 7 and Zechariah 12:10. Jesus' exalted state at the second coming has been true since he ascended. Revelation 14:14, by contrast, refers to the "son of man" reigning now (just as in Dan 7) and doing so as "seated on a cloud."

Third, the universal authority conferred on the "son of man" in Daniel 7:14 is reminiscent of Psalm 110:1 ("The LORD says to my lord:

'Sit at my right hand until I make your enemies a footstool for your feet'"), Isaiah 9:6-7 ("For to us a child is born, to us a son is given, and the government will be on his shoulders. . . . Of the greatness of his government and peace there will be no end"), and Revelation 11:15 ("The seventh angel sounded his trumpet, and there were loud voices in heaven, which said: 'The kingdom of the world has become the kingdom of our Lord and of his Messiah, and he will reign for ever and ever'"). This authority can reside only in a man who is God.

Fourth, Revelation 5:11-13 portrays the worshipers of the ascended, exalted Son in similar terms to Daniel:

> Then I looked and heard the voice of many angels, numbering thousands upon thousands, and ten thousand times ten thousand. They encircled the throne and the living creatures and the elders. In a loud voice they were saying:
>
> "Worthy is the Lamb, who was slain,
>   to receive power and wealth and wisdom and strength
>   and honor and glory and praise!"
>
> Then I heard every creature in heaven and on earth and under the earth and on the sea, and all that is in them, saying:
>
> "To him who sits on the throne and to the Lamb
>   be praise and honor and glory and power,
> for ever and ever!"

Finally, the title "Son of Man," which Jesus uses, is not just an indication of his humanity but is primarily a title that, in light of Daniel 7 and its canonical interpretation, communicates his cosmic rule, his majesty, and thus his deity.

In addition to Old Testament *prefigurings*, there are several New Testament *affirmations and inferences* of the deity of the ascended Christ. In his Gospel account of the ascension, Luke sets the tone by inference, "Did not the Messiah have to suffer these things and then enter his *glory*?" (Lk 24:26).

Pauline affirmations. Paul, in his great christological hymn in Philippians 2, signals that the one who has been highly exalted by the ascension receives a "name that is above every name" (Phil 2:9). Only God can have a name above which there is none higher. In addition, Paul adds, "every knee should bow" (Phil 2:10) before this exalted one. Since humans are to bow down to no one except God, the exalted one must be God of very God. Further, every tongue is to confess, presumably at the second coming, that he is "Lord." In light of the background of this text in Isaiah 45:23, where it refers to Yahweh, this must be God we are talking about. But to what end is this universal acclamation of the Son as God? "The glory of God the Father" (Phil 2:11) is how Paul ends this great christological hymn. This is an answer to the Son's desire expressed in the first breath of his high-priestly prayer: "Glorify your Son, that your Son may glorify you" (Jn 17:1). The ascended one, we may safely say, is God of very God, and from him emanates the magnificence of the glory of God, the glory of the Father in him, and the answering glory of the Son in the Father.

Paul further testifies to the divine, regal glory that had physically blinded and spiritually awakened him in his encounter with the ascended Jesus on the road to Damascus. In 2 Corinthians 4, no doubt recalling that experience, he speaks of "the glory of Christ, who is the image of God" (2 Cor 4:4), and of the light that awakens benighted sinners so that they can see "God's glory displayed in the face of Christ" (2 Cor 4:6). In Colossians 3, where Paul makes a direct reference to the session of Jesus at "the right hand of God" (Col 3:1), he describes this realm into which every person who participates in Christ's life will enter by the phrase "in glory" (Col 3:4). No one sits at the right hand of God unless he is God. There the Son irradiates with the glory of one who is God.

Affirmations of the writer of Hebrews. This author is especially anxious to describe the Son as God in Hebrews 1. In the center of the seven great phrases that describe him are these two: "The Son is the *radiance of God's glory* and the exact representation of his being" (Heb 1:3). The exalted Son does not merely reflect divine glory; he radiates it from his essence as God. As such, his essence is shared with the Father, since he is the Father's "exact representation." These statements by the writer are in harmony with the church's later affirmation that the Father, the Son, and the Spirit are one in essence (*ousia*) while distinct in person (*hypostasis*). The "one in essence" is the emphasis here and is the basis for saying that the Son is the radiance of God's glory. The Son possessed this deity and glory for all eternity; it was veiled in his incarnate state on earth and once again unveiled in heaven following his ascension.

Johannine affirmations. John may be described above all others as the theologian of glory. In the opening chapter of his Gospel, he declares, "The Word became flesh and made his dwelling among us. We have *seen his glory*, the *glory* of the one and only Son, who came from the Father, full of grace and truth" (Jn 1:14). Where had he seen evidence of such divine glory in the only begotten Son? No doubt, the moral glory of Jesus had been seen throughout his life. But the regal, divine glory had been hidden until John (and James and Peter) saw it at the transfiguration. Peter confirms that this event was all about glory: "He received honor and *glory* from God the Father when the voice came to him from the *Majestic Glory*, saying, 'This is my Son, whom I love; with him I am well pleased'" (2 Pet 1:17). There is a connection between the transfiguration and the ascension. Apart from the transfiguration involving an ascent, it was characterized by the presence of a cloud, just as the ascension was. Tabernacle, temple, transfiguration, ascension, and parousia all involve a cloud. Therefore, we may, with some assurance, say that what the three apostles saw by way of glory on the Mount of Transfiguration, they understood to be the case for the ascension. The glory of the only begotten to which John refers is spoken of at the transfiguration: "This is my Son, whom I love; with him I am well pleased" (Mt 17:5). We do not have Scripture to confirm this, but it seems logical to assume that as Jesus ascended, he heard these words again.

Jesus' way of expressing the ascension in John's Gospel (Jn 14:12, 28) is to speak of it as "going to the Father." This is in the context in which Jesus indicates that he is in the Father and the Father in him perpetually, even while in his incarnate, kenotic state on earth (Jn 14:9). In response to Philip's desire to see the Father, Jesus answers, "Don't you believe that *I am in the Father, and that the Father is in me*?" (Jn 14:10).

Therefore, the Son's "going to the Father" would not make him something he was not already eternally before his incarnation and during his time on earth. Rather, it would be a public manifestation of who he had always been, first in heaven and then at the second coming on earth. His speaking of his "going to the Father" is in the context in which Jesus is anticipating his imminent ascension and the subsequent sending of the Spirit. In John 14:20, John records that Jesus said, "On that day you will realize *that I am in my Father*, and you are in me, and I am in you" (see also Jn 16:28). Jesus' ascension is his return to the Father's immediate presence in heaven, and by the Spirit the disciples will *realize* that he is eternally in union with the Father ("I am in my Father").[16] This reality will be made manifest by his ascension.

Further, the ascension reveals that this manifest union between the Father and the Son—*a glorified human* and our representative before the Father—is the basis of the union of all believers with God.[17] Jesus assumed their human nature and carried it with him into the fellowship of the triune Godhead. "You are in me" implies that he has assumed humanity at the incarnation so that the disciples might be

---

[16] John Gill (1746–1763) writes, "in his bosom, in union with him, partaker of the same nature, perfections, and glory with him, and equal to him." Gill, *Exposition of the Entire Bible: New Testament* (Springfield, MO: Particular Baptist Press, 2003), 478.

[17] Gill again states, "And you in me: that they were in union with him as the branches in the vine, and as the members are in the head, and how they were loved in him, chosen in him, righteous in him, risen with him, and made to sit together in heavenly places in him" (Gill, *Exposition of the Entire Bible*, 478).

in union with him, and "I am in you" anticipates the coming of the Spirit to establish that union subjectively. The Spirit, by his new and permanent indwelling (Jn 14:17) of them, will mediate the presence of Jesus to them by coinherence. Christ will be in heaven as the human-divine Son of God with a ubiquitous divine nature but a humanity that is limited to heaven (Calvin).[18] Yet, his real presence will be in every regenerated human person by the Holy Spirit. In the Eucharist, too, though the bread remains bread, and wine remains wine, Christ is there by the Spirit so that the people of God can feed on him spiritually and find themselves caught up afresh into his ascended presence.

The homoousion. Drawing the discussion of the deity of the ascended one to a climax, we may speak of the great Athanasian word *homoousion*. This term is used for the three persons of the Trinity who share eternally the divine *ousia*, or essence, of God. However, this is the glory of the gospel of God, who is for humanity, and it is also used to show how the Son, who is God, entered into union with humanity by the incarnation. Speaking of the *homoousion* relationship within God and between God and humanity in Christ, Douglas Farrow speaks of the impossibility of narrating the inner, hidden, divine part of the story of redemption: "There is no story to be told, in Arian fashion, of a first and best creature setting out on a mission to the lower reaches of the cosmos. There is only God himself, God the Son, who, by the power of the Spirit appears in our midst as a man, and yet remains, even as he does so, God in the heights as well as God in the depths."[19] This is especially true of his ascension. Just as we cannot see or know what happened in the hidden depths of the incarnation event, neither can we know it fully in the ascension event. Farrow follows up by asserting that this is all in keeping with the "protagonist of the narrative portion" of the second article of the creed.

---

[18]John Calvin, "Last Admonition to Joachim Westphal," (1557) in *Tracts: Part 2*, ed. and trans. Henry Beveridge, *Selected Works of John Calvin: Tracts and Letters* (Grand Rapids, MI: Baker, 1983), 2:382.

[19]Douglas Farrow, *Ascension Theology* (London: T&T Clark, 2011), 148.

Here he emphasizes that Christ's nature as God, along with his humanity, is crucial in the ascension and has salvific power in raising humanity to its destiny within the very life of God. That is to say, as a result of the ascension of humanity in God,

> Man is no longer man by himself or for himself, as he had made it his ambition to be. He is once again, but this time much more fundamentally and indeed, irrevocably, man with and for God. Since God has invested himself in man, man is no longer merely man, with his own creaturely interests and responsibilities under God. Man is now an internal communicant in the very life of God, for God has made himself internally communicant in the life of man.[20]

At one point, Farrow seems to contradict the idea that he ascended as God: "The ascension of Jesus Christ is not the return of God to God. It is the ascension of the God-man to his rightful place, the place of glory, that Adam and Eve never knew, but are yet destined to know."[21] It is safe to assume that Farrow means that since the Son of God was always in complete and mutual communion with the Father even while on earth, his ascension as God was not really an ascension. While the emphasis of the ascension event is on his humanity, as Farrow suggests here, Jesus is nevertheless a divine person in divine-human oneness, making it difficult to miss altogether the Godness of the Son as he ascends. Only a man who is God, fully God, can ascend into the presence of God without cleansing. Only the Son of God, who has become human for us, can take us with him into that divine presence to sit on the divine throne.

What is being honored by the ascension and session of the Son is indeed the completion of the Son's work that his Father gave him to

---

[20]Farrow, *Ascension Theology*, 149. African theologian Mercy A. Oduyoye brings out the consequences of the life of Trinity for that of the church when she states, "The divine economy (oikonomia, the way God operates) ought to be approximated in human relations." Mercy A. Oduyoye, *Hearing and Knowing: Theological Reflections on Christianity in Africa* (Ossining, NY: Orbis, 1986), 139.

[21]Farrow, *Ascension Theology*, 150.

do in eternity past. There is surely a place for honoring the Second Person of the Trinity, who alone became flesh and died. He is surely honored in the communion of the Trinity as he ascends and sits, hearing the Father's delight and the Spirit's acclaim. The Father's assurance prior to the cross that he would glorify the Son must surely have this elevation and session of the Son as its answer. It was as God, in the presence of God, that one aspect of the atonement was ratified. Christ offered himself without spot to the triune God, of whom he is a coinherent person. It makes perfect sense that his ascension was as the God-*Man* for humanity, but it was simultaneously an ascension as the *God*-Man offering his completed work to the Father by the Spirit. One clear message of the ascension event is that the identity of Jesus is both fully human and emphatically divine.

4

GLORY CONCEALED, GLORY REVEALED

CONTINUING THE FOCUS ON Christology in the ascension, this chapter focuses not on the deity of the ascended one but on his *humanity*, on how the Son's glory, veiled at the incarnation, was unveiled in the ascension. This will lead to development of the themes of the glory of Christ the anointed one in his offices as prophet, priest, and king in chapter five.

REGAL GLORY CONCEALED AND REVEALED: INCARNATION-ASCENSION SYMMETRY

If the ascension is accomplished by a person who is intrinsically God, it is emphatically an event that exalts him as *man*, so that, as the God-Man, he once again reveals the glory that accompanies deity. The ascension brings symmetry to the story of Jesus: his exaltation is the reversal of his humiliation. Although the glory of God was revealed and acknowledged remarkably by what transpired at the birth of Jesus—hear the angelic choir in Luke 2:14, "Glory to God in the highest, and on earth peace to those on whom his favor rests"—the personal glory of the divine Son was actually veiled in his incarnate state on earth. At the ascension, it was unveiled. The ascension was the occasion of the return of the Son to a state in which he irradiated the visible divine glory, that which he had in his pre-incarnate deity, as expressed by his own words in John 17:5: "And now, Father, glorify me in your presence with the glory I had with you before the world began." What is new about his state in ascension is that this divine glory is manifested in his now perpetually incarnate-but-exalted state as the God-Man in heaven. He always possessed full divine glory, even as the humble, incarnate Jesus, but that regal glory was mostly not visible when he was on earth. He perpetually reflected a *moral* glory visible for those with eyes to see, but mostly the regal, divine glory was not seen.

Glory may be defined as the outshining of inward excellence. As such, this was veiled in the incarnate Christ, as Paul's poem in Philippians 2:6-8 suggests: "Who, being in very *nature* God, did not consider equality with God something to be used to his own advantage; rather, he *made himself nothing* [emptied himself] by taking the very *nature* of a servant, being made in human likeness. And being found in appearance as a man, he humbled himself by becoming obedient to death—even death on a cross!" The nature of the emptying these verses portray ("he made himself nothing" is literally "he emptied himself," employing the Greek verb *ekenōsen*, from which the term *kenosis* has arisen in English theological parlance) is decidedly *not* an emptying of deity. Kenosis, in other words, is not ontological but has to do with the outshining of his inward deity. The state in which his divine glory is veiled on earth is a mode of being for Christ, not his essence.[1] The term *nature* (*morphē*) in this passage refers to his being as God *and* his being a servant, as if to say that his becoming a servant was not contrary to his being God. It is crucial to revelation that in his humanity, the Son is still God, for as Athanasius taught us, only God can reveal God. Or, as Torrance said, "Nothing else will suffice for a revelation of God than God Himself."[2] The forceful message of the text is rather to say that the kind of God that God is, is a servant God. A

---

[1] See Gottfried Thomasius, "Christ's Person and Work. Part II: The Person of the Mediator," in *God and Incarnation in Mid-nineteenth Century German Theology*, ed. Claude Welch, A Library of Protestant Thought (New York: Oxford University Press, 1965), 48-50.

[2] Cited in Alister E. McGrath, *T. F. Torrance: An Intellectual Biography* (Edinburgh: T&T Clark, 2006), 148.

God of intratrinitarian mutual love reflected in extratrinitarian love for humanity.

In emptying himself to become fully human, it was his glory, not his intrinsic deity, that the Son laid aside.[3] In becoming a servant, he did not cease to be God, since Godhood and servanthood are not incompatible. It was his visible, effulgent glory as God that was veiled, not his essential Godness. "Veiled in flesh the Godhead see" are the apt words of Charles Wesley describing the incarnation in his carol "Hark the Herald Angels Sing."[4] In his time here, Jesus was, as Louis Berkhof says, the "divine incognito," which was removed when he arose and ascended.[5] If you bumped into Jesus when he was here on earth, you wouldn't know by his appearance that he was God. The disciples are given one glimpse of his glory on the Mount of Transfiguration, but it was only a glimpse. Most of the time if you looked at Jesus, you wouldn't know he was God, because his glory was veiled.

German Lutheran Gottfried Thomasius (1802–1875) speaks of this kenosis of glory, but he associates this not just with a veiling of glory but with the loss of the use by Jesus of the relative divine attributes of omniscience, omnipresence, and omnipotence, while retaining the essential attributes. This, however, runs contrary to the prevailing sentiments of the tradition.[6] The Son, though fully present in located human form, is not as to his deity circumscribed by his humanity. Thus he did not lay aside his intrinsic deity in any sense. The only kenosis is with respect to the *visibility* of his deity, that is, his *glory*, which is veiled from his incarnation until his ascension.

---

[3] This is not the only way New Testament scholars have interpreted this text. For a summary of views, see Lynn Cohick, *Philippians*, Story of God Bible Commentary (Grand Rapids, MI: Zondervan Academic, 2013), 108-10. The glory approach seems to account best for all the exegetical data and go with conciliar theology.
[4] Charles Wesley, "Hark! The Herald Angels Sing," Hymnary.org, accessed June 24, 2024, https://hymnary.org/text/hark_the_herald_angels_sing_glory_to.
[5] Louis Berkhof, *Systematic Theology* (Louisville, KY: GLH, 2017), 292.
[6] See Athanasius, e.g., *The Incarnation of the Word* 3.17, Christian Classics Ethereal Library, www.ccel.org/ccel/athanasius/incarnation.iv.html.

Jesus received that glory again, the glory he asked his Father for in John 17:5, when his earthly journey was over, his mission was accomplished, and the Father raised and exalted him to his right hand. Peter Atkins describes the ascension as "the other end of Incarnation doctrine."[7] This means that the incarnation continues, and we, as believing humans in Christ, can enter God's life. Gerrit Dawson argues that this is "the essential meaning of the ascension." He explains, "The fully human one has gone within the veil in our name and even in our skin. United to him by the Spirit, to the one who remains united to us, we may follow where he has gone."[8]

The essence of the gospel, of the ascension, is that glory is ascribed to someone who is not only God of very God but someone who, since the incarnation and after the ascension, is perpetually human. Karl Barth insists that the Son of God perpetually maintains our humanity "to all eternity. . . . It is clothing which he does not put off. It is his Temple which he does not leave. It is the form He does not lose."[9] Here Barth is faithfully reflecting the church fathers, who understood that if the one who sits at God's right hand for us were not perpetually and fully human as well as divine, then humans in Christ would not be able to perpetually enter the holy of holies and be seated with him in heavenly places, in prayer now and fully at the parousia. In Barth's paragraph "The Homecoming of the Son of Man," he describes many of the nuances associated with the mystery of the hiddenness and revealedness of the ascension. At one point he states, "In his identity with the Son of God, when he was lifted up into heaven, He was not deified, or assumed into the Godhead (for this was unnecessary for him as the Son of God and impossible for him as the Son of Man), but placed

---

[7]Peter Atkins, *Ascension Now: Implications of Christ's Ascension for Today's Church* (Collegeville, MN: Liturgical Press, 2001), 71.
[8]Gerrit S. Dawson, *Jesus Ascended: The Meaning of Christ's Continuing Incarnation* (Phillipsburg, NJ: P&R, 2004), 7.
[9]Karl Barth, *Church Dogmatics*, ed. G. W. Bromiley and Thomas F. Torrance, trans. G. W. Bromiley (London: T&T Clark, 2009), IV/2, 101.

as man at the side of God, in direct fellowship with Him, in *full participation in His glory*."[10]

One might quibble over Barth's assertion that Christ's humanity did not require deification.[11] Christ's body requires deification not because it is sinful—that is, not for moral reasons—but for metaphysical reasons. His resurrection body was already deified in that sense. He remained truly human in resurrection and ascension, but his humanity had capacities that could be attributed to deification. It was, as Paul might say, a "spiritual body," a body corresponding to the "heavenly man" (1 Cor 15:44, 48). For one thing, that body was now incorruptible, which could not be said of his preresurrection body. This aside, Barth's idea of a man who is perpetually man at the right hand of God "in full participation in the glory of God" captures the essence of the ascension as the reversal of the incarnation in its glory-emptying perspective. It is the beginning of the mediating ministry of Christ in the perpetuity of his humanity *for us*, in the presence of the Godhead. What Barth wishes to stress is that in the event of the ascension, "his divine Sonship was also revealed, but it was *the divine Sonship of this man, this man as the Son of God*."[12] He came from his death and resurrection, and it was "in his coming from the place, from which none other has ever come, that they knew him as the One he was, and is, as the exalted Son of Man and

---

[10]Barth, *Church Dogmatics* IV/2, 153, emphasis added.

[11]This is unsurprising given that the Reformed tradition as a whole has shown a certain squeamishness about theosis or deification of the Christian (let alone Christ), preferring the term *sanctification*, and the inclusion of both justification and sanctification as graces flowing from union with Christ. In the broader tradition, deification does not mean that humans become God but rather that humans become godlike in character and so become more fully human as image-bearers. Athanasius, who articulates this doctrine clearly, is far too intelligent a theologian to permit the idea of the confusion of God and humanity. There has in the past twenty years been a growing interest in deification on the part of Protestant theologians, coupled with a revival of the notion of participation in God within which deification occurs, which I discuss in a later chapter. See Paul L. Gavrilyuk, "The Retrieval of Deification: How a Once-Despised Archaism Became an Ecumenical Desideratum," *Modern Theology* 25, no. 4 (2009): 647-59.

[12]Barth, *Church Dogmatics* IV/2, 152, emphasis added.

in him the humiliated Son of God, in all his power and glory, and in this unity the Lord, the One who did the will of God, and accomplished the act of God, the Reconciler of the world with God."[13]

In addition to making it clear that the resurrection and ascension were distinctive events, these sentiments also suggest the reality that Jesus returned to heaven to bring us there and that he did so "still wearing our flesh, 'the self-same body,'" declares John Knox in the Scots Confession, "in which he had been born, lived, died and rose."[14] In support of this statement, Dawson cites T. F. Torrance, who affirms that the Son's taking up of our humanity "is a final reality enduring endlessly into eternity."[15] The writer of an ancient hymn reflects on what this reality means for humanity:

> Ascending to the sapphire throne,
> thou claim'st the kingdom as thine own;
> and angels wonder when they see
> how *changed is our humanity*.[16]

The strangeness of the idea of a human being in the Godhead comes from the incipient gnosticism that still prevails in our Western thought. Church fathers such as Irenaeus, Tertullian, Augustine, and John Chrysostom spent much of their time combating such thinking in light of the incarnation and ascension of Jesus. Tertullian, for example, assured his hearers, "Jesus is still sitting there at the right hand of the Father, man, yet God—the last Adam, yet the primary Word—flesh and blood, yet purer than ours."[17]

---

[13]Barth, *Church Dogmatics* IV/2, 152-53, emphases added.
[14]Gerrit S. Dawson, "Recovering the Ascension for the Transformation of the Church," *Theology Matters* 7, no. 2 (2001): 3.
[15]Thomas F. Torrance, *A Passion for Christ: The Vision That Ignites Ministry* (Lenoir: PLC, 1999), 15.
[16]"O Lord Most High, Eternal King," hymn 245 in *Common Praise* (Toronto: Anglican Church of Canada, 1998), verse 2.
[17]Tertullian, *On the Resurrection of the Flesh*, Christian Classics Ethereal Library, www.ccel.org/ccel/schaff/anf03/anf03.i.html.

EVEN GREATER GLORY?

A question arises about the glory Christ received in heaven, as the veiled season on earth gave way to his unveiling in heaven. Is it feasible to say reverently that his glory in his postearth existence as the ascended, superexalted (Phil 2:9) one is even greater than that of his pre-incarnate glory, given that he has accomplished the work of redemption and has brought glory to his Father? This thought may be entertained in light of his words to the Father in John 12. As Jesus anticipates the cross, he says, "The hour has come for the Son of Man to be glorified" (Jn 12:23). In what would this glorification subsist? First, he states that it is in what the cross would bring about by way of the salvation of many people: "Very truly I tell you, unless a kernel of wheat falls to the ground and dies, it remains only a single seed. But if it dies, it produces many seeds" (Jn 12:24). This is a reference to many human believers who were justified and adopted as sons and daughters after Jesus accomplished their salvation in his death and resurrection. Isaiah speaks in Isaiah 53—the most vivid depiction of the sufferings of the Messiah and the glories to follow in the Old Testament—of this fecundity when he says, "Though the LORD makes his life an offering for sin, he will see his offspring and prolong his days, and the will of the LORD will prosper in his hand. After he has suffered, he will see the light of life and be satisfied; by his knowledge my righteous servant will justify many" (Is 53:10-11). The writer of Hebrews speaks of this same aspect of the glory as he writes that Christ brings "many sons and daughters to glory" (Heb 2:10). In John 12, Jesus feels keenly what this will mean as the one who will die: "Now my soul is troubled, and what shall I say? 'Father, save me from this hour'? No, it was for this very reason I came to this hour" (Jn 12:27). But as he faces this hour, he says, "Father, glorify your name!" And a voice reverberates from heaven, "I have glorified it, and will glorify it again" (Jn 12:28).

Undoubtedly, the event of the cross was in mind in this promise of the Father to glorify the Son. For that event would honor the justice of God in accomplishing the justification of the world (Rom 3:24-26) and so bring increased glory to the Son and the Father. The paradox is that the hour of his deepest suffering and shame would thus be the hour of his greatest glory. The result of that event was resurrection and then his ascension into glory—the glory of the Son's exaltation to the Father's right hand. This must surely be included in what the Father meant. This glorification through ascension may be why, on each occasion that Luke references the ascension, it is expressed passively concerning Jesus and actively on the Father's part.

Isaiah 53 also expresses the theme of the glorification of the suffering Messiah. One can hear the Father's voice to the Son in this passage:

> Therefore I will give him a portion among the great,
>   and he will divide the spoils with the strong,
> because he poured out his life unto death,
>   and was numbered with the transgressors.
> For he bore the sin of many,
>   and made intercession for the transgressors. (Is 53:12)

The hymn writer once again catches the essence of this journey from suffering to glory:

> Ev'ry mark of dark dishonor
> Heaped upon Thy thorn-crowned brow,
> All the depths of Thy heart's sorrow
> Told in answering glory now![18]

How are we to understand that the Son of God, who is the full radiance of the glory of God (Heb 1:3), in full possession of the iridescent glory of God eternally, who veils his glory on earth, who when his time of

---

[18] Centra Thompson, "Gazing on Thee, Lord, in Glory," Hymnary.org, accessed June 25, 2024, https://hymnary.org/hymn/CHoF1944/271.

suffering and shame is over is unveiled in heaven to radiate the divine glory again, is yet also to be further glorified?

Glory must be understood as the outshining of inward excellence, for one thing, not the inward excellence itself. It is what is revealed and seen. It is never a question of what God innately possesses, for he is eternal and unchangeable in the harmony of all the attributes. Instead, glory is what God chooses to reveal. God has the prerogative to decide when he will reveal it and when he will hide it. And glory is what is seen by other agents, human and angelic, as it is revealed. Furthermore, God cannot help but glorify himself in all his acts, for he is God. As T. F. Torrance asserts, "We cannot know God except through His acts, except by His acts, except in His acts."[19] God's glory is revealed in all of his self-revelatory acts by which he makes himself known. It must be so if he is God.

In God's saving disposition and the whole course of God's saving acts toward humanity, as glimpsed first in the ascension and then one day manifested fully at the consummation of all things, and in the complete dependence of the human person on God in all this, God is and will be glorified. This is an important theme in the theology of Jonathan Edwards. In a 1731 lecture on 1 Corinthians 1:29-31, Edwards says, "What God aims at in the disposition of things in the affair of redemption, viz. that man should not glory in himself, but alone in God; 1 Cor. 1:29, 31. That no flesh should glory in his presence,—that, according as it is written, He that glorieth, let him glory in the Lord." The trinitarian centeredness of Edwards is reflected in this lecture when he states, "So much the greater and more absolute dependence we have on the divine perfections, as belonging to the several persons of the Trinity, so much the greater occasion have we to observe and own the divine glory of each of them."[20] As he sums up his argument, Edwards speaks of the glory into which God has lifted fallen sinners

---

[19]Cited in McGrath, *T. F. Torrance*, 148.
[20]Jonathan Edwards, "God Glorified in Man's Dependence" (*WJE* 17:200-201, 210).

in Christ but acknowledges immediately that the sole source of this is the trinitarian glory of God:

> Though God be pleased to lift man out of that dismal abyss of sin . . . and exceedingly to exalt him in excellency and honor, and to a high pitch of glory and blessedness, yet the creature hath nothing in any respect to glory of; *all the glory evidently belongs to God, all is in a mere, and most absolute, and divine dependence on the Father, Son, and Holy Ghost. And each person of the Trinity is equally glorified in this work*: there is an absolute dependence of the creature on every one for all: all is of the Father, all through the Son, and all in the Holy Ghost.[21]

This glorifying of the persons of the Trinity in the economy flows naturally from Edwards's view of the immanent Trinity, in which the Father views the Son eternally with beatific, glorying delight, the Son returns this beatific, glorying delight, and the Holy Spirit is this delight or mutual love of the Father for the Son. As Kyle Strobel asserts, "The Trinity is religious affection in pure act. Personal beatific-delight is simply a way to highlight the key features of religious affection as the very life of God."[22] This is undoubtedly true, yet the notion of each beatifying the other has at its heart the idea of glory redounding and emanating from the Trinity, the sum of all the excellencies of God in perfect harmony. Thus, the glorifying of the Son by the Father in the ascension is in keeping with that disposition that has pertained to the Godhead for all eternity and is evident in John 17:4-5.

---

[21]Edwards, "God Glorified in Man's Dependence," 212, emphasis added.
[22]Kyle Strobel, *Jonathan Edwards's Theology: A Reinterpretation*, T&T Clark Studies in Systematic Theology 19 (London: Bloomsbury, 2013), 90-91. Edwards's favored model of the Trinity is Western, Augustinian in its roots, yet with a strong emphasis in places on personhood. For a full discussion, see Ross Hastings, *Jonathan Edwards and the Life of God: Toward an Evangelical Theology of Participation* (Minneapolis: Fortress, 2015).

THE TRANSFIGURATION

The glorifying of the human-divine Son by the Father in the ascension is actually prefigured by the transfiguration.[23] In his detailed study of Luke's account, Davies reaches this conclusion for several reasons. The first comes from a comparison between Luke's account of the transfiguration in Luke 9:28-36 and his account of the ascension in Acts 1:1-11. The events are both on a mountain, and the mention of clouds is common to both. This "complex of ideas" is so similar as to convince Davies that the first is the prefigurement of the other.[24] The second piece of evidence lies in Luke's reference to the ascension in the immediately following context of the story of the transfiguration: "As the time approached for him to be *taken up* to heaven, Jesus resolutely set out for Jerusalem" (Lk 9:51). This word for "taken up" (*analēpsis*), in context, is not just a reference to his passion as a whole but specifically to the ascension.[25]

The third reason relates to how Luke nuances the Markan account: the specific mention of glory, and the detail that the conversation on the mountain was about the "exodus" that Jesus would accomplish, a term that, even if it included the death and resurrection of Jesus, also included the ascension. Fourth, since all three of the Evangelists saw the transfiguration as a foreshadowing of the parousia, including Luke, this must logically first implicate the ascension, which Luke does mention (Lk 9:51). It is also interesting that the author of the Apocalypse of Peter uses the events of the transfiguration to embellish his account of the ascension: Jesus leading his disciples to the Mount of Olives, the presence of Moses and Elijah, Peter's proposal to build three tabernacles, and Christ's rebuke.[26]

---

[23]John G. Davies, *He Ascended into Heaven: A Study in the History of Doctrine*, Bampton Lectures (London: Lutterworth, 1958), 39-40.

[24]Davies, *He Ascended into Heaven*, 39.

[25]Davies, *He Ascended into Heaven*, 40. Davies believes the reference to the disciples calling down fire gives the context an Elijah typology. Since calling down fire was Elijah's last act, Davies sees in this act a signal of the imminent ascension of Jesus.

[26]Davies, *He Ascended into Heaven*, 79-80. Other noncanonical sources also show that the ascension was "a definite element in the generally accepted *regula fidei* (rule of faith)" (81).

In light of both the canonical evidence and noncanonical suggestion, we may surmise that in the symmetry of glory hidden in the incarnation and glory revealed in the ascension of Jesus, a proleptic glimpse is given in the middle to three apostles on the Mount of Transfiguration. It is a glimpse of his regal glory in the human body with which he would be raised from the dead and ascend. Peter's description clarifies that it was a glory moment, for he describes himself as one of the "eyewitnesses of his majesty" (2 Pet 1:16). As the mature Peter reflects on the event on "the sacred mountain," on the temporary unveiling in the season of veiling, he comes to understand that it was all about the revelation of glory Christ had before the incarnation and would have again at the ascension: "He *received honor and glory from God the Father* when the voice came to him from the Majestic Glory, saying, 'This is my Son, whom I love; with him I am well pleased'" (2 Pet 1:17). It is not hard to imagine the words that came from the Father, and the grandeur of the glory he endowed on the Son after the cross and the resurrection, when the departure (Lk 9:31) spoken of on Tabor had been fulfilled, and the atonement of the cosmos had been accomplished, and he ascended on high and sat at his right hand. The Father's acclamation of the Son at the beginning of his public ministry (Lk 3:22), and then in the middle (Lk 9:35), cries out for an affirmation after the cross, and it happens at the ascension, where the Son, in Luke's words, "was taken up into heaven" (Lk 24:51). The writer of Hebrews provides more detail: "After he had provided purification for sins, he sat down at the right hand of the Majesty in heaven" (Heb 1:3). So, no ascension means no declaration of the restored glory of Jesus, and an asymmetry to his salvific story remains.

THE ASCENSION EXPLICATES THE TITLE "SON OF MAN"

Two titles of Jesus, "Son of Man" and "Messiah," further develop the theme of the ascension as the revealing of the glory of the Son after concealing that glory while here on earth. They are titles implying glory. The first, "Son of Man," was Jesus' preferred title for himself. While implying his humanity, this title declares his supreme kingship and his full deity. The ascension is the occasion when that identity is fully revealed. Without the ascension, we would not fully know the identity of Jesus as the Son of Man in glory, first prefigured in Daniel (Dan 7:13). This text was appropriated by Jesus at his trial when in response to the high priest's question about his identity he said, "You will see the Son of Man sitting at the right hand of the Mighty One and coming on the clouds of heaven" (Mk 14:62). The ascension and the second coming are here linked together. Earlier, in Mark 8:38, Jesus had said, "If anyone is ashamed of me and my words in this adulterous and sinful generation, the Son of Man will be ashamed of them when he comes in his Father's glory with the holy angels." Here Jesus seems to differentiate his state in his earthly ministry ("me") from who he will be after he has ascended when he comes again as the Son of Man in glorious splendor.[27] In Mark 13:26, Jesus again uses the exalted term "Son of Man" when referencing the second coming: "At that time, people will see the Son of Man coming in clouds with great power and glory."

Despite Jesus' frequent use of this title while on earth, Davies suggests that it is always proleptic.[28] That Mark uses "Son of Man" even when speaking of the suffering and death of Christ (Mk 9:31; 10:33, 45; 14:21, 41) signals the reality that even in his passion we must not forget his true identity and the destiny the ascension would fulfill. Suffering was the path by which the Son of Man was led into the divine presence of the Ancient of Days. In other words, the title "Son of Man" on every occasion anticipates the fullness of the meaning that will be apparent once he has ascended and has

---

[27] Davies, *He Ascended into Heaven*, 38.
[28] Davies, *He Ascended into Heaven*, 38.

returned as the ascended and glorified one to reign in the manner Daniel anticipated. The title is triumphant, even as it depicts the suffering Savior. This makes sense because the road to triumph and into the divine presence is through the suffering that atones for the sin of humanity, which the title also implies, and the conquering of death. Davies concludes: "It was not until Jesus had triumphed over sin and death *and* ascended that he received the dominion and glory inseparable from that status. Thus, the presence of the title 'Son of man' in Mark must be regarded as evidence of a belief in the Ascension."[29] So, no ascension, no Son of Man.

THE ASCENSION EXPLAINS THE TITLE "MESSIAH" ("ANOINTED ONE")

The second title that embodies the glory of the Son is "Messiah." Norwegian Old Testament scholar Sigmund Mowinckel points out that in Jewish thought, the Messiah would only be such in its fullest sense when he had accomplished the work of salvation. He states, "Before that time we may say that he is but *Messias designatus*, a claimant to Messianic status."[30] Just as someone who has qualified to be president by winning an election is the president designate but is not actually prime minister until the day of her inauguration, so Jesus was Messiah designate until the day of his ascension, when he was crowned such by the Father. This mirrors how Mark does not describe Peter's confession that Jesus was the Christ without directing our attention to his passion, a concept Peter did not understand then (Mk 8:29-31). During his trial, when Jesus admits he is Christ, he does so only because he is now in the throes of fulfilling the work that will make him Messiah (Mk 14:61-62). This is also congruent with Peter's sermon on the day of Pentecost:

---

[29]Davies, *He Ascended into Heaven*, 38, emphasis original.
[30]Sigmund Mowinckel, *Psalmenstudien III. Die Kultprophetie und Prophetische Psalmen* (Kristiania: Jacob Dybwad, 1923), 303.

"Therefore let all Israel be assured of this: God has *made* this Jesus, whom you crucified, both Lord and Messiah" (Acts 2:36). Jesus was, of course, already Lord and Christ, but his ascension was the occasion when he was manifestly that, no longer a designate. So, no ascension, no Messiah.

5

THE GLORY OF HIS THREEFOLD OFFICE AS PROPHET, PRIEST, AND KING

THE LITERAL MEANING OF *Messiah* as "Anointed One" naturally entails the offices that in the Old Testament were inaugurated by literal anointings with oil. These offices—prophet, priest, and king—find their fulfillment in the Messiah (Hebrew) or Christ (Greek). With a continued christological focus, this chapter will explore how Christ's ascension, session, and intercession in heaven inform his titles and mediatorial offices as prophet, priest, and king (commonly known as *munus triplex*). Treatments of the *munus triplex* are found in the work of Reformed theologians who seek to harmonize Old and New Testament perspectives. I will use this concept modestly and critically to develop a profile of the richness of the person and work of the ascended Christ, especially in light of how these titles are either explicitly used or implied in Hebrews—prophet implied in Hebrews 1:1-3; 3:1-6; priest and king, in the order of Melchizedek, used explicitly in Hebrews 7–10. What follows is a brief exposition of the three offices of our Lord in the order king, priest, prophet, an order suggested by T. F. Torrance.[1] We may say that as King, he *models* divine glory; as Priest, he *mediates* it to his people especially through the Eucharist and prayer; and as Prophet, he *declares* the glory to his church, and through his church to the world, in this era between the ascension and the parousia.

---

[1] T. F. Torrance, *Space, Time, and Resurrection* (Grand Rapids, MI: Eerdmans, 1976), 106.

KING

Christ's function as king is certainly evident before his ascension, as he pronounces the kingdom and outlines its character. Matthew invests in presenting Christ as the anointed King who fulfills the Old Testament prophecies and promises of the messianic King. However, the kind of king that Jesus was, was a source of confusion for the disciples until the day he ascended, as Luke indicates in Acts 1. Similarly, the priesthood of Christ—particularly his offering up of himself on a cross—eluded the disciples until after his resurrection and the ascension. It was only in retrospect and in light of the exaltation of Jesus as King by the ascension that Paul, Peter, and especially the writer of the Hebrews grasped the fullness of the offices of Christ as prophet, priest, and king.

In *The Ascension of Christ*, Patrick Schreiner argues that the saving work of Christ would not be complete without his kingly ascension to the right hand of God. It is a key event in the Gospel story since it prepared the way for his ongoing ministry in the church and through the church in mission. Schreiner argues, "Jesus' residence in heaven marks a turning point in his three-fold offices of prophet, priest, and king. As prophet, Jesus builds the church and its witness. As priest, he intercedes before the Father. As king, he rules over all."[2] Although the traditional order of the *munus triplex* is prophet, priest, king, Torrance insists that within "the period inaugurated by the ascension, it is evidently with another order that we have to work: King, Priest and Prophet."[3] That is, the order must begin with the ascended Christ as *King*. The coronation and sovereignty of the exalted King must come first, qualifying his priesthood and prophesying.

For Torrance, this has to do with the obvious reality that Christ's elevation and installation to a kingly office is implicit in the very act of ascension. The ascension, for Jesus, is a coronation (Ps 2; 24; 68—the

---

[2]Patrick Schreiner, *The Ascension of Christ: Recovering a Neglected Doctrine* (Bellingham, WA: Lexham, 2020), back cover.
[3]Torrance, *Space, Time, and Resurrection*, 106.

enthronement psalms; Heb 2:9). This understanding is in keeping also with the relationship between Psalm 110:1, "The LORD says to my lord: 'Sit at my right hand until I make your enemies a footstool for your feet,'" and Psalm 110:4, "The LORD has sworn and will not change his mind: 'You are a priest forever, in the order of Melchizedek.'" Thus, Torrance understands that the priesthood of Christ is a *royal* priesthood, and the proclamation of Christ is a *royal* proclamation. Torrance shows that all the words used in the New Testament for the ascension have a royal, cultic meaning—that is, they are words associated with the installation and function of a king, and that this therefore means that the predominant kingly nature of the ascended Son shapes Christ's roles as priest and prophet.

A few specific passages in *Space, Time, and Resurrection* will demonstrate Torrance's insistence on the priority of the kingly office. He states, "Christ ascends to the throne of God in order to fulfil his saving work and fill all things with his sovereign presence and power—yet, as we shall see, the ascension involves the veiling of his divine majesty and power, or the holding back, from our visible and physical contact in space and time, of his unveiled majesty and power." It is in his ascent to the throne that salvation is accomplished. What is meant here is not Christ's *atoning* work accomplished in his earthly life, death, and resurrection but salvation in its ongoing aspect and extension to humanity and the creation. Based on his reflection on Revelation 5:1-14, Torrance comments, "Even in ascension the power of Christ is *exercised through his sacrifice*, through his atoning expiation of guilt, through his priestly mediation before God." But the sacrifice Christ made on earth can be applied only by the power of the crowned King. Torrance also speaks of the ascension of Jesus as Son of Man as "the ascension of representative Man in whom all humanity is gathered up and made participant in his self-offering, so that in his ascension Christ is installed as Head of the New Humanity, the Prince of the New Creation, the King of the Kingdom which he has won and established through his incarnate life and passion." This approach reflects a *Christus Victor* approach to the atonement, or one might say, the recapitulation approach of Irenaeus. Torrance concludes that from the ascension onwards, "all things are directed from the mercy-seat of God, by the enthroned and exalted Lamb, who reigns not only over the Church but over all creation."[4] The sacerdotal seems to be in the employment of the royal.

While understanding Torrance's approach, I might suggest that the order of these offices varies depending on the biblical texts in question and their particular contexts and intent. For example, Hebrews 10:12-13 reveals a different order and a complete integration of the offices of king and priest: "But when this priest had offered for all time one sacrifice for sins, he sat down at the right hand of God [an allusion to Ps 110:1], and since that time he waits for his enemies to be made his footstool." Similarly in Hebrews 1:3, it is when Christ has "provided purification" for our sins that "he sat down at the right hand of the Majesty in heaven." The priestly function has already begun in Jesus' history on earth, particularly in his sacrifice on the cross. In consequence of his offering up of himself on the cross and completing the work of atonement, he is exalted as king.

Any ordering of these offices actually seems inappropriate, as there is no way of separating the concepts, as Hebrews 7 shows. When the writer discusses the order of Christ's priesthood, he invokes the kingly nature of the unique king-priest Melchizedek, mentioned in Genesis 14:18-20 as the prototype, not Aaron or Levi. The writer does this since the orders for priesthood and kingship were separate in Israel—from Aaron and David, respectively—Jesus being in the royal line but not the priestly one. The writer clarifies that the priesthood of Jesus derives not from Aaron but from Melchizedek, who was both a king and a priest, which are therefore inseparable offices.

---

[4]Torrance, *Space, Time, and Resurrection*, 112.

Scholars conjecture as to whether Melchizedek was merely a historical figure with both of these offices whom the writer of Hebrews takes up randomly as a prototype of kingly priests, or whether he employs Melchizedek because he was a Christophany, an appearance of Christ before the incarnation. The latter option has in its favor that an obscure Old Testament king-priest can hardly establish a divine order of kingly priesthood or priestly kingship. Furthermore, Abraham's paying tithes to Melchizedek in Genesis 14 argues for the latter's divine nature. Only God is to be worshiped. This was the basic creed of the Old Testament. However, lest we miss the point here—having invoked Melchizedek to explain the order of Christ's inseparable kingship and priesthood, the writer of Hebrews exposits Christ's priesthood in the rest of Hebrews 7. The kingly office he has established in Melchizedek is in the service of his priesthood. Thus, his kingship does not overshadow Jesus' priestly function.

This interweaving of these offices is evident also in how Christ's exaltation includes his being lifted up on the cross. In Luke 9:51, for example, one of the four verbs used for the ascension describes his movement toward the ascension via the cross: "As the time approached for him to be *taken up* to heaven, Jesus resolutely set out for Jerusalem."[5] Similarly, John uses another Greek word for the ascension, a word translated "exalted," to indicate the lifting up of Jesus at his death: "'And I, when I am *lifted up* [exalted] from the earth, will draw all people to myself.' He said this to show the kind of death he was going to die" (Jn 12:32-33; see also Jn 3:14; 8:28). Thus, the kingly exaltation includes the priestly, and the kingship is qualified as a servant kingship, not one of sheer power. The pathway to the exalted state is through the humble offering of himself. The cross is before the crown, and the

---

[5]This is the verb *analēmpseōs*, "take up," derived from the verb *anabainō*. There are four Greek words in the New Testament that are used to describe the ascension. They are *anabainō* (literally "to go up"), *kathizō* ("to sit down"), *analambanō* ("to take up," often expressed in the passive voice, e.g., "he was taken up") and *hypsoō* ("to exalt," often expressed in the passive voice, e.g., "he was exalted").

efficacy of the cross carries over into the exercise of the crown. Peter and the apostles keep these offices together: "God exalted him to his own right hand as *Prince and Savior*" (Acts 5:31).

It may be tempting to think of Jesus as a seated King, as if he were passively waiting for his enemies to be made his footstool. On the one hand, the primary agent in the outworking of salvation and kingdom purposes on earth is the Holy Spirit. The Father tells the Son to sit on his throne and anticipate the day when all humanity and all creation will come under his full sway (Ps 110:1; Heb 1:13; 10:13). However, the session in heaven is not merely "a resting place from which his completed work can be viewed passively," for, as Fergusson indicates, "while the ascent completes a pattern or movement that began with the descent of the Son of God, it does not signal the ending of the work of Christ." "Instead," Fergusson insists, "we should view the ascension as the commencement of his kingly ministry, which now moves forward in anticipation of his *parousia*."[6] Fergusson does think that the kingly dimension sets the context for Christ's prophetic and priestly ministry and should precede these in exposition.[7] This seems to accord with Jesus' prefacing the Great Commission with his kingly words, "All authority in heaven and on earth has been given to me. Therefore go and make disciples of all nations" (Mt 28:18-19), in anticipation of the "end of the age" (Mt 28:20). This also aligns with how his exaltation is described: "Therefore God exalted him to the highest place and gave him the name that is above every name, that at the name of Jesus, every knee should bow, in heaven and on earth and under the earth, and every tongue acknowledge that Jesus Christ is Lord, to the glory of God the Father" (Phil 2:9-11).

What is clear is that in his unrivaled sovereignty as the ascended one, he is actively at work, not passive. This does not eliminate or even deemphasize the work of the Spirit on earth while Christ is in heaven.

---

[6]David Fergusson, "The Ascension of Christ: Its Significance in the Theology of T. F. Torrance," *Participatio* 3 (2012): 95.
[7]Fergusson, "Ascension of Christ," 95.

It merely suggests the differentiation of roles. The works of the Trinity are undivided, but the doctrine of appropriations suggests a legitimate differentiation of function-related roles. The Son is Lord in heaven, and his sovereignty over all things on earth, including the mission of the church, is accompanied by and in harmony with the work of the Spirit who is Lord on earth (2 Cor 3:17-18; 1 Cor 12:1-11), the sovereign Spirit who regenerates and empowers his people for mission. Their work is coinherent. This is the concept that each of the divine persons is in the other, yet each is not the other. Each works in the working of the other, yet each has their own particular work. Thus, whatever comfort Christ offers through his priesthood does not remove the compelling call for his disciples to participate in his kingly reign.

The idea of Jesus as a king raised a concern for Torrance. He worries that the idea sounds "anthropomorphic or even Arian" in depicting the relationship between the Father and the Son. It is as if the ascended Jesus were the chief executive officer, working on behalf of the chairman of the board (Father). The idea of Christ's priestly intercession before the Father invites the same critique. This is to miss the point by a country mile. The point of Christ's mediation and intercession, and his reign "under" the Father, is that he does this as the person in the Godhead who is also human. As a human, he reigns for redeemed humanity; as the human Christ Jesus, he is a mediator between God and humans. As the human and the Second Person of the Trinity, he is in complete communion with the Father. Again, the two axioms of trinitarian life are at play: the doctrine of the *indivisibility* of the external works of the Trinity, which is grounded in a coinherence of being in which each is mutually internal to the other, and the doctrine of *appropriations* of specific roles to each person, differentiated by hypostatic function. The Father does have a functional priority in the Trinity, as the tradition has noted for centuries. However, his description as the font of the Trinity does not imply an ontological priority since each person shares the divine essence eternally. It is a recognition that the Father has eternally generated the Son and filiated the Spirit, but since this is an eternal, never-beginning generation and filiation, the priority of the Father must be seen as logical, not chronological. The three are equal in essence and honor but differentiated as hypostases.

The Father does therefore have an originating and therefore a functional leadership within the Trinity, which explains the Son's mediatorial function. The Son's role as the incarnate human prepared him as fitting for mediation, intercession, and reign on behalf of humanity. These roles involve presenting himself to the Father on our behalf as priest and as king. However, as the coequal Son who is God, he participates coinherently with the Father in mediation and reconciliation. Just as the Son, on the cross, is both *the judged* as man and *the Judge* as God, so the Son as a priest, in intercession with the Father, is both God with the Father, in the indivisibility of deity, and man, representing his people with whom he became one at the incarnation.

Another way to say this is that we must not separate the person and the work of Jesus on our behalf as king and priest. This explains why Torrance believes we can use the risky imagery of the Son as a chief executive regarding the kingly function and the Father as some board chair "if we are properly to integrate the person and work of Christ."[8] The work of Christ, he states, is "never detachable from descriptions of his person, and therefore with the ascension of his person we must continue to think of his action as continuing, albeit in the enactment of the eternal significance of his once-for-all work in history."[9] There is a parallel relationship between his "once-for-all work in history" and what he continues to do at the right hand of the Father, both in terms of the Father-Son relations and regarding the fact that the first,

---

[8] Fergusson, "Ascension of Christ," 95-96.
[9] This commentary on Torrance's work on the ascension in Torrance, *Space, Time, and Resurrection*, 270-73, is by Fergusson, "Ascension of Christ," 95-96. The analogy of the CEO and board chair is Torrance's.

historical work of atonement is extended to the second, though in a "different mode."[10] The mode in the intercessory phase of his priesthood, his kingship, and God's mission to the world and creation is one of *application* of the completed atonement to humanity, not a continued work of atonement. This mode includes how Jesus' disciples apply the atonement in their witness to the world, not by adding to the atonement but filling up "what is lacking" (Col 1:24) by way of the cost of proclaiming and living it.

The notion that the truly human Christ is King is also crucial from the perspective of the beginning and end of the biblical story, as well as the eternal decree of God concerning humanity and creation. A sizable strand of traditional Christology suggests that the advent and work of Christ should be viewed not merely as "sin management" or a forensic atoning mission. Instead, the primary lens should be ontological, with forensics considered within that purview. In other words, God's primary intent for humanity, within his decree, was that his Son would reign with humanity on earth.

This brings an appropriate bookend to the *biblical* narrative of Genesis 1–2. The first humans are to be in intimate fellowship with God, ruling over the created order in a caring way. They were to be priestly kings in and with the King. John Calvin is more specific about the situation and state of the first humans. They could only be what God wanted them to be—stewards of creation on behalf of and with God—through participating in the Son in his pre-incarnate state. Even before the fall, they needed mediation since they were at a metaphysical remove from God. They could only be image-bearers in participation with the pre-incarnate Christ.[11] The last Adam recapitulates what was lost in the first Adam because of his sin. Sin must be atoned for, but the aim of that reconciliation is not merely forensic but the recovery of humanity's essence and first intended

---

[10]Fergusson, "Ascension of Christ," 95-96.
[11]John Calvin, *Institutes* 2.12.6.

function in union with Christ—the first intended role of humanity to be coheirs and corulers of the earth with Christ.

This view reflects the instincts of Irenaeus's doctrine of recapitulation, which states that Jesus came not merely to reconcile humanity with God but to head up a new humanity. He participated fully in humanity and accomplished, in his person, what was needed to create a new humanity under his headship. God's original intent for humans to reign with him as vice regents has been fulfilled and surpassed by what reconciled humanity has become in the last Adam, the true Regent, the King of kings. Thomas Doughty has recently argued that the primary purpose of the Son's incarnation was logically prior (*supra*) to the fall of humanity into sin. Therefore, God's original intent and motivation for his creation was that there would be within it a divine-human co-dominion shared between the Son and his people (*Christus Dominus*).[12] Thus, as T. F. Torrance asserts:

> The ascension means the exaltation of man into the life of God, and on to the throne of God. In the ascension, the Son of Man, New Man in Christ, is given to partake of divine nature. There we reach the goal of the incarnation, in our great *Prodomos* or Forerunner at the right hand of God. We are with Jesus beside God, so we are gathered up in him and included in his own self-presentation before the Father.[13]

He emphasizes that this exaltation of humanity into the life of God is not pantheism or mysticism: it is not the "disappearance of man or the swallowing up of human and creaturely being in the infinite ocean of the divine Being, but rather that human nature, remaining creaturely and human, is yet exalted in Christ to share in God's life and glory," and to share in the reign of Christ with his people on earth.[14]

The kingship of the Son is vital to this theological, biblical, and eschatological perspective. The visions of Revelation are filled with

---

[12] Thomas G. Doughty, *Supralapsarian Christology and the Progressive Work of Christ: Christus Dominus* (Lanham, MD: Lexington, 2024).
[13] Torrance, *Space, Time, and Resurrection*, 135.
[14] Torrance, *Space, Time, and Resurrection*, 135.

glorious images of Christ as King, celebrating the triumphant atonement he accomplished: "You are worthy to take the scroll and to open its seals, because you were slain, and with your blood you purchased for God persons from every tribe and language and people and nation" (Rev 5:9). The destiny of the international people he has purchased by his redemptive work is "to be a kingdom and priests to serve our God, and they will reign on the Earth" (Rev 5:10). The redemptive work does not make the redeemed persons merely forgiven and justified but also kings and priests.

PRIEST

If Christ as King models and radiates divine glory, his priesthood mediates his grace and glory to his people by his once-for-all atonement and his intercession in perpetuity. Though aspects of his priesthood occur before it, the ascension and what follows it is are vital to the understanding of the office of the Son as priest. As noted, the priestly ministry of the Lord Jesus, which begins during his time on earth, continues perpetually. His priesthood has a once-for-all sacrificial dynamic and an eternally ongoing intercessory dynamic. Hebrews confirms the earthly beginning of Jesus' priesthood by emphasizing that he offered himself up as a sacrifice precisely and already as a priest. Only a priest offers sacrifices; in fact, a priest must "have something to offer" (Heb 8:3) if he is to be a priest. Utterly remarkable in Christ's case is that "through the eternal Spirit [he] offered *himself* unblemished to God" (Heb 9:14). He offers his *own* blood (Heb 9:12).

The once-for-all dynamic of that offering is expressed in verses such as Hebrews 7:27: "Unlike the other high priests, he does not need to offer sacrifices day after day, first for his own sins, and then for the sins of the people. He sacrificed for their sins *once for all* when he offered himself." Similarly, in Hebrews 9:12, the writer affirms, "He did not enter by means of the blood of goats and calves; but he entered the

Most Holy Place *once for all* by his own blood, thus obtaining eternal redemption." Hebrews 9:26 is emphatic: "Otherwise Christ would have had to suffer many times since the creation of the world. But he has appeared *once for all* at the culmination of the ages to do away with sin by the sacrifice of himself." There is a cluster of references to this once-for-all dynamic in Hebrews 10 (Heb 10:1-2, 10). Hebrews 10:10 emphasizes that there needed to be no repetition of the sacrifice because it was perfectly efficacious the first time. The writer states, "And by that will, we have been made holy through the sacrifice of the body of Jesus Christ once for all."

The reference to "that will" points to the *framework* within which the offering of Christ is made: the will of God decreed in the eternal past in God's covenant of grace but expressed in history in the new covenant (Heb 8:7-13). The *locality* of this offering is the holy sanctuary of God, answering to the type of the most holy place in the tabernacle or temple, where atoning blood was sprinkled seven times in front of and once on the mercy seat. This is where matters of cosmology arise as well as some of the recent controversies as to where the atoning work of Christ happened, spatially speaking. Take Hebrews 9:12, just quoted above, where the writer states, "He did not enter by means of the blood of goats and calves; but he entered the Most Holy Place *once for all* by his own blood, thus obtaining eternal redemption." Hebrews 9:14 and other New Testament texts (such as 2 Cor 5:18) abundantly clarify that the Son enacted the atonement in the presence of the triune God—there is no other God than the triune God. There is no mysterious God behind the back of the Father, Son, and Holy Spirit. Whatever we may make of the cry of dereliction made by Jesus on the cross, we cannot conclude that the Trinity was broken up, for this is impossible. It was the cry of the human Christ as he felt the weight of his sin-bearing role. But as the man who is God, he was in the presence of the Godhead. He was both the judged and the Judge in that mysterious moment. Whatever went on within the

Godhead is a mystery beyond our comprehension, a dark mystery rather than a light one.

Hebrews 9:25-26 indicates that what transpired on the cross transpired "in heaven." The writer states, "Nor did *he enter heaven* to offer himself again and again, the way the high priest enters the Most Holy Place every year with blood that is not his own. . . . But he has appeared once for all at the culmination of the ages to do away with sin by the sacrifice of himself." This text would seem to suggest that the offering made by Christ was made in heaven. Does this imply that the atonement was not complete until the ascension, when Jesus presented himself in heaven, or that his offering made on the cross was presented to the Father at his ascension and session, and not before? The context contradicts this. It is the act of the "*sacrifice* of himself" when he "appeared once or all at the end of the ages" that does away with sin (Heb 9:26). I suggest that the entering heaven implied in Hebrews 9:25 is precisely what happened when Jesus was on earth, on the cross—that heaven and earth are one on the cross. This is in the spirit of the cosmology implied throughout the epistle. All is sacred space in this epistle. Furthermore, in Romans 6:10, there is clarity about the location of the once-for-all act by which sin is atoned: "The death he died, he died to sin *once for all*; but the life he lives, he lives to God." It was in his death that atonement was procured, not in his ascent. The ascent was the Father's acceptance and celebration of what was accomplished in Jesus' vicarious life, his death on the cross, and the resurrection. The ascension is vital to *salvation* but is not part of the *atonement*.

This acknowledging of the sacrificial and forensic aspect of the atonement is necessary, and it does not take away from the filial priority. The Son's history on earth serves the primary objective of his incarnation, which was to create children of God, sons destined for glory, and human image-bearers in co-dominion with Christ on earth. The ascension of the man Jesus was vital to that ontological purpose.

The recapitulation of humanity in the *eschatos* Adam is the telos of the atonement. God's first intent for the incarnation is a new creation managed by his high-priestly Son united with his royal priesthood. This is what comes first in the eternal purposes of God. Atonement for sin, with all its facets, vital in itself, serves that overarching purpose: creating a humanity in union and coregency with his Son. The ascension is in keeping with that purpose and is therefore salvific. But it is not atoning per se. We may even say it is part of the order of the history of Jesus (*ordo historia*) that becomes his people's saving order (*ordo salutis*), but it is not part of the atonement per se.

Furthermore, the ongoing work of the High Priest in Hebrews is contrasted with an already *completed* work. The session of Jesus, spoken of repeatedly in Hebrews (Heb 1:3; 8:1; 10:12; 12:2), is the sign of a completed atonement and also the beginning of a new phase in the Priest's existence that will last forever. What follows the session is the intercession. These are highly symbolic actions, to be sure. How can he be seated at the right hand of God and at the same time be actively interceding for his people? A likely possibility is that the intended contrast of postures emphasizes a finished objective atonement on the one hand and the unfinished application of the atonement, subjectively speaking, forever, on the other.

There is, of course, more than the atonement's application in his intercessory work. There is empathy with the suffering people of God, the hearing and mediation of their worship and prayers to the Father, the mediation of his presence by the Spirit in the Eucharist, and so on. I will expand on these themes of the session and intercession of the great High Priest in the following chapter.

PROPHET

Christ as Prophet *declares* the glory of God to his church, and through his church to the world in this era between the ascension and the parousia. Jesus, as the *Word made flesh*, was *the* prophet predicted in

Deuteronomy 18:18. Hebrews, an epistle primarily focused on the exposition of Christ as king and priest, actually first establishes his role as a prophet: "In the past God spoke to our ancestors through the prophets at many times and in various ways, but in these last days he has spoken to us by his Son" (Heb 1:1-2). His prophetic role is related to his identity as the Son. Jesus, as a prophet, stands in continuity with all the prophets before him but also in a glorious discontinuity with the other prophets that reflects his superiority to them as Son. This revelation "in Son" is not just another revelation: it is final, one of fulfillment, one of divine speech embodied in the incarnate person of the Trinity, the Word (*Logos*). The remainder of the writer's opening exposition in Hebrews 1:2-3 is a variation on the theme of his sonship and therefore his prophetic function. These verses answer the questions: Who is this Son, what is his destiny, his relation to creation, and who is he in the essence of his being?

I suspect that the writer is employing a chiasm, as depicted below:[15]

> whom he appointed heir of all things,
> > and through whom he also made the universe.
> > > The Son is the radiance of God's glory and
> > > the exact representation of his very being,
> > sustaining all things by his powerful word.
>
> After he had provided purification for sins, he sat down at the right hand of the Majesty in heaven.

The opening statement of the chiasm is a statement that the Son has been "appointed the heir of all things," and the final statement is, "After he had provided purification for sins, *he sat down at the right hand of the Majesty in heaven*" (Heb 1:2-3). In other words, there is no full understanding of the Son as prophet without the ascension and rule of the cosmos. He was destined to be the heir of the whole creation, and his ascension after his atoning work fulfilled that

---

[15] I offer this tentatively, not having seen it in commentaries on Hebrews.

kingship. We don't know who the Son is until we see his ascension, through which he sits down at the right hand of the Majesty in heaven.

The second part of the chiasm reveals the relationship of the Son with creation. It declares he is both the divine person who is the agent of creation, "through whom also he made the universe" (Heb 1:2), and the one exercising providence over the creation, "sustaining all things by his powerful word" (Heb 1:3). The ascended Son speaks with authority because of his existence prior to creation, his agency in creation and his providential care of it, by which he leads it to fulfill its purpose. That purpose involves the glory of humanity recovering its regency of the cosmos in co-dominion with Jesus, the recapitulated human person, the incarnate and ascended Son.[16]

The third part of the chiasm reveals why the Son is the ultimate prophet of God, God's perfect spokesman. The two statements in the inner core of the chiasm are these: "The Son is the radiance of God's glory" and "the exact representation of his being" (Heb 1:3). They indicate that he is qualified to speak about God and for God because he *is* God—God the Son. He cannot *not* speak in light of who he is. On the one hand, he is the "radiance of God's glory," the theme of this chapter. In his eternal being, the Son does not merely reflect glory. It comes from within his own being as God. It is a radiated, iridescent glory. It is the beauty of the divine being as three persons in complete union and harmony of being and act. It is the outshining of the inward excellencies of all the attributes of God. The ascension spoken of in the final statement of the chiasm speaks to each statement; in this case, it is the evidence of his intrinsic glory.

The Son is also *the exact imprint of God's very being*. This strikes at the very heart of the superiority of the revelation of the prophet Jesus as Son. As Son, he is the authentic representation of God's nature (*hypostaseōs*) because he is God. He is not just the image, as if a mere

---

[16]John's association of the Word with his agency in creation has a similar pattern (Jn 1:1-4). On the glory of humanity, see Irenaeus, *Against Heresies* 4.20.7 (*ANF* 1:490): *Gloria enim Dei vivens homo*. The *ANF* translation renders this, "For the glory of God is a living man."

reflection of God, like a stamp, a die, or an engraving. Such an analogy fails because it suggests that the Father is the real thing and the stamp is a distinct replica and therefore second class. This phrase indicates an exact correspondence between the Father and the Son with respect to the very essence of deity. They share the same essence. No wonder the revelation of the Prophet-Son is superior to that of all other prophets. There is nothing that the Father is that the Son is not, except that the Son is not the Father. There is a personal distinction between the Father and the Son related to origin and economic function, but none that diminishes the eternal divine essence of either. The Son is truly and fully God.

The Father and the Son are one not just in essence but also in communion. The Prophet-Son spoke as God, particularly as the Son in communion with his Father. This intimate communion of the Son with the Father in his prophetic ministry is clarified in John's Gospel, as Jesus affirms that he speaks only what he hears the Father speaking (Jn 8:28). The Son's prophetic function also emerges out of his close communion with the Spirit. Jesus begins his public ministry with words cited from Isaiah 61: "The *Spirit of the Lord* is on me, because he has *anointed* me to proclaim good news to the poor" (Lk 4:18). Therefore, as the Man who is God, the superior Prophet, he is fully qualified to speak for God.

The final descriptor in this christological masterpiece in Hebrews 1:2-3 is an action, Christ's completed action in making purification for sin, evidenced in his sitting down "at the right hand of the Majesty in heaven." This statement is climactic because it completes the first statement in the chiasm (the heir of all things sits down). However, the two statements taken together, his act of purification and his session upon ascension, are climactic also in that they have a bearing on all the statements before it. This is where the whole description has been heading. These two significant acts of the Son, purifying and sitting, anticipate the epistle's theme. They actually imply all three offices of Christ: First, they echo the first statement that he has been appointed heir of all things, by speaking of his session as *king* over all the creation, at the right hand of the "Majesty in heaven," sharing it, as Hebrews 2 reveals, with those who will share in his glory (Heb 2:10) and be in co-dominion with him (Heb 2:5-18). Second, they contain the idea of *priesthood* as it references his sacrificial purification of sins in ways that will be expanded on in the epistle. It also speaks of his session, which both implies a completed atoning work and anticipates the ongoing priesthood in which he saves his people completely since he "always lives to intercede for them" (Heb 7:25). Third, they imply also his *prophetic* office, for this action of the Father in elevating his Son communicates volumes—it vindicates his identity as God, for only God sits with the Father in this manner, and most remarkably, it highlights the presence of a Man in that place and so declares the very heart of the gospel. A man who represents the new humanity has been taken up into Majesty so that all in him may find themselves in the presence of God.

There is another implicit reference to the prophetic nature of Jesus in Hebrews 3. The titles of Jesus in this passage are "apostle and high priest." However, the comparison made in this context is with Moses as a prophet. In Hebrews 3:1, the writer urges believers to fix their thoughts on this Jesus because they "share in the heavenly calling," which he has opened up for them by his ascension into heaven on their behalf. This emphasis on Christians' heavenly calling echoes similar passages in the New Testament, such as Colossians 3:1-3. Although the final venue of the redeemed church is on earth, according to Revelation 21—and from this we can safely assume that the new humanity will fulfill its image-bearing co-dominion with Christ—it must not be forgotten that this is first a heavenly community that comes down to earth. Sometimes, in the appropriate emphasis on the earthiness of the eschaton, the notion of a heavenly transformation and orientation is missed in current scholarly evangelicalism. One should not neglect care of creation and the reality that heaven does come to earth in the fullness of the eschaton. But how does the writer of Hebrews motivate his people who are suffering persecution fatigue, having lost homes and suffered a great deal for the gospel? His focus is what is upward, or, better, *who* is upward. Jesus, the apostle who fulfilled his mission for the world, is urging his missional people similarly. Jesus, the high priest, can salve their wounds and impart strength for the journey.

The writer then introduces a comparison in Hebrews 3:2-6 between Jesus and Moses that seems to imply his prophetic character. Moses is spoken of as a prophet from the time of his calling in Exodus 7:1 and as a great prophet in Deuteronomy 34:10. The comparison by the writer of Hebrews is not without respect for Moses. The author describes Moses as "faithful in all God's house" (Heb 3:2), encouraging the Hebrew saints to persevere in their calling within God's house in their time. However, he intends to paint a picture of Jesus that far outstrips Moses, and so to head off the inclinations of some in his audience to defect back to the Jewish faith. So, the greatest encouragement would come from the one greater than Moses.

Jesus' greatness over Moses is related first to the origination of the house in which Moses operated: "Jesus has been found worthy of greater honor than Moses, just as the builder of a house has greater honor than the house itself" (Heb 3:3). The house being a reference to the covenant people of God, the writer points out that Jesus built that community of which Moses was a part. Second, the author equates Jesus irreducibly with God: "God is the builder of everything" (Heb 3:4). Third, Jesus and Moses have different roles within God's house: Moses was faithful in his role as "a servant in all God's house" (Heb 3:5), whereas Jesus is faithful as "*the* Son *over* God's house" (Heb 3:6). Fourth, Moses was merely a type or figuration of Christ, "bearing witness to what would be spoken by God in the future" (Heb 3:5). Jesus is greater since he is the antetype of the type. In

Hebrews 3:6, the writer declares, "And we are his house, if indeed we hold firmly to our confidence and the hope in which we glory." Here he includes the readers in "the house" and calls them to be faithful as Moses was, especially in light of who Jesus is, who he is for them, and what he enables them to be.

In so doing, the author hints that the readers are also in the prophetic role, just as Moses was and as Jesus is as the supreme Prophet. This agrees with the prophetic mantle imparted in one sense to the whole people of God through the Spirit's empowering, as in Acts 2:17 (referencing Joel 2)—"your sons and daughters will prophesy." It also resonates with the specific role of preachers in the church who speak the "oracles of God" (1 Pet 4:11 KJV) or the "very words of God" (NIV). This reflects a high view of preaching, that when preachers truly expound the Word, Christ is preaching. Therefore, while there is a uniqueness to the prophetic office of Jesus Christ, given he is the Word, there is also a continuity between his prophetic ministry and that of his church in general witness (Jn 20:19-23) and through gifted prophet-preachers, both through their participation in his ministry. Patrick Schreiner stresses the continuity between the earthly prophetic ministry of Christ and its heavenly role. He recognizes that Jesus' "commission" has been "realized in a new way . . . thrust into a higher gear" by his ascent: "[Jesus] empowered his people and unified them under his sovereign voice. He gave them his Spirit and authorized him to go forward in his prophetic work. . . . His people are empowered to carry on his prophetic work because Christ's presence is mediated to them by the Spirit."[17]

Thus, Christ's prophetic ministry, in which his prophetic people participate, is a continuing ministry in the same manner as his priestly ministry, which also continues "enabled by his ascension and royal enthronement."[18] This is what enables the prophetic speaking of the

---

[17] Schreiner, *Ascension of Christ*, 20-21.
[18] Fergusson, "Ascension of Christ," 98.

church, and it is primarily through his church that the ascended Christ speaks:

> Now, as Christ is absent from his disciples, they proclaim him as Lord. This proclamation, however, is one in which Christ is not only object but also subject. The church speaks of him, but in this action he speaks through the church to the world. In other words, through the Spirit, Christ himself is present and active in the church's *kerygma*. In the ministry of proclamation, Christ as the true Word of God, is again heard.[19]

Though Christ's ongoing prophetic office is primarily through the preachers in the church, it also includes the proclamation that is the Lord's Supper or the Eucharist in the church: "For whenever you eat this bread and drink this cup, you proclaim the Lord's death until he comes" (1 Cor 11:26). Thus, Word and sacrament are together a prophetic speaking of Christ through his church to the world, a sentiment Fergusson expresses: "In the ministry of proclamation, Christ, as the true Word of God, is again heard. Similarly, in the eucharist, Christ as our incarnate, crucified, risen, and ascended Lord becomes sacramentally visible and tangible."[20]

We may summarize by saying that the ascension is Christ's accession into the fullness of his messianic identity as prophet, priest, and king. He is King, Priest, and Prophet in one person, and each office influences the other. However, the ascended Christ is not there alone. He is there as one who has come into irrevocable union with humanity, and his offices are shared with his people on earth by the work of the Spirit, who is coinherent with the Son, mediating his presence to the church and its persons. He is there as one who has been his people's atoning sacrifice and now sits in God's presence and on his throne for them. The ascension is thus the celebratory climax or symbol of acceptance of the atonement of humans in Christ. They are reconciled

---

[19]Fergusson, "Ascension of Christ," 98.
[20]Fergusson, "Ascension of Christ," 98.

and justified in him. But their ongoing sanctification or theosis until glorification continues by means of their corporate eternal existence in Christ and his ongoing intercessory priestly ministry.

These realities anticipate the following soteriological and eschatological themes developed in subsequent chapters: the ascension of Jesus in a glorified, deified body as anticipation of the theosis toward glorification of redeemed humanity; the event of the giving of the Holy Spirit triggered by the ascension; and the event anticipated by the ascension—the second coming. Before developing these themes, however, it is essential to clarify further two ontological or christological themes: first, what the session and intercession of Christ mean for him and therefore for us, and second, to identify and clarify some of the mysteries of the ascension and the ascended Christ.

6

THE GLORY OF A COMPLETED ATONEMENT, THE GLORY OF AN ETERNAL SALVATION

Atonement Accomplished in the Session, Atonement Applied in the Intercession of Christ

IN THIS CHAPTER, I consider first the glory of the kingly priesthood of Christ. In the punctiliar event of his session, his sacrifice as Priest offered on earth is acknowledged and celebrated, and his kingly coronation is enacted. Second, I reflect on his continuing *intercession* for his church, paying attention to the security he gives his people, the absolution he grants them, the prayers and worship that he leads on their behalf, and the strength and the sympathy he communicates to them in their suffering as one who has suffered and suffers with them. This chapter is *christological* but has *soteriological and cosmological* repercussions. It will focus on Christ's session, but in getting there, it journeys through the categories of the atonement on earth, in his person, through his incarnation, vicarious humanity, death, and resurrection. It will interpret the session of Jesus as the sign of an *atonement* accepted as complete.

THE SESSION OF THE ASCENDED GREAT HIGH PRIEST: ATONEMENT ACCOMPLISHED

The nature of the ascended Christ's person—that he is God and the God-Man—is his glory. Nevertheless, equally vital for the gospel is that he ascends as the glorified *man* who is God. The reality that a human person entered the presence of God in heaven assumes the union of the Son with humanity by his incarnation—a union anticipated from eternity and one that will continue throughout eternity (Heb 7:16-25). Thus, because the Son became one with our humanity, he acted vicariously on our behalf. Stephen Seamands affirms that the church fathers believed that "the major movements in Christ's life were now movements they were caught up in too."[1] Having believed in Christ, they understood that they were "in Christ," meaning that what Christ had accomplished in these major movements had become true for them, including the ascension. This affirms that the *ordo historia* of Christ—the historical order of Christ's existence—becomes the *ordo salutis* of his people—the order of their salvation.

Colossians 3:1-4 reflects some of these movements in the history of Jesus in which we participate: "Since, then, you have been raised with Christ, set your hearts on things above, where Christ is, seated at the right hand of God. Set your minds on things above, not on earthly things. For you died, and your life is now hidden with Christ in God. When Christ, who is your life, appears, then you also will appear with him in glory." We are one with him in the historical events of his death, resurrection, ascension, and appearance at the second coming. His death means that we died, his resurrection that we live, his ascension that we sit as risen ones with him at the right hand of God, his appearing that we will appear with him. Our destiny in all this is clear: it is glory, a glory in which we already participate now as those present in him at the right hand of God, and a glory we will reflect more fully

---

[1] Stephen A. Seamands, *Give Them Christ: Preaching His Incarnation, Crucifixion, Resurrection, Ascension, and Return* (Downers Grove, IL: InterVarsity Press, 2012), 142.

when we are present as his bride at the second coming in glory. In 2 Thessalonians 1, Paul speaks of the second coming as "the day he [Christ] comes to be *glorified in his holy people and to be marveled at among all those who have believed*" (2 Thess 1:10). The New Testament speaks of both the ascension and the second coming as events when Christ is glorified but also of how his people, joined to him forever, will reflect that glory.

Hebrews 1, as noted, describes the eternal Son as the "radiance of God's *glory*" (Heb 1:3), and Hebrews 2 speaks of his bringing "many sons and daughters to *glory*" (Heb 2:10). Their glory is *reflected*, whereas his glory is *radiant*, inherent to who he is as God. His is "unborrowed light," whereas ours is borrowed by participation in him.[2] This notion of the inherent glory of the Son given to his people with whom he is in union is present throughout the New Testament.

For example, on the one hand, when Paul describes the ascension in his proto-creed of 1 Timothy 3, it is Jesus' glory that is the focus: he "was taken up in *glory*" (1 Tim 3:16). At the second coming, we are told we will see "the Son of Man coming on the clouds of heaven, with power and great *glory*" (Mt 24:30), and it is safe to assume that he already radiates this glory in heaven as a result of the ascension. On the other hand, the New Testament speaks of the glory of the ascended and coming Christ as shared with and in his people, progressively now as they contemplate his glory (2 Cor 3:18) and more fully after they have seen his face and been beatified (1 Jn 3:2). Thus, Paul assures us that "our present sufferings are not worth comparing with the *glory* that will be revealed in us" (Rom 8:18), that Christ in us is "the hope of *glory*" (Col 1:27), that Christ's glory at the second coming will not be good news for those who do not believe (2 Thess 1:8) but that his glory will be seen "in his holy people" and "be marveled at among all those who have believed" (2 Thess 1:9-10).

---

[2] A phrase from Joseph Armitage Robinson's transfiguration hymn "'Tis Good Lord to Be Here," in *Hymns, Ancient & Modern* (Atlanta: Canterbury, 2022), 318.

The salvation accomplished by the ascended Christ is accompanied "with eternal *glory*" (2 Tim 2:10).

These thoughts perhaps inspired the words of another hymn, one written by Count Zinzendorf, the founder of a United Brethren community in Herrnhut, Germany:

> Jesus, thy blood and righteousness,
> my beauty are, my glorious dress;
> 'midst flaming worlds, in these arrayed,
> with joy shall I lift up my head.[3]

Having surveyed some non-Hebrews texts on the session of Christ in glory and its implications for his people, let us consider four texts from Hebrews.

Hebrews 1:3. "After he had provided purification for sins, he sat down at the right hand of the Majesty in heaven." Implied in this verse is a royal coronation, which signals a completion. The session is the crowning of the king, returning after his triumphant conquest of sin, death, and the devil on behalf of humanity. The regal overtones are suggested, as already indicated, from the corresponding opening phrase in the chiasm of Hebrews 1:1-3: he was "appointed heir of all things" (Heb 1:2). The description of the location of Christ's session as "the right hand of the *Majesty in heaven*" further suggests royalty and coronation. He is enthroned in majesty, a majesty he shares with the Father and the Spirit.

However, a priestly dynamic is also at work in this passage, suggested by the phrase "after he had made purification for sins." The atonement, spoken of here as "purification for sins" *in the past tense* ("after he had provided," NIV), is completed, and therefore the *sitting down* of Jesus is a sign of this.[4] Jesus offers himself to the Father as he ascends, but this is not an atoning action but a triumphant one—an

---

[3] Nikolaus Ludwig von Zinzendorf, "Jesus, Thy Blood and Righteousness," trans. John Wesley, in *Common Praise*, 111.
[4] "After he had provided" translates an aorist middle participle, *poiēsamenos*.

act by which the Son gives to the Father his devotion and a scarred body indicative of a finished work of atonement, leading to the Father's seating him by his side. This scarred body is the basis of John's depiction of Jesus as a Lamb before God, perpetually as freshly slain. Commenting on Revelation 5:6, Watchman Nee writes of the "eternal freshness of the cross" to God:

> In heaven at the time of the ushering in of eternity, the Lord will still be the One who is freshly slain! Oh, the eternal freshness of the cross! . . . In the future when the heavenly glory breaks forth, the glory of the cross will prove unfading! When God's redeemed ascend to heaven, they will find the redemption of the cross still as fresh as before! . . . In Revelation, He is mentioned as the Lamb twenty-eight times! The glory of the Lord's cross will outshine all ages! . . . The wound is still there! The eternal wound guarantees eternal salvation. The crucifixion of the Lamb becomes our eternal memorial. God can never forget this. The angels can never forget this, and those ascended and saved ones can never forget the redemption of the cross.[5]

This idea of an eternal wound that guarantees eternal salvation is in keeping with the sentiments of Revelation 13:8, which states that the Lamb was "slain from the creation of the world." The predetermined nature of the death of Jesus (see also Acts 2:23) and its efficacy is fulfilled by the presence of Jesus in "the power of an indestructible life" (Heb 7:16) at the right hand of God, based on a redemption accomplished in his death and resurrection, a presence and an event that is both retrospective and prospective in its effects.

Hebrews 8:1-2. "Now the main point of what we are saying is this: We do have such a high priest, who sat down at the right hand of the throne of the Majesty in heaven, and who serves in the sanctuary, the true tabernacle set up by the Lord, not by a mere human being." This passage expresses the distinction between the punctiliar session ("sat

---

[5]Watchman Nee, *The Christian*, Collected Works (Anaheim, CA: Living Stream Ministries, 1975), 1/6:832.

down") and the ongoing serving of the royal priest ("serves in the sanctuary"), the contrast between a throne and a tabernacle or sanctuary—the first referencing the office of Christ as King and the second his office as Priest, in close juxtaposition. The tenses also justify one as an event and the other as an ongoing process. On the one hand, the content is unsurprising given that the author in Hebrews 6–7 has discussed the offices of Priest and King in the order of Melchizedek. On the other hand, the scope of these statements is mind-boggling: a king in the "true tabernacle," a priest on a throne.

This verse confirms the punctiliar session as an event signifying the pleasure of the Father with what the Son had accomplished through victory over evil and satisfaction for sin. Thus, royal and sacerdotal themes combine even in the act of his session. The relative passivity of *being seated* is also contrasted with the activity entailed in the intercession. As in Psalm 110:1, cited in Hebrews 1:13, the Son is seated passively by God, who then begins the processive subjugation of his enemies. There is no hint that the Son effects further atonement during his session. It is a celebration, an honoring, an exaltation in light of the mission accomplished.

Hebrews 10:12–14. "But when this priest had offered for all time one sacrifice for sins, he sat down at the right hand of God, and since that time he waits for his enemies to be made his footstool. For by one sacrifice he has made perfect forever those who are being made holy." This text, which also has Psalm 110:1 in mind, further justifies the connection between the atonement as accomplished and the session of Jesus, indicating both the punctiliar nature of the sacrifice made by Jesus and its eternal efficacy. This text emphasizes the *priestly* and emphatically once-for-all nature of his sacrifice and therefore of his session. His sacrificial work as a priest is over, and the Father rewards it in his session. The "one sacrifice," referred to as perfecting forever "those who are being made holy," in light of how sacrificial language is used in Hebrews and elsewhere, must refer to the cross event as an offering or sacrifice to the Father, not to a further atoning event when he offers himself to God at his ascension. Ephesians 5:2 similarly describes Christ, who "gave himself up for us as a fragrant offering and sacrifice to God." It is unlikely that this would refer to something other than what transpired on the cross.

It is not necessary to assume that the offering up of the Son to the Father happened at the ascension. It was enacted in the presence of the Father on the cross. The Father and the Son are always present to each other (Jn 10:30, 38), mutually internal, in perfect communion. There is no reason to assume that this is not the case when Jesus goes into the garden of Gethsemane, prays for any possible alternative to the cross, with his *human will* wrestles with a possible way out, with his *divine will* submits to the Father, and in his one person goes to the cross in obedience and love. The prayer of Matthew 26:36-46 is a communion between the Father and the Son, with no hint of a rift between them, a voluntary commitment of the Son to the Father, not cosmic child abuse. And the Trinity did not break up when Jesus suffered for our sin on the cross, not even when he as a man let out the cry of dereliction, "My God, my God, why have you forsaken me?" (Mt 27:46; see Ps 22:1). This was the cry of the Man for all humanity recapitulating true humanity in his act of obedience, bearing humanity's sin, in the presence of the Trinity, of which he is a person. This is the one divine-human person who is both judged and the Judge, the judged as a man representing all humanity, and the one who is also the Judge as God with the Father and the Spirit. This is a voluntary act of the Son, who from beginning to end is in communion with the Father (Lk 23:34, 46). The Trinity can never be severed.

This reality of the presence of the Father—indeed, the whole Godhead together—in the climactic sacrificial event of the cross may evoke an alternative to David Moffitt's recently expressed notion that the ascension/session event was an atoning act, indeed, the climactic one.⁶ I will say more about Moffitt's important new perspective in chapter eight. Suffice it to say here that his desire to keep the atonement always within the person of Jesus Christ is commendable, as is his understanding that the atonement is not punctiliar but within the whole history of Jesus. This is based on his exposition of Hebrews 1–2, which makes the deity and humanity of Christ the window from which to view the later passages concerning the atonement.⁷ This understanding brings the ontological or filial aspects of atonement to bear on the forensic, sacrificial dynamics. However, this does not necessarily lead to the conclusion that all the events in Jesus' history are efficacious in the same way with respect specifically to the atonement. There are clear assertions in the epistle to the Hebrews to the effect that atonement had been accomplished on earth before his ascension to heaven. Thus, to make the Son's ascension, coronation, and then his intercession part of the objectively accomplished atonement, as Moffitt does, is, I think, a mistake precisely because Hebrews speaks of an efficacious purification of sin before he sits down at the Father's right hand (Heb 1:3; 10:12).

In fairness, this locating of atonement by Moffitt appears to have some precedence, for example, in the work of T. F. Torrance, who, following the lead of John Knox, insisted that the "ascension is not just an addendum to the story of Jesus . . . but it is one of the great salvation events."⁸ The notion that the ascension of Jesus is evidence of the deification of the vicarious humanity Jesus assumed, leading to the theosis of redeemed humanity, is a strong theme in Torrance. However, whether he viewed the ascension as an *atoning* as opposed to a *saving* event seems unclear.

Atonement, for Torrance, is always accomplished within the person of Christ, as it should be.

---

⁶David M. Moffitt, *Rethinking the Atonement: New Perspectives on Jesus's Death, Resurrection, and Ascension* (Grand Rapids, MI: Baker Academic, 2022), 159-80.
⁷Moffitt, *Rethinking the Atonement*, 138-41.
⁸T. F. Torrance, *Theology in Reconstruction* (Grand Rapids, MI: Eerdmans, 1965), 151.

However, the offering of the Son's person to God on the cross does not contradict the notion that the work of Christ was accomplished within the person of Christ. Nor does it suggest that his work on the cross was carried out outside of God's presence. The writer of Hebrews sees all space as sacred, including in the cross event, removing the need that Moffitt sees for the ascension as the moment when Christ offers himself as a sacrifice in the presence of the Father. Rather, when Christ offers himself as a sacrifice to God on the cross, he does so in God's presence. Heaven and earth are one in that event as the locus of the presence of God. The need Moffitt sees for Jesus' atonement to be in the ascension is based on the figurations in the Levitical offerings and those on the Day of Atonement, which he points out were first slain before they were offered up and accepted as atonement by God.[9] This is to press the figuration too far. With respect to the antetypical offering up of Christ on the cross and his being slain, these are intertwined and inseparable. The timing is less important than the factuality of both. Michael Morales has it that the significance of the atonement depicted on the Day of Atonement was that "it makes possible life in the divine Presence."[10] The accomplishing of that is through blood, which connotes life, sprinkled before and on the mercy seat. This is quite evidently a figuration of atonement or reconciliation in the cross event, not the ascension.

A passage in Hebrews that must be reckoned with is Hebrews 9:1-26, where the atonement is described as being accomplished by Jesus in the "sacrifice of himself," in the immediate presence of God, on earth, on the cross. Although Christ is on earth, as he offers himself up and dies, what he enacts occurs in the heavenly tabernacle: "But when Christ came as high priest of the good things that are now already

---

[9]Moffitt, *Rethinking the Atonement*, 167-70, 179. See Christian Eberhart, *The Sacrifice of Jesus: Understanding Atonement Biblically* (Eugene, OR: Wipf & Stock, 2018), for insights into the Levitical sacrifices and their interpretation within the whole history of Jesus.
[10]L. Michael Morales, *Who Shall Ascend the Mountain of the Lord? A Biblical Theology of the Book of Leviticus* (Downers Grove, IL: IVP Academic, 2015), 82.

here, he went through the greater and more perfect tabernacle that is not made with human hands, that is to say, is not a part of this creation" (Heb 9:11). Where is Christ as he dies to accomplish eternal redemption? The writer of Hebrews is clear: "He entered the *Most Holy Place* once for all by his own blood, thus obtaining eternal redemption" (Heb 9:12). In his offering himself up to God, in his shedding of blood, in his enacting redemption, he is on earth on a cross, but he is also in heaven. All is sacred space here.

This passage continues with an unequivocal acclamation of the efficacy of this offering of Christ to God, enacted within God's "greater and more perfect tabernacle." This tabernacle has been in heaven eternally as the prototype for the earthly tabernacle of the Old Testament. However, when Christ ascends the cross, that tabernacle is his body (Jn 1:14; Heb 10:20) and as such the very presence of God where atonement is accomplished. This is expressed in Hebrews 9:14: "How much more, then, will the blood of Christ, who through the eternal Spirit offered himself unblemished to God, cleanse our consciences from acts that lead to death, so that we may serve the living God!" The ascension is thus not needed to finish the atonement. Instead, it is the occasion to celebrate the atonement and the coronation of the King-Priest.

Hebrews 9:26 goes on to reference his appearing "once for all at the culmination of the ages," which in context clearly means his life on earth, which culminates in his "do[ing] away with sin by the sacrifice of himself." He does not have to "suffer many times" but only once. There can be no continuance of atonement in heaven, for there can be no suffering in heaven. That appearing on earth is then contrasted with his entry into "heaven itself," not just heaven in earth but the actual abode of God, where the homilist speaks of his appearing "for us in God's presence." His ascension, session, and intercession there in God's immediate presence signals a completed atonement and its perpetual application in all aspects of our salvation. But clearly, it is his presence there, not a continuous atoning work there involving suffering, that perpetuates our salvation.

Appreciating the value of the ascension in our time is timely. However, it must not be forgotten that what Jesus commands his church to do as the center of its life is the Eucharist, which commemorates his death, not the ascension; his body given on the cross, his blood shed for us. A body now ascended, yes. But a body first sacrificed (Heb 10:10). In the Eucharist envisioned by Calvin, for example, the people of God are caught up afresh in Christ's ascension, but this is only after they have fed spiritually on Christ and his sacrifice for us. This event in the life of the church is the weekly re-intervention of God by the Spirit, which feeds the church afresh with what his historic intervention into human history effected and then draws us up into his presence with the ascended Christ.

Hebrews 12:1-2.
Therefore, since we are surrounded by such a great cloud of witnesses, let us throw off everything that hinders and the sin that so easily entangles. And let us run with perseverance the race marked out for us, fixing our eyes on Jesus, the pioneer and perfecter of faith. For the joy set before him he endured the cross, scorning its shame, and sat down at the right hand of the throne of God.

The contrast drawn by the writer here is clearly between the cross endured and the throne accessed. A cross endured for salvation with a "joy" awaiting, not further atonement. A cross endured so that atonement was accomplished ("originator") and would then be applied to the end of their pilgrimage ("perfecter"). The nature of the joy awaiting Jesus is not specified precisely here but seems to be appropriately defined by being in parallel with the phrase "sat down at the right hand of the throne of God." It may include the joy of enthronement by God, the endowment of glory (1 Tim 3:16), the gift of the Holy Spirit from the Father (Jn 14:16; 15:26; Acts 1:4; 2:33), the reward of a church, his body and bride (Is 53:10; Ps 22:22), and universal acclaim (Ps 22:27-28; Phil 2:10-11). All this following his impalement of the cross, where shame and aloneness were his lot.

The notion suggested in Hebrews 12:2 of Jesus as the perfecter of the faith triggers the second half of this consideration of Jesus the great High Priest in his *intercession* for his people.

THE INTERCESSION OF THE ASCENDED GREAT HIGH PRIEST: ATONEMENT APPLIED

The distinction between Christ's session, signaling completion, and his intercession, implying an incomplete and ongoing work, is made clear by their juxtaposition in Hebrews 8:1-2, as noted above: "Now the main point of what we are saying is this: We do have such a high priest, *who sat down* at the right hand of the throne of the Majesty in heaven, and *who serves* in the sanctuary, the true tabernacle set up by the Lord, not by a mere human being." What does it mean to "serve" his people in—a locale significantly different from a manger or on a cross but in a sanctuary—the true tabernacle? What does he do in that prototypical sanctuary where God and humans meet? From the immediate and overall context in Hebrews, we may discern the following aspects of the intercessory ministry of Christ.

He guarantees eternal security. The eternal security of Christ's people is the great theme of the second half of Hebrews 6. Whatever the first half means, it cannot infer the loss of eternal security since the second half makes it abundantly clear that true believers (as opposed to those who merely profess to be believers) have eternal security, grounded in the life and character of the ascended Christ. The believer's eternal security is grounded first on the "unchanging nature of [God's] purpose," as expressed in the promise given to Abraham, and then God's oath, which reinforces the promise (Heb 6:17-18). On top of these two "unchangeable things" that were uttered in the past for the assurance of God's people, the writer adds that true believers have "fled to take hold of the hope set before us" (Heb 6:18). They can thus look forward, not just backward, for the guarantee of their security. And then, to seal the matter, the writer urges an upward look to anchor the soul. The object of that contemplative look upward is to the one who has entered the "inner sanctuary behind the curtain" (Heb 6:19), our "forerunner, Jesus" (Heb 6:20), the one who has gone on before us into God's presence and who will ensure we will follow after him, the one who is a "high priest forever, in the order of Melchizedek" (Heb 6:20).

This last phrase anticipates the further reinforcement of eternal security gained by the writer's exposition of the Melchizedekan high priesthood of Christ in Hebrews 6, in phrases such as these:

> one who has become a priest not on the basis of a regulation as to his ancestry but *on the basis of the power of an indestructible life.* . . .
>
> "The Lord has sworn
>   and will not change his mind:
>   'You are a priest forever.'" (Heb 7:16, 21)
>
> Because of this oath, Jesus has become the *guarantor of a better covenant.* (Heb 7:22)
>
> But *because Jesus lives forever, he has a permanent priesthood.* (Heb 7:24)
>
> Therefore he is *able to save completely* [right on to the end] *those who come to God through him, because he always lives to intercede for them.* (Heb 7:25)

Eternal security is God's work, the work of the ascended Christ. It has a corresponding phenomenology in the lives of those who are secure. Hebrews is full of warnings for those who have made a profession of faith but have not continued or are contemplating defecting from the faith. In so doing, they would show themselves as not truly in the faith. The only guarantee of eternal security from a human perspective, therefore, is the perseverance of the saints. Even Jesus distinguished between those who truly believed and those who only professed to be believers: Many "believed [*episteusan*] in his name. But Jesus would not entrust [*episteuen*] himself to them, for he knew all people" (Jn 2:23-25). There are several exhortations in the New Testament toward self-examination concerning the genuineness of faith. However, the assurance of salvation is the greatest in those who look away from themselves to the ascended Christ.

He cleanses and forms his people. Christ, in his ongoing priestly ministry, cleanses and sanctifies his people, granting them absolution in response to their confessions. This ongoing work of salvation is the application of atonement, not its objective accomplishment. Its focus is restoring fellowship, not a fresh work of judicial expiation or propitiation. It is not a repetition of justification but rather the continuance of progressive sanctification as sins are confessed and slowly overcome. It is what Jesus meant when he educated Peter in John 13 about the difference between having his whole body washed and just his feet. Peter was already clean, meaning he possessed salvation in Christ by a once-for-all act of God's grace. He was justified, we might say, in Pauline parlance, although we recognize this was not a concept he fully grasped in John 13. He was forgiven his sin and was in a saving relationship with God. Nevertheless, he would continue to commit sins, including denying his Lord. As Peter's compatriot John would later say in his first epistle, he would need to confess those sins, not for a new salvation but for restoration of fellowship to the Father: "If we claim to be without sin, we deceive ourselves and the truth is not in us. If we confess our sins, he is faithful and just and will forgive us our sins and purify us from all unrighteousness. If we claim we have not sinned, we make him out to be a liar and his word is not in us" (1 Jn 1:8-10). What does the High Priest do in heaven, in the true sanctuary? He hears confession, restores fellowship, and purifies "us from *all* unrighteousness." He is at work in his people to restore when sins have compromised relational fellowship with his Father and to purify them of their sins and sinful tendencies—sins of ignorance and willful sins. This is the work of the Son and the Spirit in making his people holy. The sacrifice of Christ not only sets apart God's people, which is a fait accompli, but in its application results in their ongoing sanctification: "For by one sacrifice he has made perfect forever those who are *being made holy*" (Heb 10:14).

The passage that follows this in Hebrews 10 speaks of the new covenant within which the High Priest operates, where the possibility of cultivating holiness in the new covenant people of God unfolds. Holy living is related to the internalization of the work of Christ in human hearts and minds: "I will put my laws in their hearts, and I will write them on their minds" (Heb 10:16). This pursuit of holiness of the regenerate people in Christ is grounded in an already granted forensic forgiveness ("Their sins and lawless acts I will remember no more," Heb 10:17), accomplished by one sacrifice for sin forever ("And where these have been forgiven, sacrifice for sin is no longer necessary," Heb 10:18). In Paul's words, justification, expressed as a fait accompli in Romans 5:1 ("since we have been justified through faith") for those who are in union with Christ, accomplished through the propitiating, redeeming, sacrifice of Christ (Rom 3:25-26), does not lead to license or antinomianism ("Shall we go on sinning so that grace may increase?" Rom 6:1) but rather to the living out of the history of Christ in his death and resurrection, in the sanctified life.

Similarly, John Calvin argues that union with the ascended Christ (*unio cum Christo*) is the grounding for the twin graces (*duplex gratia*) of the believer—justification and sanctification—and perseverance.[11] Calvin argues that Christ, who is made to us righteousness (1 Cor 1:30), is likewise said to have been "made to us sanctification . . . because he has, so to speak, presented us to his Father in his own person, that we may be renewed to true holiness by his Spirit."[12] Julie Canlis clarifies that the union with Christ that leads to justification and sanctification

---

[11] J. Todd Billings, *Calvin, Participation, and the Gift: The Activity of Believers in Union with Christ* (Oxford: Oxford University Press, 2007), 15, 57-61.

[12] See Calvin's commentary on Jn 17:9 in John Calvin, *Commentary on the Gospel According to John*, trans. W. Pringle, Calvin's Commentaries 2 (Grand Rapids, MI: Baker, 1979), 181.

is a relational one: "In the wide world of *koinonia*, imputation has a central place by being the direct result of *unio cum Christo*, a distinctively participative category."[13] As such, it is more than just imputation. It is impartation of cleansing and holiness.

Undergirding the believer's union with Christ (*unio cum Christo*) is the union that was effected at the incarnation and has continued into the ascended life of Christ—the hypostatic union of the two natures of Christ (*unio hypostatica*), the union through which the eternal Son as a person took into himself a truly human nature. Having taken this *anhypostatic* human nature and having acted vicariously for humanity, he cleansed it. On that basis, he continues to do so as he intercedes for his redeemed people. His participation in humanity is the foundation for our participation in Christ, facilitated by the Spirit. Such participation in Christ facilitates the transformation of believers in holiness. His union with us and our union with him continues. These two unions continue as he intercedes for us in his ascended status.

Hebrews 12 also uses a participatory term to describe how believers grow in holiness: "we . . . share in his holiness" (Heb 12:10), meaning we are participants in the holiness of God. The verse following indicates both the divine agency and the human response in sanctification or theosis, implying a concurrent agency of the human responding in the working of God: "No discipline seems pleasant at the time, but painful. Later on, however, it produces a harvest of righteousness and peace *for those who have been trained by it*" (Heb 12:11). For discipline in the life of believers to be productive, they are to be "trained by it." The adversities encountered under the providence of God lead them to spiritual practices that will train them in holiness: introspective practices, leading to confession, repentance, and soul knowledge; contemplative practices, leading them to look

---

[13]Julie Canlis, *Calvin's Ladder: A Spiritual Theology of Ascent and Ascension* (Grand Rapids, MI: Eerdmans, 2010), 144.

away from themselves and their circumstances to the ascended Christ; mortification practices that are receptacles for entry into the reality of union with Christ in his death; vivification practices that renew them in the reality of his resurrection and ascension.

The Pauline teaching on cleansing and sanctification is clearly grounded in participation in the history of Jesus Christ, in his death, resurrection, and ascension. Colossians 2:20–3:4 begins with encouragement to live out what is already a reality for believers, their death in Christ's death: "*Since you died with Christ* to the elemental spiritual forces of this world, why, as though you still belonged to the world, do you submit to its rules?" (Col 2:20). Then, in Colossians 3:1-4, the theme of union with Christ in his resurrection emerges, motivating contemplation of the ascended Christ: "Since, then, *you have been raised with Christ*, set your hearts *on things above, where Christ is, seated at the right hand of God*. Set your minds *on things above*, not on earthly things. For you died, and your life is now hidden with Christ in God. When Christ, who is your life, appears, then you also will appear with him in glory." An important dimension in the cleansing from vices, negatively speaking, and the development of virtue, positively speaking, is the practice of contemplation. As the believer gazes on Christ, there is an awareness that the old life lived independently of God has died, and there is a new life emerging from hiddenness in that Christ. There is also encouragement to live in light of the return of the ascended Christ, when the struggle for sanctification will be over, when there will be a sharing in his glory.

Paul further teaches sanctification in all its aspects, through contemplation, at the end of 2 Corinthians 3. He emphasizes, on the one hand, the work of the Spirit, articulating his deity and the divine freedom he brings to regenerated people: "Now the Lord is the Spirit, and where the Spirit of the Lord is, there is freedom" (2 Cor 3:17). However, there is a focus on contemplation too: "And we all, who with unveiled faces contemplate the Lord's glory, are being transformed into his image with ever-increasing glory, which comes from the Lord, who is the Spirit" (2 Cor 3:18). The text focuses on "the Lord's glory," which infers his ascended state. The KJV has a certain cadence that can be captured by emphasizing the main verbs: "beholding . . . are changed."

I fear that *contemplation* is much neglected in Christian life today. We do not have time for it, not even in our church services, which must run like clockwork. The central practice that facilitates contemplation is the Lord's Supper. There we are to remember and contemplate the one we remember. There we are to perceive his obedience, cross, shame, and suffering. There we are to sense his presence as the ascended one and gaze on his triumph and his dazzling glory, and so be transformed. The repeated practice of the Eucharist is critical to the formation of the Christian self as an other-oriented person, in a manner that reflects the Trinity. As David Ford writes, "Who can tell in advance what sort of self is being shaped year after year as these practices are interwoven thoughtfully with all the rest of life?"[14] In habitual eucharistic facing of the ascended, glorified Christ, we are to feed on him spiritually. There we are caught up afresh by the Spirit into the heavenlies in Christ. And we are cleansed and formed.

There is also a place for contemplation in our personal life with God. The well-known practice of lectio divina has, as its climactic stage, the merging of meditation on the written Word into contemplation of the living Word, Christ. But whatever method one uses for systematic Bible reading, the goal must be to seek the Spirit's leading so that the living, ascended Christ is encountered. "Beyond the sacred page, I seek Thee, Lord," the old hymn goes.[15]

He leads his people's prayers and worship. The great High Priest leads a priestly community in worship and intercessory prayers. Christ's ongoing work of prayer on our behalf is possible because of

---

[14]David S. Ford, *Self and Salvation* (Cambridge: Cambridge University Press, 1999), 165.
[15]Mary A. Lathbury, "Break Thou the Bread of Life," Hymnary.org, accessed July 4, 2024, https://hymnary.org/text/break_thou_the_bread_of_life.

the ascension, not just the atonement. The believer has access to the presence of God because of the atonement, but active engagement in prayer is enabled by the ascended High Priest. We noted concerning Hebrews 8:2 that Jesus "serves in the sanctuary, the true tabernacle set up by the Lord, not by a mere human being." "Serves" (Greek *leitourgos*) is a priestly, liturgical term. In Hebrews 9:14, another priestly, liturgical word describes what we, his people, are privileged to do as a result of the self-offering of the Son on our behalf: "so that we may serve [Greek *latreuein*] the living God!" So Christ is the one Priest, the liturgy leader, the leader of the church's worship, presenting the priestly worship of the many, in a way that is perfect and fragrant to the Father. Priestly ministry for the priests in the Priest has to do first with liturgical life. Christ is the worship leader, offering up his people's Spirit-evoked praises and prayers in his intercessory work to the Father.

The role of Christ's high priesthood in the church's worship is greatly neglected in the life and worship of the evangelical church. The idea that the primary worship leader in the church's services is not the worship pastor, senior pastor, or priest but Jesus, the high priest, is not superspiritual talk. Worship is possible only through participation in the Son's communion with the Father by the Spirit.[16] This is not just because we are distracted sinners as we come to worship but because of the metaphysical remove between us and God. Because the Man for all humanity has entered the throne room of God for us and represents us to the Father, we can and must invoke his presence and his aid whenever we begin a service. Prayers of invocation and epiclesis must be scattered throughout our liturgy, not just because he is, with the Father and the Spirit, the object of our worship, but because he is the subject of our worship, presenting our worship with us to the Father.

---

[16]See Robin A. Parry, *Worshipping Trinity: Coming Back to the Heart of Worship* (Carlisle, UK: Paternoster, 2005).

In some traditions, by the prayer of epiclesis at the Lord's Supper, the pastor or priest invites the Spirit to come and make real the spiritual presence of Christ in the bread and the wine so that Christ may gather us up afresh and transport us into the presence of the Father. Christ is also the subject and object of the preaching of the church. This motivates the preacher to rely profoundly on Christ in the exegetical preparation of the Word and its delivery. But this is not onerous or overwhelming for the preacher: What greater delight is there than knowing that as you preach, Christ is preaching?

The public and private prayers of the people of God are also impossible without the gracious intercession of the ascended Priest. In Hebrews 4:14-16, his first great statement concerning Christ's high priesthood, the writer asserts that Christ "has ascended into heaven," that he is both "Jesus," the human, and "the Son of God," the divine, and that he can "empathize with our weaknesses." All these realities are in preparation for the great invitation: "Let us then approach God's throne of grace with confidence, so that we may receive mercy and find grace to help us in our time of need" (Heb 4:16). What has made prayer possible is all the Christology that has gone before in the previous verses. We can pray and cry out to God in our crisis "time of need" only because of what Christ has done and what he is doing as we pray. This idea of our prayer as participation in Christ's prayer does not mean we have no agency. The opposite is true. We are never more our authentic selves than when we are in communion with Christ. There is nevertheless what Karl Barth would have called a concursus in this process: Who is praying? I am praying—in his praying, and he is praying—in my praying.

When asked about their prayer lives, Christians often express a sense of failure. It is good news to know that Christ is praying as we pray, translating what we think are feeble prayers and infantile utterances and presenting them to the Father as fitting and beautiful. This awareness takes prayer away from the achievement category and places it in the realm of grace and engracedness, if there is such a word. It is a great comfort to know that the outcome of our prayers is in Jesus' hands, as the Prayer of St. John Chrysostom indicates: "Fulfill now, O Lord, our desires and petitions *as may be best for us*."[17] God always answers our prayers, but not in the way we may expect or want.

James Torrance has reminded the Protestant world in recent years of the reality of engraced and trinitarian prayers in the high priesthood of the ascended Christ. His book *Worship, Community and the Triune God of Grace* exposes much of what passes for worship in Protestant churches in our time as unchristological or Arian, Pelagian, and unitarian. For Torrance, "the real agent in all true worship is Jesus Christ. He is our great High Priest and ascended Lord, the One true worshiper who unites us to Himself by the Spirit in acts of mercy and a life of communion, as He lifts us by word and sacraments into the very triune life of God."[18]

Similarly, J. J. von Allmen's trinitarian description of the human response to God speaks of the worship of God offered by Jesus Christ. He emphasizes that Jesus' whole life was an act of priestly worship to God—"The true glorification of God on earth, which is the perfect worship, has been fulfilled by Jesus Christ in his ministry"—and that his earthly life of worship is included as integral to his Melchizedekan priesthood now:[19]

> If the title of sovereign high priest (after the order of Melchisedek) is clearly supremely appropriate after His ascension, it still remains true that His whole life also must be seen in this liturgical perspective. Moreover, it is probable that Jesus Himself understood His ministry in

---

[17]"The Prayer of St. John Chrysostom," in *The Book of Common Prayer*, by Anglican Church in North America (Huntington Beach, CA: Anglican Liturgy Press, 2019), 52, emphasis added.

[18]James Torrance, *Worship, Community and the Triune God of Grace*, Didsbury Lectures 1994 (Downers Grove, IL: InterVarsity Press, 1996), 17.

[19]Jean-Jacques von Allmen, *Worship: Its Theology and Practice* (New York: Oxford University Press, 1965), 21.

this way; since He came to destroy the works of the devil (1 John 3: 8) and to reconcile men with God through His death (Rom. 5:10 etc.).[20]

Von Allmen also comments that this worship is ongoing and is now rendered by Jesus to God in heaven: "The present of the history of salvation is the heavenly offering which Jesus Christ renders to His Father in the glory of the Ascension."[21] We participate in that worship.

Another way we learn participatory prayer is to pray the prayer Jesus taught his disciples. "When you pray, *say* . . ." was Jesus' response to the disciples for teaching on prayer (see Mt 6:5-13). The content of that prayer is as comprehensive and beautifully ordered as prayer can be and is meant to be prayed by all of Jesus' disciples daily. "Give us today our *daily* bread" infers this (Mt 6:11).[22] When Jesus says "Our Father," he includes himself, and the inference is that he is praying it with his disciples. Paul provides another example in Ephesians 3:17, where addressing the Father of glory leads to the invocation of the Spirit's strengthening in order that the Son may "make his home" (NLT) in our hearts so that, gloriously immersed in the immeasurable love of God, we will be filled with the fullness of God. This is a prayer to be prayed often, with God, for the people of God.

Beyond but never isolated from worship and prayer are other priestly duties to which the many, in the one Priest, are called. Peter's use of the term "holy priesthood" in 1 Peter 2:5 describes worship and prayer *within* the church, the "spiritual house": "offering spiritual sacrifices acceptable to God through Jesus Christ" (1 Pet 2:5). The mediation of Jesus is indicated by the phrase "through Jesus Christ." Though the distinction is not completely clear, the function of royal priests has a more outward or missional orientation: "But you are . . .

---

[20] Von Allmen, *Worship*, 21.
[21] Von Allmen, *Worship*, 35, cited in John D. Witvliet, "The Doctrine of the Trinity and the Theology and Practice of Christian Worship in the Reformed Tradition" (PhD diss., University of Notre Dame, 1997), 206.
[22] For a description of the breadth and the nuances of this prayer, see W. Ross Hastings, "The Gospel Orientation of God in Karl Barth's Exposition of the Lord's Prayer," *Crux* 59, no. 1 (2023): 10-32.

a royal priesthood . . . that you may declare the praises of him who called you out of darkness into his wonderful light" (1 Pet 2:9). This reflects the kingly priesthood of Jesus. Peter's language here is strongly covenantal, suggesting God's intent that the people of Christ are the new Israel, the new priesthood. The calling of royal priests involves missional service outside the church, including their daily work, the pursuit of justice in society, life in marriage, and singleness in community, as well as their verbal witness to Christ—all of this in communion with the ascended King. He empowers the priestly activity of the whole people of God.

A fresh realization emerges, in light of their identity as the many priests in the family of the one ascended Priest, that *all* of God's people are holy and royal priests, not just pastors. This invites a new reformation of the church's life and witness, not incentivizing activism but action that flows from the deep life of the church in the ascended Christ and his Holy Spirit. Christ has set apart some to be ministers in the church, but they are not at an ontological remove from the rest despite the tendencies of some congregants to elevate them and some leaders to believe their own press. They are called to high ethical and characterial standards. However, they are mere humans, persons called by Christ to function as apostles, prophets, evangelists, pastors, and teachers, functioning in response to the gifts and calling of the one ascended head of the church (note the connection between the giving of the gifts and the ascension of Jesus in Eph 4:7-10), in participation with *his* mission and ministry. Moreover, they are called primarily in these offices to equip the whole people of God for ministry, not to do the ministry (Eph 4:12). Their aim is that the church would attain the "whole measure of the fullness of Christ" and become the "mature body of him who is the head, that is Christ," and thus be for the glory of Christ, not their own glory (Eph 4:13, 15).

He comforts his people in suffering. The ascended Christ's intercessory ministry includes the comforting reality that he communicates sympathy and strength to God's people in their suffering and temptation, as the one who has already suffered temptations and now continues to suffer sympathetically with them.[23] Hebrews 4:14-16 emphatically expresses Christ's capacity to suffer with and sustain his people, which raises the theological question: Can God suffer? Classical theism or the *actus purus* tradition insists that God cannot suffer and frowns on patripassianism, the idea that the Father can suffer, because suffering means a change in the God assumed to be immutable. Thomas Weinandy, for example, states, "The sin and evil that deprive human beings of some good and so cause them to suffer is contained wholly within the created ontological order and cannot reverberate or wash back into the uncreated order where God alone exists as absolutely good."[24]

How, then, does the Son of God suffer with us? His humanity provides the answer. His divine and human natures exist in an unconfused union. It is in his humanity that he suffers. Yet, we may venture to say that the divine nature of the one person of the Son experiences suffering in a mediate way (as indeed perhaps the Father also), whereas in his humanity, he suffers in an *immediate* sense. We are referring to mediate and immediate in a spatial sense, not in a temporal sense. Hence, Hebrews emphasizes his humanity when considering the sympathy and ongoing intercession of the Priest who lives in the power of an indestructible life (Heb 7:16; see Heb 2). The acknowledged mystery in the ascension's language and the Priest's ascended work should not lead us to spiritualize or demythologize the event or his intercessory ministry.

On the other hand, we must not forget that this Priest is truly God (Heb 1). His priesthood functions because his divine person and his humanity are hypostatically united. He offers his life as a perfect

---

[23] There is a range of opinion on the meanings and appropriateness of empathy and sympathy in sociological and psychological literature.

[24] Thomas G. Weinandy, *Does God Suffer?* (Notre Dame, IN: University of Notre Dame Press, 2000), 153.

sacrifice to God and becomes a true priest for us as God and man. Bringing his deity together with his humanity and history as the incarnate one, T. F. Torrance states:

> The ascension means that our relation to the Saviour is only possible through the historical Jesus, for the historical Jesus is the one locus within our human and creaturely existence where God and man are *hypostatically united*, and where man engulfed in sin and immersed in corruption can get across to God on the ground of reconciliation and atonement freely provided by God himself. The ascension thus means that to all eternity God insists on speaking to us through the historical Jesus. Just because it is the historical and risen Jesus who is ascended, what Jesus says to us, the Jesus whom we meet and hear through the witness of the Gospels, is identical with the eternal Word and Being of God himself.[25]

Torrance asserts that "the ascension . . . sends us back to the incarnation, and to the historical Jesus, and so to a Word and Act of God inseparably implicated in our space and time." He deduces, therefore, that "all contact with the majesty of God as of the glorified Lord is in and through the crucified One," not "some kind of *theologia gloriae* reached by direct speculation of the divine majesty." The ascension, he insists, necessarily "sends us back to a Gospel which is really accessible to frail creatures of earth and history, and a Gospel that is relevant to their bodily existence day by day in the structures and coherences of space and time."[26] Therefore, he concludes,

> Through the historical and crucified Jesus, we really meet with the risen and ascended Lord, we really meet with God in his transcendent glory and majesty, and we really are gathered into the communion of the Son with the Father and of the Father with the Son, and really are taken up through the Spirit to share in the divine life and love that have overflowed to us in Jesus Christ.[27]

---

[25]T. F. Torrance, *Space, Time, and Resurrection* (Grand Rapids, MI: Eerdmans, 1976), 133.
[26]Torrance, *Space, Time, and Resurrection*, 134.
[27]Torrance, *Space, Time, and Resurrection*, 134-35.

Thus, within this understanding of the humanity of the historical Jesus, in continuity with the now-ascended Jesus, we can speak of Christ in his capacity for suffering and sympathy.

Hebrews 4:14-16 emphatically expresses Christ's capacity to suffer with and sustain his people in several ways. First, the passage grounds this in the assurance that the suffering people of God have a great high priest "who has ascended into heaven." His ascension did not imply a loss of the Savior for God's people but the gain of a King-Priest. Second, the identity of that priest is suggested by two contrasting names, "Jesus the Son of God." Alexander B. Bruce observes, "Jesus is the historical person, the tempted Man; and this part of the name laid the foundation for what is to be said in the following sentence concerning his power to sympathize." He adds that the title "Son of God" "justifies what has been already said of the High Priest of our confession" and rather quaintly comments, "If our High Priest be the Son of God, he may well be called the *Great*, and moreover there can be no doubt whither he has gone. Whither but to his native abode, his Father's house."[28] Another way to speak of this is to say that this high priest is sympathetic and strong to save his people. One of the agonies of pastoral care is that often, as we stand beside a terminally ill person, we may do our best to empathize, but we are incapable of saving them. This high priest is acutely sensitive to the hurts and pain of the sufferer, and we are assured that he is strong enough to heal them if he chooses or to accompany them into his presence as they pass on.

Third, Jesus' capacity to suffer with and sustain is expressed robustly using a double negative, which seems to suggest the writer is in a defensive mode, countering with strong assertions, "as if there were someone maintaining the contrary."[29] Bruce offers two possibilities for objections to the reality that Christ can suffer. The first relates to his dignity precisely as the Son of God and the second to his sinlessness.

---

[28] Alexander B. Bruce, *The Epistle to the Hebrews: The First Apology for Christianity* (Edinburgh: T&T Clark, 1899), 169.

[29] Bruce, *Epistle to the Hebrews*, 170.

The writer of Hebrews responds not with an elaborate philosophical argument but with a strong assertion. Bruce argues, "'We have *not* a high priest, who *cannot* be touched with sympathy'—this part of his assertion disposing of doubt provoked by Christ's dignity—'but one who has been tempted in all respect, says we are, apart from sin'—this part of the assertion meeting doubt based on Christ sinlessness."[30] Those prone to denying Christ's real humanity (Docetism) need to be assured of his true humanity, and others who are worried that Jesus must have been able to sin if his temptation was indeed temptation need to be assured of Christ's sinlessness. Bruce does not rationalize it by using theological categories or the Augustinian distinctions concerning Christ being "able not to sin" (Latin: *posse non peccare*) or being unable to sin (*non posse peccare*) but asserts that temptations do not threaten the sinlessness of Christ.

Fourth, based on Christ's capacity to suffer, the writer exhorts the people to appropriate what Christ offers by way of sympathy and strength: "Let us then approach God's throne of grace with confidence, so that we may receive mercy and find grace to help us in our time of need" (Heb 4:16). Note that we are not passive. There is something for us to do in order to access the sympathy and strength of the ascended priest. We must approach the throne in prayer. As Albert B. Simpson writes, "Christ ascended to the right hand of God, that he might lift us up into an ascension life."[31] The incentives for this intercessory life on our part are superabundant. Approaching the throne of grace where Christ intercedes for his people with confidence (Gk. *parrēsias*) is the very "doctrinal keynote of the epistle."[32] It is a place of grace, not just because of the access through the amazing grace embodied in the person of Christ but also because of what is dispensed in prayer: "mercy and grace." In the relationality of prayer, the ascended High Priest pours out compassion for every vicissitude of life's pilgrimage

---

[30]Bruce, *Epistle to the Hebrews*, 170-71.
[31]Albert B. Simpson, *The Christ of the Forty Days* (New York: Christian Alliance, 1868), 305.
[32]Bruce, *Epistle to the Hebrews*, 171.

and undeserved, superabounding grace for every circumstance, including the "time of need." This term connotes a time of crisis, such as the Hebrews were experiencing, as described in Hebrews 10:32-35. They had "endured in a great conflict full of suffering" (Heb 10:32), been insulted, persecuted, and accepted confiscation of property. They knew all about the "time of need," and they are exhorted not to throw away their confidence (*parrēsian*), which will be richly rewarded (Heb 10:35).

The Old Testament image of the Levitical priesthood helps to sum up the intercessory work of the great High Priest Jesus—its strong, sympathetic character and personal nature. The high priest wears an ephod on his shoulder, on which are written the names of the twelve tribes of Israel on two onyx stones (Ex 28:11). Then they were to "mount the stones in gold filigree settings and fasten them on the shoulder pieces of the ephod as memorial stones for the sons of Israel." Why? So that he would "bear the names on his shoulders as a memorial before the LORD" (Ex 28:11-12). The high priest also wore a chest piece that contained twelve gemstones, one for each of Israel's twelve tribes, enabling him to "bear the names of the sons of Israel over his heart on the breastpiece of decision as a continuing memorial before the LORD" (Ex 28:29). How expressive this figuration is of Jesus, our great High Priest, who bears us in the presence of God on his shoulders, implying strength that carries us, and holds each of us near to his heart as he presents us to the Father, implying sympathy. This beautifully represents the description of our great high priest in Hebrews 4—the "Son of God," strong to save, and "Jesus," the man who can and does sympathize with us.

7

THE GLORY OF GOD IN THE ASCENDED HUMAN

Implications for All of Human Life

HAVING EXPLORED THE CHRISTOLOGY implicit in the ascension, the question concerning Jesus' humanity, and therefore the rest of humanity, arises. How does the presence of a man in the Godhead in heaven affect humanity as a whole? In the ascended Son there is the true and permanent humanity. It is humanity glorified, humanity emanating fully the glory of God, as was God's first intent for humanity. Since Jesus is the recapitulated human (Irenaeus), the representative human person, the last Adam, what does his ascended, deified humanity say about humanity as an entity? The reality that the Son has participated in humanity and taken it into the Godhead reaffirms humans in the nondegreed image of God, and it enables the regeneration of believing humans so that they might grow in the degreed image of God.[1] What does this have to say concerning the important anthropological issues of our time—issues such as personhood, human rights, political theology, identity, transhumanism, artificial intelligence, sexuality, and embodiment in education? Not all of these issues can be addressed in detail here. Rather, I offer the

---

[1]This nondegreed/degreed way of speaking of all humans and believing humans is a nomenclature introduced by Christa McKirland. See Christa L. McKirland, "The Image of God and Intersex Persons" (paper presented at Logos Institute, St. Mary's College, University of St. Andrews, October 12, 2016). Irenaeus similarly speaks of all humans even after the fall being in the image but not the likeness of God. Whether viewed as "nondegreed" (McKirland) or "image" (Irenaeus, *Against Heresies* 4.20.7), all humans are image-bearers and therefore have full human rights and responsibilities.

framework of a theological anthropology shaped by the ascension as a guiding framework for ethical discernment.

PERSONHOOD

In the previous chapter I observed that human beings are persons analogous to the trinitarian persons, in whose image humans are made. The most compelling evidence comes from seeing Jesus' divine-human person ascending to the Father's right hand. He is the eternal, incarnate, divine-human person of Christ. He provides the vindication of the dignity of human personhood understood not according to human individualism and the obsession with *self*, the narcissism of the "Big Me" movement of our time, but in accordance with a trinitarian understanding of persons-in-relation.[2] As Oliver O'Donovan says, "In a body that represents 'the perfection' of man's nature, we see the first fruits of a renewed mankind and a sign of the end to that 'futility' which characterizes all created nature in its 'bondage to decay' (Rom 8:19-21)." That new creation does not eliminate the old but recovers its lost integrity and splendor. Humanity's restoration to caring lordship of creation and freedom from death in the last Adam was not his only accomplishment. Union and intimate communion was also restored.[3]

Acknowledging the inseparable but distinct events of resurrection and ascension, O'Donovan describes their triumph as divided into two moments, "a moment of recovery and a moment of advance." In the resurrection, the restoration of humans to persons is signaled, and in the ascension, of humans to persons-in-relation. Correspondingly, O'Donovan observes that the Western church has focused heavily on the restoration dynamics (forensics) of the death and resurrection of Jesus, whereas the Eastern church has spoken "more commonly of

---

[2]On the "Big Me," see David Brooks, *The Road to Character* (New York: Random House, 2015), 103.

[3]Oliver O'Donovan, *On the Thirty Nine Articles: A Conversation with Tudor Christianity*, Latimer Monograph (Exeter, UK: Paternoster, 1986), 28.

theosis or 'divinisation,' emphasising the advance beyond simple restoration to communion with the divine nature." With ecumenical sensitivity, he argues that both are essential and are "differentiated in the two steps of Christ's exaltation. Differentiated, but not therefore torn apart." The inevitability of the ascension after the resurrection is conveyed by Jesus' words to Mary on resurrection morning: "for I have not yet ascended to the Father. . . . 'I am ascending to my Father and *your* Father, to my God and *your* God'" (Jn 20:17). Speaking specifically to what the ascension has accomplished for human persons and their destiny, O'Donovan articulates a profound anthropology: "This transition from the earth to Heaven is more than a reversal of the incarnation, at which God 'came down'; it is the elevation of man, physical, spatio-temporal man, into an order that is greater than the physical and the spatio-temporal, and which is not his native habitat." Not all questions of what exact form the body will take outside of space and time are answered, just as the cloud enveloped Jesus on the Mount of Transfiguration. However, O'Donovan asserts, "we know that the path has been taken, and that we are to take it too."[4]

This destiny anticipated by the ascended Christ recalls the glory of the human person fully alive, which Irenaeus envisioned. What is true of the one man who recapitulated the image of God and true humanity becomes the destiny of redeemed humankind in him. In sum, we may say that the dignity of human personhood is both ectypal (mirroring the person of the Trinity analogically) and eschatological. But what does such a high view of persons-in-community have to say to the big anthropological questions of our day?

HUMAN RIGHTS

This view establishes an ontological grounding for human rights. All human beings are made in the image of God, even after the fall

---

[4]O'Donovan, *On the Thirty Nine Articles*, 28-29, 32.

(Gen 9:6). Palestinians as well as Israelis have human rights and must be treated as fully human persons and communities. The New Testament's intention for the church, the new humanity, is for it to *be* a winsome model of humanity, equality, and reconciliation and therefore to *speak* to the world on these issues, calling it to acknowledge the one throne in the universe above all others and to live out respect for its neighbor. Paul makes it abundantly clear that in this era of human history, there is "neither Jew nor Gentile" (Gal 3:28) in the community of Christ and that this should be the norm for humanity.

This perspective, established at the creation of humans, made in the image of God, and reaffirmed by the ascension of the one who is the image of the invisible God, has repercussions for politicians and political theology. Human rights have no ontological or even epistemological grounding apart from the reality of a common Creator and Lord who reigns in heaven as the paradigm for true humanity. The lordship of the Creator is the intended model and the sovereign standard for political leadership guided by upholding human rights and justice.

POLITICAL THEOLOGY

The ascended Christ, crowned as the supreme King of kings and destined to universal reign, is also O'Donovan's basis for acknowledging the qualified authority of governments, since Christ is over every power and authority. This is an understanding that all the authority of political leaders is derived, provisional, and anticipative of the government and judgment of the ascended and returning Christ. O'Donovan explains that by Christ's ascension and coming judgment, "political leaders are not simply denied their authority, but are constituted, on these new terms, as a secondary theatre of witness to the appearing grace of God, attesting by their judicial service the coming reality of God's own active judgment." Thus, in light of Christ's ascension, political authorities are not sovereign or justified as mere exhibitions of pride and lust for power. O'Donovan argues that the moral order is reaffirmed by Christ's resurrection and ascension, and "political authority in all its forms—lawmaking, war-making, welfare provision, education—is to be re-conceived within this matrix and subject to the discipline of enacting right against wrong."[5] Human leaders are capable of some level of ethical discernment as they manage nations in this "now but not yet new" era of the kingdom. Political leaders are capable of ethical judgment at the horizontal level such that even "just wars" can be a provisional witness to God's judgment. Whether they know so or not, political leaders are influenced by salvation history and to some extent can reflect the moral order of the risen Christ and the glory of the ascended Christ.

O'Donovan insists that our human vocation, in light of the office of the ascended King Jesus, is that "we are called to a final destiny in the life of the new Jerusalem, subject to the throne of God and the Lamb," and therefore "all other thrones need further justification." That is, "their role is subordinated to the task of preparing the way for that final one." O'Donovan asserts that "this was the ground of the distinction that arose within a Christian view of history between secular and spiritual authority, this worldly and ultimate rule." In the meantime, "the authority of government resides essentially in the act of judgment"—an assertion derived from Romans 13 and the general view of the New Testament that any authority that inheres in human government after the ascension "forbids human rule to pretend to sovereignty, the consummation of the community's identity and the power of its ruler."[6]

What does O'Donovan mean by *judgment* as the role of government? He means the type of act that enacts justice and moral transformation. He likens it to the Hebrew Old Testament prophetic word *mishpat*, stressing its "active force." What since the ascension is *new* about this

---

[5]Oliver O'Donovan, *The Ways of Judgment* (Grand Rapids, MI: Eerdmans, 2005), 5.
[6]O'Donovan, *Ways of Judgment*, 4-5.

way of relating human government to that of Christ? It is that "the triumph of God in Christ has not left these authorities just where they were, exercising the same right as before." O'Donovan insists that this ascended triumph of Christ "imposes the shape of salvation-history upon politics." He is confident that the "operations of the Holy Spirit," sent by the ascended Lord and working in coinherent unity with him, "drive the political leaders back upon the tasks of justice, and so effect a transformation," thus offering "a distinctive perspective on the evolution of political forms in history."[7]

What does the ascended triumph of Christ have to say to our current world? It invites our political leaders towards a spirit of humility, evokes submission to the principles of God's natural law, urges dependence, and invites servant leadership of the people they serve. It also invites the realization that the issues they grapple with, including the assuring of human rights for all, are present in society due to a Judeo-Christian heritage that provides an ontological basis for moral judgments. It invites leaders to see the ancient principles of justice as the basis for right moral judgments. Above all, the ascension commands the awareness of humanity's glory as derived from the glory of the one Man for all humanity.[8] Naturally, in post-Christian secular governments, political leaders are not generally aware of the origin of these impulses. It is the role of the church to be the harbinger of the new humanity by its inner being and in its outwardly oriented evangelical (as opposed to legal) speech in the public square.

The role of Christ's ascension in O'Donovan's political theology is thus of profound importance. While acknowledging O'Donovan's assertion that "the identity of the church is given wholly and completely in the relation of its members to the ascended Christ," Nicholas Wolterstorff queries his insistence that membership in Christ replaces

---

[7] O'Donovan, *Ways of Judgment*, 5-6.
[8] Just war theory condemns retaliative measures that are not commensurate with the acts of aggression committed, and also any war for the purpose of plundering another nation's resources.

all other political identities.[9] Wolterstorff, by contrast, acknowledges the common grace in political identities, in which one sees evidence in a political regime of how God ruled over Israel or how Christ rules over the church since the ascension, that is, where political leaders are protecting the people, ensuring their national or ecclesial identity, and rendering justice within the people. Wolterstorff believes there to be a lacuna in O'Donovan's thinking: his lack of emphasis on what moves beyond mere justice to the human flourishing that good political leaders engender.

The differences between the political theologies of these two theologians and their understanding of the nature of the kingdom of God have to do with their theologies of providence and common grace. Wolterstorff reflects a more standard Reformed view:

> The state is a manifestation of God's providential care for humanity—of God's common grace—with the same task now that governmental authority has always had. Ever since God's call to Abraham to leave Chaldea, God's kingly rule of humanity has come in two forms: a providential form in "secular" governmental authority, and a redemptive form in Israel and the church. Neither of these is to be assimilated to the other.[10]

For Wolterstorff, the state, not just the church, is "a manifestation of God's providential care" for humanity.[11] Believing that O'Donovan differentiates too much between the origin of the church and state, Wolterstorff preserves a place for the state in its own right:

> Christ is not beating the state back to the margins of human existence; the state is not waning. It remains what it has always been: an indispensable component of God's providential care for humanity. Slowly, episodically, but inexorably, the gross malformations of the state are being cured, so that it comes closer to doing what it's always

---

[9] Nicholas Wolterstorff, "A Discussion of Oliver O'Donovan's *The Desire of the Nations*," *SJT* 54, no. 1 (March 2001): 104.
[10] Wolterstorff, "Discussion of Oliver O'Donovan's *The Desire of the Nations*," 108.
[11] Wolterstorff, "Discussion of Oliver O'Donovan's *The Desire of the Nations*," 108.

been meant to do in God's providential order. But that's different from being beaten back so that it does only what its supposed re-authorization permits it do so.[12]

Wolterstorff provocatively states, "It's possible resolutely to deny all common grace and insist that God's concern is solely the health of the church; most of the time, that appears to be O'Donovan's view."[13] This seems to misconstrue and underrepresent O'Donovan's repeated reaffirmation of humanity and creation as a consequence of the resurrection and ascension of Christ in a created human body. O'Donovan does not deny common grace but asserts its origin in Christ—it is not something natural or inherent in creation.

When Wolterstorff asserts that "the state must be viewed as authorized to promote the health of various institutions and communities . . . since the health of such institutions and communities is indispensable to that life of finding joy in the goods of creation to which the church is called," he assumes that this is a result of a common grace grounded in creation, something the fall has not affected.[14] O'Donovan's view is that the health of "institutions and communities" that provide "joy in the goods of creation" is a consequence of God's reaffirmation of creation in the resurrection and ascension of Jesus. Community and the arts should begin through the church's influence and be modeled in the church.

While O'Donovan is at times rather inscrutable in his expression, it must be said in his favor that the resurrection and the ascension of Jesus make a difference to his political theology. The history of Jesus Christ and the whole salvific history of God for humanity in the world determine his theology. His is a theology not just of creation but of creation *and* redemption—indeed, the redemption of creation in the ascended, reigning Christ.

---

[12] Wolterstorff, "Discussion of Oliver O'Donovan's *The Desire of the Nations*," 109.
[13] Wolterstorff, "Discussion of Oliver O'Donovan's *The Desire of the Nations*," 105.
[14] Wolterstorff, "Discussion of Oliver O'Donovan's *The Desire of the Nations*," 105.

CONTEMPORARY ETHICAL AND MISSIONAL ISSUES

The most startling significance of the ascension of Jesus Christ is what it says about the importance of the human body. God preserves his incarnate, embodied Son forever. Christ's physical body endures in the life of God and his creation. It persists with a continuity with respect to his earthly body. Even the discontinuous aspects of his body, resulting from its glorification and orientation to the spiritual, heavenly realm, occur without loss of the identity of his body. This further emphasizes the biblical teaching that the human body matters. The participation of believers in the humanity of Christ by faith ensures also the continuance of their bodies, and a continuity of identity despite the discontinuity that transformation to a spiritual body brings (1 Cor 15:44) when it is received at the occasion of the resurrection and glorification in the eschaton.

The biblical norm for human persons is *embodiment*. Biblical ethics is grounded on the fact that we are bodies, that our bodies matter, and that what we do with our bodies matters. Thus, biology trumps psychology in matters of human sexuality. How we feel or think about ourselves is secondary to our biology. It also means that having sex is the uniting of persons, not just the benign exchange of bodily fluids, and hence is reserved for persons within the covenant of marriage between a man and a woman. All forms of intercourse outside that cannot bring shalom and flourishing. This also means that single people cannot find sanctification and wholeness by ignoring their bodies and their sexual desires. Rather, as humans with bodies, they are to be in touch with those desires, realizing that the meaning of sex transcends having sex. The meaning of sex is contemplative.

The dignity of the body also means that we must be vigilant in how we use technologies (artificial intelligence, iPhones, Zoom calls, social media). Their effect on our brains makes us the most distracted human generation of all time. We must be wary of any attempt to make us *more* than the embodied, limited human persons we are. We are humans, not subhuman and not superhuman, just humans. The move toward increasing the online portion of education experiences may have some benefits, but this challenges the power of embodied, communal learning in one place. There are complexities associated with each of the ethical issues alluded to here, and biblical hospitality (not postmodern alterity) on the part of the church and pastoral care is needed.[15] Accounts of these ethical and pastoral issues belong in works on Christian ethics. The following comment may sum up the moral state of things in the culture of the West: gnosticism has recurred in human history in subtle ways that often cause it to escape detection.

The embodied state of the Son in heaven, specifically the locatedness of that body in heaven (as per Calvin), contrasted with his ubiquitous divine nature, also has implications for a theology of place for humans. Mission therefore must address the loss of place that many refugees are undergoing in our time. Old Testament scholars such as Brittany Melton and Megan Alsene-Parker have drawn attention to this issue of the loss of place of Judahites in Lamentations, for example.[16] They cite J. Gordon McConville's statement that "the Bible gives good reason to see placedness as an essential aspect of our being human."[17] In drawing in New Testament perspectives on this, one is immediately reminded that Jesus had "no place to lay his head" (Mt 8:20) during his earthly pilgrimage. He stands in solidarity with all refugees and those who through migration have a sense of

---

[15] See W. Ross Hastings, *Theological Ethics: The Moral Life of the Gospel in Contemporary Context* (Grand Rapids, MI: Zondervan Academic, 2021); Hastings, *Pastoral Ethics: Moral Formation as Life in the Trinity* (Bellingham, WA: Lexham Academic, 2022).

[16] Brittany N. Melton and Megan D. Alsene-Parker, "Lamenting Placelessness: The Deconstruction of People and Place in Lamentations" (paper presented at Society of Biblical Literature annual meeting, San Diego, CA, November 26, 2024).

[17] J. Gordon McConville, *Being Human in God's World: An Old Testament Theology of Humanity* (Grand Rapids, MI: Baker Academic, 2016), 101.

homelessness. When at the ascension Jesus rises to his "home," the right hand of the Father in heaven, he does not do so before telling his disciples, "I am going there to prepare a *place* for you" (Jn 14:2).

Although, in the "now" of the kingdom come, Christians must do all they can to address the structural reasons that lead to the tragedy of refugeeism and do their level best to offer hospitality to refugees, there is an ultimate eschatological hope. In his ascension, Jesus is preparing a place for his pilgrim people that will be a heavenly home come down to earth. I have personally struggled most of my life with a lack of a sense of belonging. The longing for home drives me to my home in the triune God (Eph 3:17), but place continues to elude me on earth, and restlessness has been my tendency. The desire for place is important even if it drives us to think of a place, a room (Jn 14:2), where our embodied persons may one day be at home. So many displaced persons highlight the world's fallenness. The norm for our stable embodied existence is our place.

The value of the body, spoken eloquently in the ascended body of Jesus, also speaks to the nature of the church's mission. Whereas the church's missionary efforts have often been undergirded by an unfortunate dualism of body and soul, leading to tension between those promoting a social gospel and those who collapsed mission into evangelism-only approaches, a fully biblical approach shows deep concern for the whole person. This involves seeing the Great Commission under the rubric of the Great Commandment and the cultural mandate, to love one's neighbor and nurture people toward what it means to become fully human in the totality of their being, body, soul, and spirit. *Mission* involves evangelism and the conversion of whole persons: recovering the health of bodies through proper nutrition and health care, helping to provide safe accommodation and a place to call home, developing minds through education, nurturing family life, and helping to provide meaningful work.

IN TRANSFORMATION AND GLORIFICATION

To be like Christ is the eschatological hope of the human person in Christ, and this involves the body as integral to theosis and the pursuit of ecclesial and personal practices in that direction. Paul discusses the glory of Christ reproduced in the Christian in 2 Corinthians 3:7-18. He contrasts the bright but transitory nature of the glory in the face of Moses in the old covenant with the "surpassing glory" (2 Cor 3:10) and the permanent nature of transformation facilitated under the new covenant. This intense and lasting glory results from two spiritual orientations involving the two hands of the Trinity, the communion enabled by the Lord who is the Holy Spirit, and the contemplation of the face of the Lord who is the Son: "And we all, who with *unveiled faces* contemplate the Lord's glory, are being transformed into his image with ever-increasing glory, which comes from the Lord, who is the Spirit" (2 Cor 3:18). Note that the body, specifically the face, is involved in this contemplative gazing that must characterize the Christian life. And its end is the beatific vision when we are face to face with Christ. The transformation will truly reflect the glory of Christ.

Douglas Farrow describes this transformational, anaphoric work of Christ as involving three distinct movements, each with descent and ascent phases.[18] These movements contextualize the ascension's place within Christ's saving work. In the first movement, Farrow speaks of Christ's birth and baptism (his descent) and then of his passion and death, an act of ascent since he is "lifted up on the cross, in demonic mockery of the destiny of man." The second movement involves his descent to the dead and his restoration to life, "God's verdict reversing man's," which entails the ascension. The purpose of Christ's ascent is the setting of heaven in order, followed by the third movement involving his descent to judge the earth. He then brings about the ascent of the church "with him into the Father's presence."

---

[18]*Anaphora* is the most central and solemn part of the Divine Liturgy, and it refers to the lifting up of the elements for the epicletic work of the Spirit. It may also refer to the central aspects of Christ's atoning history.

Farrow argues: "[Christ] glorifies God by leading *many sons to glory*, and by offering up the whole creation to be the kingdom of God. It is to that consummate offering that his ascension already tends, for by it he presents himself to God as the first fruits, that God may in turn present him to us as the guarantee of a full harvest."[19]

There is also a coinherent working of the Holy Spirit in each movement of this salvific work of Christ by which humanity is recapitulated and ascends in Christ. Irenaeus's account of the anaphoric work of Christ is epicletic, meaning that it invites and evokes the intermingling work of the Spirit in the same way that the priest invites the work of the Spirit in the bread and wine.[20] The Spirit hovered over the union of the divine and human natures of Christ at the incarnation. The Spirit led and empowered the Son in his human pilgrimage, even during his postresurrection ministry (Acts 1:1-3). The Son offered himself to God on the cross through the eternal Spirit (Heb 9:14), and the Spirit raised the Son from the dead (Rom 8:11). The same Spirit who was involved in every act that accomplished our salvation, objectively speaking, now acts in the subjective application of these to believing persons. The Spirit unites persons to Christ so that they are thereby in union with him in his death, resurrection, and ascension (Eph 2:1-7), regenerating them since in Christ they are already risen. The Spirit makes men and women holy, perfecting in them the divine image and likeness (2 Cor 3:17-18). The Spirit as Gift is, most importantly, the seal of Christ's salvation in every believing heart and the earnest of their whole-personed ascension when Christ returns (Eph 1:13-14). The Spirit's work in us now prepares us for *our* ultimate ascension.

The living Word, who has by the incarnation brought us into "resolute companionship" with himself, "is capable," says Farrow, "both of recalling man to the Spirit's ministrations and of recalling the Spirit to the aid of man; that is, of habituating man to the Spirit and the

---

[19]Douglas Farrow, *Ascension Theology* (London: T&T Clark, 2011), 128-29, emphases added.
[20]Farrow, *Ascension Theology*, 129.

Spirit to man." He adds, "When this is achieved, when through the invocation of the Spirit man has ascended with Christ into the presence of the Father, it is not only the condition of man that will be changed, but the condition of all creation." Citing Romans 8:19-21, he concludes on a doxological note that "this makes possible the new man, and with the new man a new world order, in which the glory of God shines forth in all things."[21]

As Romans 8:19-21 indicates, the liberation of the creation from its "bondage to decay" is contingent on the revealing of the children of God. The glorification of earthly things, which is all of creation, therefore is for the benefit of humanity. As Irenaeus asserts, "For if there are to be real men, there must also be a real establishment [*plantationem*], that they vanish not away among non-existent things, but progress among those which have an actual existence."[22] "Progress" here signifies "both continuity and discontinuity between the old creation and the new."[23] Irenaeus was the first to speak of the glorified state of humans as involving perpetual progress (Greek *epektasis*) rather than a static state of perfection. Similarly for Gregory of Nyssa, it is a "tending forward, an endlessly greater apprehension of divine glory by creatures, who 'kinetically' experience the peace of God, and finitely live in his infinity."[24] This idea is also present in Maximus.[25] Jonathan Edwards also speaks of glorification as eternal, asymptotic progress in union with God and toward being like God in his communicable but infinite attributes, especially his glory, "infinitely nearing but never collapsing into identity with one another."[26]

---

[21] Farrow, *Ascension Theology*, 129.
[22] Irenaeus, *Against Heresies* 5.36.1 (*ANF* 1:566).
[23] Farrow, *Ascension Theology*, 129.
[24] David Bentley Hart, *The Beauty of the Infinite: The Aesthetics of Christian Truth* (Grand Rapids, MI: Eerdmans, 2003), 110. Farrow comments that Gregory's version retains unhelpful Platonist traces of Origenism (*Ascension Theology*, 130).
[25] See Paul M. Blowers, "Maximus the Confessor, Gregory of Nyssa, and the Concept of 'Perpetual Progress,'" *Vigiliae Christianae* 46, no. 2 (June 1992): 151-71.
[26] W. Ross Hastings, *Jonathan Edwards and the Life of God: Toward an Evangelical Theology of Participation* (Minneapolis: Fortress, 2015), 314 with reference to Jonathan Edwards,

"Continuity and discontinuity" is an apt framework to describe the future of the redeemed human person after the parousia, for it is an apt framework to describe the ascended Christ. Continuity, in that after his resurrection and ascension, he is still a man, "this same Jesus" (Acts 1:11), and discontinuity, in that this body adapted to heavenly things and has powers beyond that of its preresurrection and pre-ascension state. Farrow describes the corresponding continuities and discontinuities of the new humanity and new creation:

> But when man has been refashioned in Christ, when the very possibility of sin is behind him, when body and soul have been fully invested with the life-giving Spirit, then he shall go forth and flourish in a world that is also incorruptible. This he will do, not laying aside his creaturely nature, but ever in reinvigorating it by means of "fresh converse with God."[27]

The primacy of Christ as the glory of God in the human in the restoration and transformation of humanity is crucial. God spoke to the first Adam in their garden communion, but in the person of the Word, God has visited humanity in an altogether different way. As Farrow states, "It was no mere theophany. It was incarnation, absolute solidarity. And in this absolute solidarity was the secret of the image-bearing creature called man, the creature who has God both as his source, and as his end."[28]

Similarly, Irenaeus says, "For in times long past it was said that man was created in the image of God, but it was not yet shown" until humanity was taken up "to the invisible Father, through means of the visible Word."[29] Since this appearance in the depths of sinful humanity, the Son has taken up humanity on behalf of humanity. Farrow comments that "things have changed for man" because

---

"Concerning the End for Which God Created the World" (*WJE* 1:102). *Asymptotic* refers to a function or line that approaches but never arrives at infinity.

[27]Farrow, *Ascension Theology*, 130-31.
[28]Farrow, *Ascension Theology*, 149.
[29]Irenaeus, *Against Heresies* 5.14-16.

"man's maker has taken up his place in and with man and as a man elevated man beyond man." Farrow adds, "God has made room in man for himself and at the same time made room in himself for man." This is not to be understood as humanity becoming God, ontologically, or the "decline and disappearance of man *qua* man." The *homoousion* must shape our thinking for what the human in Christ becomes in light of the incarnation and the ascension. The *homoousion*, when referring to the person of the Son, means that his divine nature is identical to the Father's and that his human nature is identical to ours. Correspondingly, this means that when "man's maker has taken up his place in and with man," the human stays human.[30] Humans do not become God.

However, in Christ, as participants in that union, humans do become "like God" and more than mere humans, as the ascension shows. The ascent of humanity to God in the event of the ascension, and our consequent participatory ascent in him, involves the deification or glorification of humanity. The *homoousion* assures us "that God has invested himself in man permanently," ensuring that humanity is permanently in God, relationally speaking, yet always still human.[31] In what sense is it more than mere humanity, then? There is in the ascended Son a true and permanent humanity. Yet, it is humanity glorified, humanity emanating fully the glory of God, as was God's first intent for humanity, in line with Irenaeus's famous statement, here repeated: "For the glory of God is the living man, and the life of man consists in beholding God," sometimes translated, "The glory of God is a human being fully alive."[32]

The permanence of the humanity of the ascended Christ, and its implications for the transformation and permanence of the humanity of persons in Christ, is emphasized in the ancient and modern traditions. Jesus did not cast off his human nature when he

---

[30] Farrow, *Ascension Theology*, 149.
[31] Farrow, *Ascension Theology*, 150.
[32] Irenaeus, *Against Heresies* 4.20.7 (*ANF* 1:490).

ascended to the Father. Gerrit Dawson demonstrates that Tertullian, Justin Martyr, Augustine, and John Chrysostom consistently affirmed the permanence of the humanity of Christ and its continuity of identity and discontinuity of state (no longer subject to decay) with his body here on earth.[33] Tertullian opposed those whom he said "excluded from . . . the court of heaven itself, all flesh and blood whatsoever," and declared, "Jesus is still sitting there at the right hand of the Father, man, yet God . . . flesh and blood, yet purer than ours."[34] Origen was condemned posthumously for asserting that "after the resurrection, the body of the Lord was ethereal."[35] The affirmations of Christ's perpetual humanity were essential in the battle against Gnosticism because it tended to spiritualize matter and the body.

The patristic convictions are reiterated in the works of Karl Barth and T. F. Torrance, for example. Barth insists that Christ the Son maintains our humanity:

> He ceased to all eternity to be God only, receiving and having and maintaining to all eternity human essence as well. Thus the human essence of Jesus Christ, without becoming divine, and its very creatureliness, is placed at the side of the Creator. It is a clothing which he does not put off. . . . It is His temple which He does not leave. It is the form which He does not lose. It is an organ the use of which he does not renounce. He is God in the flesh. . . . The glory and dignity and majesty of the true God, exercised and revealed in his son, consist of the fact that he is God in the flesh, and therefore that he has also human essence as his clothing and temple and organ, because and as he is also called Jesus of Nazareth.[36]

---

[33] Gerrit S. Dawson, *Jesus Ascended: The Meaning of Christ's Continuing Incarnation* (Phillipsburg, NJ: P&R, 2004), 31-33.
[34] Tertullian, *On the Resurrection of the Flesh* (ANF 3:584).
[35] "The Anathemas Against Origen" (*NPNF*² 14:319).
[36] Karl Barth, *Church Dogmatics*, ed. G. W. Bromiley and Thomas F. Torrance, trans. G. W. Bromiley (London: T&T Clark, 2009), IV/2, 100-101.

Barth shows that it is because of Christ's humanity that we can know God and have our humanity perpetuated.[37]

Similarly, Torrance argued that in the glorified and exalted state of his humanity, Christ's body did not make him less human but in fact "more fully and truly human than any other humanity we know, for it was humanity in which all that attacks and undermines creaturely being is vanquished."[38] First, the connection between Son's humanity and ours lies in his taking on our humanity in the incarnation. He therefore acted representatively of humanity. Thus, what he did in ascending and maintaining his perpetual humanity is representative and vicarious. Just as he lives, so also shall we live. Second, what is already true in the Son becomes real to the experience of those who, by the Spirit, enter into union with Christ by faith. Our particular humanity is being transformed now and will be glorified when we see Jesus. This exalted, transformed humanity will be maintained in communion with Christ throughout eternity. As Peter Toon writes:

> For now there is in heaven, in the very life of God himself, a glorified humanity belonging to the eternal Son and a humanity of the same essence as shared by the whole human race. Now created human beings can be drawn nearer to God than can the holy angels, for the former possess the same human nature as the Son possesses, and so in and through him they can draw near to God.[39]

When redeemed humans ascend at the second coming, they will also be fully human but *gloriously* human due to their participation in his incarnation and ascension. As Farrow says, "We ourselves, when in the final anaphora we are presented to the Father, in perfect union with the Son, are destined to enter his glory, and *to add our own glory to it*, the glory that comes to those who feast from the tree of life."[40]

---

[37] Barth, *Church Dogmatics* IV/2, 101.
[38] T. F. Torrance, *Space, Time, and Resurrection* (Grand Rapids, MI: Eerdmans, 1976), 127.
[39] Peter Toon, *Heaven and Hell: A Biblical and Theological Overview*, Nelson Studies in Biblical Theology (Nashville: Nelson, 1986), 58.
[40] Farrow, *Ascension Theology*, 150, emphasis added.

Our glorified humanity will answer to the surpassing of angels anticipated in Psalm 8, "for we will be like God" (but not God), no longer lower than angels or "even on a par" with them. Instead, "we will not live and move, as they do, *coram Deo*; we will live and move with Christ *in Deo*. We will be deified by the Spirit, knowing God, by way of God."[41]

Reflecting on the closing line of Dante's *Paradiso*, Farrow speaks of the divine light that Dante sees, "All impossible, to be painted with a human effigy," and expresses wonder at the fact that "it is, Beatrice, Bernard, and Mary, not Rafael, Michael, and Gabriel, whose prayers and service assist him in rising at last to his communion, with 'the Glory Infinite.'" But this is "only fitting," says Farrow, "because the way of atonement is not just any way, but the way of the incarnation. When God comes down for our salvation, he comes down 'for us men' in a way that transforms what it means to be a man. . . . The end of man, and his beginning, too, are determined from his middle, the middle that is the incarnation."[42] Farrow concludes his reflection as follows:

> It is no violation of the canons of caution to speak of having an end that is higher, not merely in degree but in kind, than that of the angels, not if the *homoousion* is true. In the heavenly city, when that "supremely cooperative, supremely ordered association of those who enjoy God, and one another in God" is finally attained, it will be the human race, fully incorporated into Christ in the eucharistic mystery that is the church, that shall reign over the new creation, participating from within in the three-personed Love that set everything in motion. The angels will see and rejoice, and nature itself shall be glad.[43]

IN EVANGELISM

A vital dimension of the ascension related to the outpouring of the Spirit and participation is the church's mission in union with the

---

[41]Farrow, *Ascension Theology*, 150.
[42]Farrow, *Ascension Theology*, 150-51.
[43]Farrow, *Ascension Theology*, 152.

ascended Christ, under his kingship, and empowered by the missional Holy Spirit, to the glory of God the Father. Though the mission is more than evangelism, it is not less than evangelism. The necessary priorities for the church in evangelism are fivefold in light of the ascension and the outpouring of the Spirit on Christ's new Israel.

First, evangelism is a priority, a vital function, of the church because in this season of eschatological reserve, between Christ's ascension and his return, the church is the sent community, in its sent Lord, by the sent and sending Spirit, under the command of its Lord to make disciples (Mt 28:18-20; Mk 16:15; Jn 20:19-23). The church does not exist for itself but first for God and his people and then for the world. Second, evangelism is an outflow of participative life in the missional God and life in the Spirit, charged by his power. In communion with the ascended Christ, the contemplative life enables us to hear his directives and discern to whom, when, and how we share the gospel. Third, evangelism must be evangelical. This means that judgment is not the first thing people need to hear but that God loves them, that he has sent his Son for them (and, yes, for their sin), that the ascended Lord is for them, that the Father awaits with open arms their prodigal return. This also means treating people with respect. Ironically, some of the evangelistic methods (such as yelling at people) some have used have dehumanized the very people whom they should be helping to become truly human.

Fourth, evangelism should be primarily declarative, not defensive. There is a place for apologetics, but rationalistic apologetics are sometimes an accommodation to modernity. Declaring as Peter did on Pentecost that God has made Jesus Lord and Christ (Acts 2:36) is the essence of gospel preaching and witness. In Isaiah, the Lord already anticipates what the gospel proclamation will be: "I will set a sign among them, and I will send some of those who survive to the nations—to Tarshish, to the Libyans and Lydians (famous as archers), to Tubal and Greece, and to the distant islands that have not heard of my fame or seen my glory. *They will proclaim my glory* among the nations" (Is 66:19). Our task is the proclamation of the Lord of ascended glory. Fifth, in our age of deep suspicion of the church, evangelism should be mainly in the context of relationships. In fact, given the biblical illiteracy of many, catechizing people in a relational context is the preferred way. Programs such as Alpha and others facilitate this well. However, it may take many years of observing our Christian lives before our friends come to faith. In all cases, discerning what the Spirit is doing is all-important.

8

THE GLORY OF A FINISHED OBJECTIVE ATONEMENT

THIS CHAPTER FOCUSES ON the significance of the ascension for atonement and our salvation. I make a distinction between the dynamics of the *objective* atonement accomplished by Christ, its celebration in heaven on the occasion of Jesus' ascension and session at the Father's right hand, and the *subjective* salvation it accomplishes in humanity (and creation). This second dimension, the application of the atonement in the eternal salvation and care of Christ's people, will be the primary focus of the following chapter. Even if the focus of these chapters is *soteriological*, it cannot help but be christological, pneumatological, ecclesiological, and cosmological. The purpose of this chapter is not to give a detailed account of the participatory nature of the atonement and its various facets or models.[1] Suffice it to say that the atonement is accomplished in the person of Christ through his incarnation, vicarious humanity, death, and resurrection, and hence the totality of his history becomes our order of salvation by participation.

One question to be addressed has to do with whether the ascension itself is atoning or alternatively a capstone celebrating the completion of the atonement. On the latter account, what happens after Christ's session leads to the unfinished work of the atonement's *application*, for the permanent salvation of his people. Is the ascension *atoning* or

---

[1] For an account of the atonement that emphasizes its ontological grounding, and participation as the primary theory, see Ross Hastings, *Total Atonement: Trinitarian Participation in the Reconciliation of Humanity and Creation* (Lanham, MD: Fortress Academic, 2019).

merely *salvific*, in that it carries his people up into the presence and life of God on the basis of the completed atonement? Another way to pose this question is to ask whether the ascension corresponds to the final appearance of the high priest on the Day of Atonement depicted in Leviticus 16—in the old Levitical order, after he had done all the sacrificial work—or whether it corresponds to the actual offering up to God of the sacrifices.

This chapter contends that Jesus' session, mentioned four times in Hebrews (Heb 1:3; 8:1; 10:12; 12:2), is the sign of an *atonement* that is already complete when Jesus is seated, and that after he is seated he implements the value of his completed atonement. I will consider the opposing view, that the ascension is in itself atoning, with reference to the work of New Testament scholar David Moffitt and that of theologian Douglas Farrow as interlocutors in this regard. One issue at stake in this discussion has to do with the distinction between the resurrection and what it accomplishes, and what is effected by the ascension.

Before engaging this controversy, we must address a foundational question. Rather than being a part of objective atonement, was the ascension actually a crucial part of God's eternal decree that preceded humanity's fall into sin? Can we therefore grant it salvific but not atoning value, in that by his ascension in union with his people, the Son paved the way for the recovery of the first intentions of God that humanity would be his sons sharing his glory, coheirs with Christ, his vice regents with him of the cosmos? In other words, does the ascension accomplish the final end, the filial or ontological purpose of the atonement, rather than being part of atonement for sin? This is in keeping with a strand of thought in the tradition that the Son would have become incarnate and ascended even if sin had never entered humanity's history.[2]

---

[2]Maximus, John Duns Scotus, Francis de Sales, and Lawrence of Brindisi are exponents of this view.

Reflecting patristic sensibilities, Thomas Doughty has recently re-emphasized that the primary intent of God's decree for the Son's incarnation was not *first* that of the reconciliation of sinners. Instead, logically prior (*supra*) to the fall, God's original intent and primary motivation was ontological—there to be, within his creation, a divine-human co-dominion shared between the Son and his people (*Christus Dominus*).[3] This way of seeing the work of Christ grounded in the biblical story includes the objective atonement, with its associated models and their contingent motivation within the work of Christ. However, the primary motivation for the work of Christ is ontological: that Christ the Lord (the last Adam), in union with his people (the new humanity, the corporate Adam), would reign on earth to fulfill the purpose of the first creation and the image-bearers mandated to steward it on behalf of God. There is much to be commended in Doughty's work: it echoes the patristic idea of Christ as the recapitulation of the first Adam; it upholds the kingpin of orthodox atonement theology—that atonement transpires within the *person* of Christ; it clarifies the ontological nature of the salvific purpose of God, placing in context the models of the atonement ("contingent motivations") without jeopardizing them; it exalts God's benevolent purpose for creation; and it makes the ascension important in this narrative.

Crucially, the ascension of Christ declares him explicitly to be King in a way that the resurrection does not. His entrance into humanity and carrying humanity into the throne room of God is the beginning of the fulfillment of God's decree regarding a "divine-human co-dominion" shared between the Son and his people (*Christus Dominus*) "over the cosmos."[4] The ascended Son is the King who has "sat down" at the right hand of God, and his people are one with him. They are "in Christ" and thus already occupy the throne with Christ. The whole

---

[3] Thomas G. Doughty, *Supralapsarian Christology and the Progressive Work of Christ: Christus Dominus* (Lanham, MD: Lexington, 2024).
[4] Doughty, *Supralapsarian Christology*, 1.

church already sits at the Father's right hand (Eph 2:6) and participates in Christ's reign over the cosmos through its participation in the Eucharist and Word, prayers, and multifaceted vocations in mission. Currently, the church is also called the kingdom of God. At a minimum, it is the primary seat of the kingdom of Christ. This provides a positive and hopeful but not triumphalist view of the church's mission. Within the biblical narrative's broader context, it fosters an understanding that mission entails the recovery of the cultural mandate of Genesis 1–2, including earth keeping and a theology of work within that. The church should be at the forefront of everything that makes us fully human.

The fullness of the divine-human co-dominion between Christ and his church is a prominent future aspect of the kingdom of Christ. The church's future in perpetual union with Christ, depicted by the bride-Bridegroom metaphor, is lived out on earth, as mentioned in Revelation 20:1-4. The church's coming down from heaven suggests it was first in heaven. That is, there has been an ascension of the church to heaven in a way that was prefigured by the ascension of Christ and enabled by it. Another way to say this is that Jesus' ascension included his people's ascension. The ascended Son has provided a place in the life of God for humanity.

Paul indicates this in 1 Thessalonians 4, reassuring believers that at the second coming, their loved ones who are dead will rise first to meet the Lord in the air. Those who are alive in Christ will then be "caught up together with them *in the clouds* to meet the Lord in the air" (1 Thess 4:17). The reference to "in the clouds" resonates with what occurred when Jesus ascended: "he was taken up before their very eyes, and a cloud hid him from their sight" (Acts 1:9). This may not be strong evidence on its own that the ascension anticipates our ascension (and then descent), but when combined with what Jesus promises for his people in John 14:2-3, for example, this notion increases in credibility. Here Jesus assures his disciples that he is going to his "Father's house," where he will prepare a place for them. Then he adds, "And if I go and prepare a place for you, I will come back and *take you to be with me that you also may be where I am.*" Given that the ascension of Jesus is in an embodied state, the ascension of the believer at the parousia is more likely in view in this passage. That it may also include what is sometimes called the "intermediate state" of the believer between death and resurrection—their ascension to be "with the Lord" when they die (see Phil 1:21-25; 2 Cor 5:1-10)—is a possibility.

Questions regarding the atoning, as opposed to the salvific, nature of the ascension arise in the work of New Testament scholar David Moffitt, as signaled above. He claims that the atonement was not completed until the ascension and that it continues with the intercession of Jesus. As we discuss the issues surrounding this view, I will contend that Moffitt conflates salvation and atonement and that the ongoing intercession of Jesus is not atoning but rather entails the *application* of the atonement and the mediation of the worship of the church.[5]

ASCENSION AS ATONEMENT IN DAVID MOFFITT

Moffitt's book *Rethinking the Atonement*, a compilation of essays that builds on his previous work, is a significant advance in Hebrews scholarship and intends to reinforce his earlier proposals by including engagement with patristic theology. For our purposes, I will engage one theological issue in this work—how the term *atonement* is interpreted in light of Hebrews and specifically *when* atonement is completed. Moffitt rightly challenges the idea that atonement is restricted to what happened on the cross. Here he is in accord with the tradition from Athanasius and Gregory of Nazianzus onward. For these Fathers, everything from incarnation to the resurrection is

---

[5]For more on this, see Ross Hastings, "Review of Rethinking the Atonement: New Perspectives on Jesus's Death, Resurrection and Ascension," *International Journal of Systematic Theology* 26, no. 1 (January 2024): 131-34.

atoning, and this has influenced theologians such as Thomas Erskine, John McLeod Campbell, Karl Barth, Dietrich Bonhoeffer, and T. F. Torrance, the latter of whom dubs the separating of the person and work of Christ in the atonement as the Latin heresy.[6] The atonement occurs in the *person* of Christ. In support of Moffitt, the resurrection as part of the death event is a given for many theologians.[7]

Nuance is crucial in this discussion. When, in chapter nine, Moffitt declares, "It Is Not Finished," this can sound jarring to the cherished tradition that when Christ expired on the cross, his triumphant cry, "It is finished," meant that the atonement was completed in his dying. Through death, he destroyed as a fait accompli the one who has the power of death (Heb 2:14). Based on his studies in Leviticus, where sacrifices are accepted by God only *after* they are killed and offered on the altar, Moffitt believes that the atonement of Jesus was not (mainly) accomplished until he ascended and offered himself up to God at his session. He believes the atonement was *inaugurated* at the cross when Jesus died but was *fulfilled* when he ascended and offered himself to the Father at his session. This de-escalation of the work of atonement on the cross may jar the orthodox, who may wonder how Jesus, in his risenness, already possessed a deified or glorified body if the atonement wasn't completed. It may be unfair to say Moffitt believes that the ascension is *the* atoning moment, given that he stresses that atonement is a process, but it is difficult to know whether the death of Christ accomplishes much, if anything at all. It is hard to imagine what the sufferings of Christ before and on the cross mean on this account, especially in light of a passage such as Isaiah 53, which affirms he was "wounded for our transgressions" (Is 53:5 KJV).

A further challenge to Moffitt's proposal is his assertion that killing of sacrifices did not even occur at the outer altar. This is unlikely,

---

[6]Thomas F. Torrance, "Karl Barth and the Latin Heresy," *SJT* 39, no. 4 (January 1986): 461-82.
[7]See Oliver O'Donovan, *Resurrection and Moral Order: An Outline for Evangelical Ethics* (Grand Rapids, MI: Eerdmans, 1994), 15, 19.

given a number of allusions in the Pentateuch to sacrifices being made on altars, famously when Abraham offered his son Isaac and "laid him *on* the altar" (Gen 22:9). Exodus 20:24 has explicit instructions from God to Moses on this matter: "Make an altar of earth for me and *sacrifice on it* your burnt offerings and fellowship offerings, your sheep and goats and your cattle." One need only to look also to Leviticus 1, where the bullock's slaying is implicitly in that vicinity. There is no reason to assume that the case of the offering of a bird ("The priest shall bring it to the altar, wring off the head and burn it on the altar; its blood shall be drained out on the side of the altar" (Lev 1:15) is any different for the bullock.

Furthermore, how Moffitt interprets the final destination of the offering or gift is open to question. He acknowledges that there was a process by which the sacrifices were carried out. This is particularly evident on the Day of Atonement, when portions of the sacrifices, that is, the blood, were sprinkled in the holy of holies. The problem is his association of this with the ascension. No blood is shed at the ascension, only on the cross. The marks in Jesus' hands and his risen life are the signals of a completed work, celebrated on ascension day.

Furthermore, to reference the Pauline concept of sanctification, this happens as believers live in union with Christ in his accomplished *death*, resurrection (Rom 6:1-11), and ascension (Col 3:1-2). The reality that Christ in death cleansed our humanity, putting sin to death, seems obviated on Moffitt's view. It is also hard to make sense of the temporal gap between the cross/resurrection and the ascension if the atonement is not effected until the ascension. One major challenge in pressing the Levitical pattern of sacrifice too far, as I believe Moffitt does, is that it does not quite correlate. Jesus offers himself up at the ascension as a living person, not a dead one. In appreciation of the Levitical pattern Moffitt has discovered, could we not rather assume that on the cross, Jesus, in the presence of the triune God, as Judge and judged, offers himself up to God, even as Hebrews 9:14 envisages?

This is not a disembodied or Docetic reality for the Son. All is sacred space (Marie Isaacs[8]) in Hebrews, and I struggle to understand why an offering up of Jesus on the cross, in the presence of the whole Trinity, is not central to his reconciling work. This would fulfill the Levitical pattern equally well.

In sum, Moffitt seems to understand the definition of atonement in Hebrews as a broader concept than the theological understanding of atonement used in contemporary and even older theological contexts. For Moffitt, atonement is a longer process than is traditionally conceived and seems better described as salvation. His contention that the ongoing priestly work of Jesus, even beyond the ascension, is necessary to complete our atonement would make more sense if the term *salvation* were applied to this rather than the word *atonement*. Hebrews 7 makes it abundantly clear that there *is* an ongoing aspect to our *salvation* that is dependent on the ongoing intercessory high priesthood of Jesus (Heb 7:25). And Hebrews 9:28 clarifies that there is a future consummation of the outworking of that salvation, in a context that makes a clear distinction between atonement, as completed by his once-for-all offering, and salvation. But does this ongoing and consummating high-priestly ministry of Jesus mean that there is no finality to the work of atonement accomplished in Christ's person? This finality is signaled and *celebrated* by his ascension to the kingly and intercessory priestly role that this passage describes. Instead of being a moment of atonement, the ascension and session seem to be a moment of celebration and affirmation of the atoning work of the Son, as expressed typically through the words of Psalm 24. The finality is implied in the opening text of the epistle: "After he had provided purification for sins, he sat down at the right hand of the Majesty in heaven" (Heb 1:3). The session of Jesus seems to be a sign of a *completed* purgation of sin. All else after that is the *application* of

---

[8]Marie Isaacs, *Sacred Space: An Approach to the Theology of the Epistle to the Hebrews* (Sheffield: Bloomsbury/T&T Clark, 1992), passim.

the atonement through the ongoing intercession of Jesus. It is salvation but not atonement.

The role that the sacrificial system of the Levitical order plays in Hebrews is important. Whereas Paul only hints at that order in his references to the atonement, this is front and center for the writer of Hebrews. Moffitt pays insufficient attention to the nonatoning aspects of this, however. What do Levitical priests do? They do not just offer sacrifices. The nature of that sacrificial function is described in Leviticus 1–7; 16. They also mediate confession, give moral judgments, enter the holy place daily to trim lamps and replace the showbread. Regarding confession and forgiveness, as Calvin noted, Christ's intercession is not a clash of wills with the Father but rather a praying for us based on the power of his atonement.[9] Forgiveness for sins confessed after conversion does not imply he is still a sacrifice. Relational absolution is granted based on the finished work of atonement, not a repetition of the bathing of the whole person but a washing of the feet (Jn 13). The Aaronic priests pray for and on behalf of the people at the golden altar of incense. Thus, there is a punctiliar action of sacrifice, *and* the priests have ongoing daily intercessory ministry. This finds fulfillment in the new covenant in a Priest who offers a sacrifice that is not merely punctiliar but complete and has forever effects (an emphatic theme in Hebrews). But this Priest also continues after his session at the Father's right hand to intercede for his people until their *salvation* is complete. Moffitt stresses that salvation is incomplete when he sits down, but he ought, I think, to stress that the *atonement is* complete when he sits down.

Hebrews points out that "by one sacrifice *he has made perfect forever* those *who are being made holy*" (Heb 10:14). The notion of an incomplete salvation, a sanctifying work, is evident from the phrase "being made holy." Nevertheless, a completed work precedes this: "We have been made holy. . . . He has made perfect forever" (Heb 10:10, 14). So, to say

---

[9]John Calvin, *Institutes* 3.20.18-22.

that our *salvation* is incomplete, a notion Peter also reflects (1 Pet 1:9), is canonical and good; to say that *atonement* is incomplete is a different matter and seems to minimize the nature of the work of Christ accomplished in his earthly incarnation, life, death, and resurrection.

The ongoing work of Jesus is a majestic theme in Hebrews. Recalling the nonsacrificial work of the Levitical priests, Jesus offers up our worship and prayers as his prayers, hears our confession, and grants absolution based on the accomplishments of his sacrificial atonement. As Hebrews 8:2 indicates, he "serves" (a priestly word) so that the people of God in *their* priestly function "may *serve* [priestly word] the living God" (Heb 9:14). He ratified the covenant by the finished work, *and* he upholds the covenant by his presence and his prayers, his unfinished work. He has made *objective* atonement once for all, but the *subjective* application of the atonement's benefits are eternal for humanity and the cosmos. If Moffitt had written, "It is finished, *and* it is not finished," the theme of his book might have been more palatable. One can certainly see how Moffitt's reading fits with the postponed sense of justification by faith in the new perspective. That the humanity of Jesus was deified already once he rose from the dead in a resurrection body, and that this is the basis for the future glorification of his people, argues in favor of a completed work of atonement, climaxed in his death and resurrection.

In Hebrews, all is sacred *space*, and divine *time* intersects human time. Much mystery remains in pursuing the wonder of the atonement/salvation of Christ, which Moffitt inspires us to pursue. As David Fergusson reminds us, it is a bright mystery, not a dark one.[10] Based on the inseparability and undifferentiated nature of the resurrection and the ascension in the Pauline epistles, O'Donovan states, "The ascension, we must judge, does not stand over against the resurrection as the resurrection stands over against the crucifixion, it does not add

---

[10]David Fergusson, "The Ascension of Christ: Its Significance in the Theology of T. F. Torrance," *Participatio* 3 (2012): 95.

a new element to the story which was not present before, but unfolds the implications of what is present already in the resurrection."[11] Further exploration of this topic in the work of Douglas Farrow is also fruitful.

ASCENSION AS ATONEMENT IN DOUGLAS FARROW

Farrow is clear that the ascension "is an act of *saving* grace accomplished by the triune God." This salvific work completed what was commenced in Jesus' baptism, his work of reconciliation, and his formation of a "royal priesthood that is Catholic in scope." Farrow also calls the ascension an act of "*perfecting* grace" in that it completed what the Holy Spirit had begun in his hovering over the waters in Genesis 1, and over Mary, who brought forth a son, the new creation. He comments that in his ascension, the Son erased "the alienation between God and man introduced by the fall," thus establishing "the communion between God and man which God was already aiming in the creation itself." The ascension completes "the formation of man and perfects his image in man. And bearing our humanity home to the Father, Jesus brings human nature as such to its true end, and to its fullest potential in the Holy Spirit. He causes it to be entirely at one with God, and so to become the object (and, for other creatures, the mediator) of God's eternal blessing." Farrow does therefore see the ascension as not just salvific but also atoning, in the filial aspect that it is "the one-ing of God and man that is the goal of the incarnation." He designates both the saving and the perfecting aspects of the ascension as both salvific and atoning. He associates the first aspect with the *purgation of heavenly things* (forensic) and the second, the teleological aspect, with the *"glorification of earthly things"* (ontological).[12] Describing these aspects of the ascension as *atoning*

---

[11]Oliver O'Donovan, *On the Thirty Nine Articles: A Conversation with Tudor Christianity*, Latimer Monograph (Exeter, UK: Paternoster, 1986), 30.
[12]Douglas Farrow, *Ascension Theology* (London: T&T Clark, 2011), 122-23.

does merit some discussion. Is it not better to differentiate between what is *salvific* and what is *atoning*?

On the one hand, one can readily agree that all acts of Jesus in his person must belong together, which is vital to understanding the atonement properly. The words of Henri de Lubac are cogent:

> Let us not break the rhythm of the Christian mysteries, which call for one another and are linked together. The Word of God, in incarnating itself, sets the first act of an unbreakable series, which is followed by death, resurrection, and finally ascension.... Accordingly, the resurrection is succeeded by the ascension, to show what it meant and to force us finally to turn our eyes upward, to go beyond the earthly horizon and all that pertains to man in his natural state. Thus the lesson of the ascension does not contradict the lesson of the incarnation: it prolongates it, deepens it. It does not set us beneath or apart from life; it obliges us to assume it fully while aiming beyond.[13]

Similarly, Farrow emphasizes that the atonement of Jesus occurred within his person and in all of his history: "Thus did he complete his earthly mission of purification, 'not despising, or evading any condition of man' but sanctifying our humanity entirely in his own person."[14] His whole life and his death were thus utterly vicarious.[15] Farrow thus quotes the words of Jesus on the cross, "It is finished," as evidence of the completion of his *earthly* mission.

However, the two aspects of ascension that Farrow specifies, purgation and certain aspects of glorification, would, I suggest, be more accurately be considered as aspects of the *application* of the atonement Christ had already finished in his vicarious incarnation,

---

[13]Henri de Lubac, *Paradoxes of Faith* (San Francisco: Ignatius, 1987), 68-69.
[14]Farrow, *Ascension Theology*, 123.
[15]Farrow here references Irenaeus, *Against Heresies* 2.22.4: "For he came to save all through means of himself—all, I say, who through him are born again to God—infants, and children, and boys, and youths, and old men. He therefore passed through every age, becoming an infant for infants, thus sanctifying infants; a child for children ... a youth for youths ... an old man for old men, that he might be a perfect master for all.... Then, at last, he came on to death itself, that he might be 'the firstborn from the dead, that in all things he might have the pre-eminence,' the Prince of life, existing before all, and going before all."

life, death, and resurrection. They may be described as *salvific* but not *atoning*. All his atoning work was accomplished in his *person*, and we cannot separate all the acts of Jesus. However, may we not distinguish them and what each accomplishes? By his resurrection, before Christ ascends, he is already the last Adam (1 Cor 15:21-22), his humanity is already deified, the new man has already been formed, and he is fully in the image of God. Therefore, the ascension is not the occasion of these affirmations but the celebration of the man already reconciled and now fit for the divine presence.

The idea of "bearing our humanity home to the Father" is valid and heartwarming, indeed salvific, but what has prepared humanity to come home is its having been cleansed and reconciled to God in the incarnation, in the vicarious humanity of Jesus and most explicitly in the cross event. The idea that the ascension erased "the alienation between God and man introduced by the fall," thus fully establishing "the communion between God and man which God was already aiming in the creation," is a valid and lofty notion, but I think to locate it in the ascension is incorrect.[16] The man who is God is welcomed there in light of all he has accomplished for humanity. He is not enacting atonement as he ascends to the Father and sits down at his right hand. He is there in light of the atonement, and he is there to apply it. So we may appropriately say it is salvific, but not strictly speaking, atoning.

In the Pauline consideration of reconciliation, for example, the death of Christ is invariably spoken of as having accomplished the "one-ing" of God and humanity. The mechanism by which reconciliation is accomplished lies in the statement, "God made him who had no sin to be sin [sin offering] for us so that in him we might become the righteousness of God" (2 Cor 5:21). Statements in Hebrews concerning the session of Jesus at his ascension make it clear that it is in light of his atoning acts of sacrifice that he ascends: "*After* he had

---

[16] Farrow, *Ascension Theology*, 122.

provided purification for sins, he sat down at the right hand of the Majesty in heaven" (Heb 1:3).

The high priesthood of Jesus is a common factor in both the atonement enacted at the cross and that deemed to have occurred at the ascension, and therefore it might be considered to be merely hairsplitting to argue where the atonement occurs. Although the writer of Hebrews sometimes speaks of the sacrificial work of the High Priest, pre-ascension, as if it were contemporaneous with his ongoing work in heaven as the coronated Priest post-ascension, there is a clear pattern in the epistle: the sacrificial work is completed before he ascends, and it is the basis of his installation as Priest and King. As Hebrews 10:12-14 reads, "But when this priest h*ad offered for all time one sacrifice for sins, he sat down* at the right hand of God, and since that time he waits for his enemies to be made his footstool. For by *one sacrifice*, he has *made perfect forever* those who are being made holy."

Farrow mentions the cry of completion Jesus utters on the cross in this very context and affirms the reality of completing his work on earth. However, his reason for speaking of atonement as ongoing relates to the work of the ascended Christ, "purifying heavenly things."[17] It is better to speak of this as atonement *applied* rather than *accomplished*. What does this purification of heavenly things in Hebrews 9:23-24 mean? The passage is as follows: "It was necessary, then, for the copies of the heavenly things to be *purified with these sacrifices*, but the heavenly things themselves with better sacrifices than these. For Christ did not enter a sanctuary made with human hands that was only a copy of the true one; he entered heaven itself, now to appear for us in God's presence." This is the first of three appearances of Christ that the writer describes in summarizing the mission of the Son in Hebrews 9. They are not in chronological order. The first appearance of Christ, chronologically, is to put away sin (Heb 9:25-28). It is expressed with a note of finality:

---

[17]Farrow, *Ascension Theology*, 123.

> *Nor did he enter heaven to offer himself again and again*, the way the high priest enters the Most Holy Place every year with blood that is not his own. Otherwise Christ would have had to suffer many times since the creation of the world. But he has appeared *once for all* at the culmination of the ages *to do away with sin by the sacrifice of himself.* Just as people are destined to die once, and after that to face judgment, so *Christ was sacrificed once to take away the sins of many*; and he will appear a second time, not to bear sin, but to bring salvation to those who are waiting for him. (Heb 9:25-28)

The phrases "once for all," the doing "away with sin," and "sacrificed once" are surely unequivocal. The purification of heavenly things has to do with his ongoing presence in heaven (Heb 9:23-24) representing his people. It has to do with the purification of their best efforts in worship and prayer. It has to do with the cleansing of sins confessed and the restoration of fellowship with the Father—not repeated atonement, not repeated justification, but sanctification. This aspect of his purification of the saints is in context in stark contrast to "do[ing] away with sin" (Heb 9:26).

In order to further clarify what the writer means by the purification of heavenly things, we must see this passage in Hebrews 9 based on the figuration of the Day of Atonement (Yom Kippur) as described in Leviticus 16 and Numbers 29. At the risk of oversimplifying the remarkable events of that feast day in the Hebrew calendar, the high priest dons the priestly linen garments to offer up sacrifices for himself (a bull) and for the people (two goats). The priest takes the blood of the first goat into the most holy inner sanctum and sprinkles it seven times before and once on the mercy seat of the ark of the covenant. This represents the offering of Christ as a sacrifice of atonement—that which satisfied divine justice (the meaning of *mercy seat* is "propitiation"). As Paul indicates, "God presented Christ as a sacrifice of atonement" (using the Greek word for the atonement cover on the ark of the covenant) so that God is both "just and the one who justifies those who have faith in Jesus" (Rom 3:25-26). One might say that the priest atones for sin.

Over the head of the second goat, the priest confesses all the people's sins, and it is sent to a deserted place. This is figural for the *substitutionary nature* of the atonement of the Son, not merely for sin but for sins. Then the high priest takes off his priestly garments and offers a bull as a burnt offering for himself and the people. That he does so without the linen garments may suggest that this offering depicts the offering of Jesus Christ as God to God rather than as man for humanity; that is, the offering of a sweet savor that brought satisfaction to the Father, the offering up within the trinitarian life of God that brought satisfaction not merely of a forensic kind. It was an offering of filial and aesthetic delight in which the Son offered himself by the eternal Spirit without spot to God (Heb 9:14). This is the focus of the atonement in the work of Anselm, whereas the substitutionary dimension found in the sin offerings, and the second goat in particular, is the emphasis in the work of Aquinas.[18] All of these offerings and sacrifices depict the multifaceted sacrificial work of Christ. And unlike the type, the sacrifice of the antetype, Jesus, was a once-for-all, fully efficacious sacrifice. This is the writer's whole point in Hebrews 9. But what then of the purification of heavenly things?

On the Day of Atonement, the high priest applies blood to the brazen altar in the outer court, the golden altar of incense, the table of showbread, and the golden candlesticks in the tent of meeting, which is the section where the priest accesses for his daily work as a priest, not the most holy place, which he enters only once a year. This is depicted in Leviticus 16:16—"He is to do the same [sprinkle blood] for the tent of meeting, which is among them in the midst of their uncleanness"—and Leviticus 16:33—"and make atonement for the Most Holy Place, for the *tent of meeting* and the *altar*, and the *priests*

---

[18]See Hastings, *Total Atonement*, 179-230.

and all the members of the community."[19] These represent all the aspects of priestly ministry. Since imperfect priests conducted these operations, they and these furniture pieces also required cleansing on the Day of Atonement.[20] This anticipated the priestly work of a future people of God in Christ, who, though reconciled once for all in light of Christ's once-for-all atoning work, are still imperfect, sinful people, who even at their best in worship need confession and absolution, and the assistance of their great High Priest for praying and worshiping in ways that bring pleasure to the Father.

The fulfillment of the applications of atonement to the furniture of the holy place in Leviticus 16 is found in Hebrews 9:23-24, where the writer states: "It was necessary, then, for the copies of the heavenly things to be purified with these sacrifices, but the heavenly things themselves with better sacrifices than these. For Christ did not enter a sanctuary made with human hands that was only a copy of the true one; he entered heaven itself, now to appear for us in God's presence." The priests in the Priest require not a new reconciliation event when they sin but rather restoration of fellowship and gracious assistance in their best acts of service and worship. This cleansing application of the atonement from heaven where the Priest functions is the continual "cleansing of the feet" rather than the "whole body" Jesus referred to when he washed his disciples' feet in John 13. They require the sanctifying influence of their Priest. They require that the Priest offer up the imperfect offerings of worship, prayer, and ministry perfect to the Father.

Farrow describes the "perfecting grace" or glorification as Jesus bringing "human nature as such to its true end, and to its fullest potential in the Holy Spirit" so that it is "entirely at one with God, and so to become the object (and, for other creatures, the mediator) of

---

[19] This is referenced also in Heb 9:21, "In the same way, he sprinkled with the blood both the tabernacle and everything used in its ceremonies."

[20] This is prefigured in the Levitical order also when priests were installed: "Then Moses took some of the anointing oil and some of the blood from the altar and sprinkled them on Aaron and his garments and on his sons and their garments. So he consecrated Aaron and his garments and his sons and their garments" (Lev 8:30).

God's eternal blessing."[21] I am prepared to concede—indeed, enthusiastically endorse—the idea that the ascension is a glorifying act; indeed, this is the primary point of my whole project. In that act of ascending, the Son of God "was taken up in glory" (1 Tim 3:16), and because he was also fully human, in union with humanity and acting for humanity, humanity was glorified in his glorification. My only contention is that this is a *salvific* act, not an *atoning* act. The New Testament speaks of Christ's ultimate work of purification and beatification (1 Jn 3:1-3) as *salvation* but never *atonement*.

The act of the exaltation of Christ, in which all believers participate, is salvific, as is the outpouring of the Spirit that flows out from it. John Milbank wishes to go as far as to call the Holy Spirit the "other atoner" for good reason: to honor the Holy Spirit, often spoken of in the tradition as merely the applier of salvation to human persons.[22] Milbank's move is understandable in light of the Spirit's regenerating and incorporating work and because the Spirit is the gift that the Son's cross accomplished. Jonathan Edwards also makes this point in his desire to honor the Spirit in his Puritan-Reformed context. The infinite cost of the cross was commensurate with the value of the Gift it procured, that of the Spirit, thus bestowing equal honor to the Spirit in redemption. Edwards states,

> But according to what has now been supposed, there is an equality. To be the wonderful love of God is as much as for the Father and the Son to exercise wonderful love; and to be the thing purchased, is as much as to be the price that purchases it. The price, and the thing bought with that price, answers each other in value; and to be the excellent benefit offered, is as much as to offer such an excellent benefit.[23]

However well-intentioned these pneumatic corrections may be, the Spirit never works in isolation but rather in coinherent togetherness

---

[21]Farrow, *Ascension Theology*, 122.
[22]John Milbank, "The Second Difference: For a Trinitarianism Without Reserve," *Modern Theology* 2, no. 3 (1986): 213.
[23]Jonathan Edwards, "Treatise on Grace," in *Treatise on Grace and Other Posthumously Published Writings*, ed. Paul Helm (Cambridge: James Clarke, 1971), 67-68.

with the Son. The atoning work of the Son is the grounding of regeneration, the incorporation of believers into the body of Christ, and the sanctification and ultimate glorification that the Spirit accomplishes. For this reason, I suggest it is safer to speak of these works of the Spirit—the ascension, and our present and future ascension in his—as salvific, not atoning. With respect to the doctrine of appropriations in the Trinity, the Spirit is better spoken of as the *other savior* rather than the *other atoner*. With respect to the indivisibility of the persons, the Spirit participates in every step the Atoner makes, including in his atoning death, for, as in Hebrews 9:14, the Son offers himself for the cleansing of our consciences and priestly ministry "through the eternal Spirit." So perhaps we are splitting hairs here?

9

THE GLORY OF THE HEAVENLY APPLICATION OF THE ATONEMENT

THIS CHAPTER WILL HIGHLIGHT the relationship between the ascended Christ in heaven in his session and intercession and the person and work of the Spirit on earth. It addresses how this indivisibility of the works of these divine persons, along with the appropriations of particular functions of the persons, is relevant to the participation of believers in Christ, in his salvation and in his glory. The central confession of the church that "Jesus is Lord" takes on new meaning in light of the ascension, in part because it inaugurates a climactic work of the Spirit.

The Spirit's ministry on earth since the ascension is a ministry in coinherent harmony with the ministry of the Son in heaven, just as the work of the Spirit was present to the Son during his ministry on earth. The Spirit's ministry now includes the Spirit's directing attention to the glory of Christ for the sanctification of his people (2 Cor 3:18). It includes the impartation of the Son's glory to the church. I will first consider these concepts theologically and then as they are expressed through the writings of Peter, Paul, John, and the writer of Hebrews, with a postlude on one theologian in the tradition, John Calvin.

THE ASCENDED SON AND THE SPIRIT: THEOLOGICAL REFLECTION

Since chapter five has already focused on the ongoing intercessory work of the great High Priest Jesus, this chapter focuses on the other hand of the Trinity, the Holy Spirit. The Spirit works in tandem with the Son, given that they are coinherent persons. This was true of the whole mission of the Son when here on earth. Cappadocian father Gregory of Nazianzus writes: "Christ is born, the Spirit is his forerunner; Christ is baptized, the Spirit bears him witness; Christ is tempted, the Spirit leads him up; Christ performs miracles, the Spirit accompanies him; Christ ascends, the Spirit fills his place. Is there any significant function belonging to God, which the Spirit does not perform?"[1] As indicated by Gregory, this coinherence is also true of the work of the Spirit in this age since Christ has ascended. Just as the Spirit was the "mediator of communion" in the life of Jesus, he is that in bringing the persons he regenerates into union and communion with Christ.[2] Adam Johnson concludes that in light of the work of the Spirit in the atonement, it "is a work not merely of the Father and the Son, the benefits of which are applied by the Spirit; the atonement is the one work of the one God: Father, incarnate Son, and Holy Spirit."[3] What the Son has done as a result of his participation in humanity (*participatio* or *unio hypsostatica*), the incarnation, something accomplished by the Spirit (Mt 1:20; Lk 1:35), enables what the Spirit does in the regeneration of human persons as they are brought into union with Christ by faith (*unio cum Christo*; Titus 3:6; Eph 1:12-14) and preserved by the Spirit, who is the earnest of salvation's fruition in fullness. The union with humanity in the incarnate Christ, by the Spirit, and his ministry all the way to his death and resurrection, by the Spirit, is also the foundation for the Spirit's work post-ascension in corporately

---

[1] Gregory of Nazianzus, *On God and Christ: The Five Theological Orations and Two Letters to Cledonius*, Popular Patristics Series (Crestwood, NY: St. Vladimir's Seminary Press, 2002), 139.

[2] This is a phrase used by George Hunsinger in describing the role of the Spirit in the soteriology of Karl Barth. See George Hunsinger, "The Mediator of Communion: Karl Barth's Doctrine of the Holy Spirit," in *The Cambridge Companion to Karl Barth*, ed. John Webster (Cambridge: Cambridge University Press, 2000), 177.

[3] Adam Johnson and Tessa Hayashida, "The Spirit of the Atonement: The Role of the Holy Spirit in Christ's Death and Resurrection," *Religions* 13, no. 10 (2022): 8-9.

baptizing and incorporating the church into Christ in glorious union (*unio mystica*; 1 Cor 12:13).

In short, what the Son does as Prophet, Priest, and King, he does in communion with the Holy Spirit. It is a consequence of Jesus' victorious, glorious ascension that the Holy Spirit is given to him by the Father and then poured out by Jesus on his church. The church also carries out the *missio Dei* in union with Christ the sent and sending one, indwelt and empowered by the sent and sending Holy Spirit (Jn 20:19-23). God's people need comfort and strength for their pilgrimages to heaven. The sympathy and strength imparted to them by their High Priest in heaven are in fact imparted by the Comforter, the Holy Spirit, who applies these directly to their hearts. From above and from within, the triune God communicates his comfort and endurance to his people. Stated differently, we may affirm the following: the participation of the Christian and the church in the kingly, prophetic, and priestly nature of the ascended Christ—that is to say, in the coinherent work of the Spirit in each aspect of that work—leads to the impartation of Christ's glory in its communicable aspects to the church and so to the world, the new humanity of kings and priests and prophets.

Christology and pneumatology are connected by Jesus himself when he states that the Spirit cannot come until he is glorified (Jn 7:39). The outpouring of the Spirit is closely related to Jesus' accession to the throne and the inauguration of his kingdom as the ascended Christ in the now. Christ's church is therefore a kingdom (Acts 1:4; 1 Pet 2:9; Rev 1:6), the sign of his kingdom on earth, and its people are *kingly* representatives of their King on earth, receiving the kingdom and living out its way of being in all realms of life. As such, they are empowered by the Spirit for Christ's mission on earth, his cultural mandate, his Great Commandment and his Great Commission. The *prophetic* nature of the ascended Christ is imparted to the church decisively by the work of the Spirit, as indicated in Acts 2:17-18 and

1 Corinthians 12–14. Paul makes it clear that those "speaking by the Spirit of God" say "Jesus is Lord" (1 Cor 12:3). The *priestly* nature of the ascended Christ is also imparted to the church, as implied in passages such as 1 Peter 2:5-9, which refers to the church as a holy and a royal priesthood. Hebrews 8:1 alludes to the priesthood of the many in light of the priesthood of the one in Hebrews 9:14, where liturgical words are used of both. The Spirit is operative in all of these aspects, and their purpose is the glorification of Christ and a growing in glory of his people.

Discussion of the relation between Son and the Spirit in the economic Trinity, and therefore in the immanent Trinity, has occurred for centuries in the life of the church. The *filioque* controversy cannot be considered here at length, but in light of what pertains in the economic Trinity, as indicated by texts such as John 16:14-15 and Acts 2:33, some resolution of the controversy may be found in the phrase *per filium* ("through the Son"), which conveys the close intertwining of the works of the Son and the Spirit. This is the idea that the Father gives the Spirit to the Son at the ascension so that the latter may Impart the Spirit to the church. The Spirit is therefore given from the Father *through* the Son. Given the revelatory correspondence between the economic and the immanent Trinity, it is then possible to suggest that in the eternal or immanent Trinity, the Spirit proceeds eternally from the Father *through* the Son. That the missions of the persons in the economy reflect the processions in the inner life of God seems to simply make good sense. This option has informed ecumenical dialogue between the East and the West.

Relevant to our purpose here, it is certainly the case that the gift of the Spirit given to the Son is a significant aspect of the glory endowed on Christ in his ascension. That he is given the privilege of giving another person in the Trinity to his church is remarkable glory. The perichoretic nature of the persons prevents this from being a subordination of the Spirit to the Son. It is rather a mutual submission, a giving and receiving that characterizes the coinherent or perichoretic life of the Trinity. The texts cited above simply affirm that the end toward which the atonement of Christ moved was in fact the gift of the Spirit to the Son, which is then poured out on the church, as recorded in Acts 2. The Son ascends in glory. The Father gives him the glory of the gift of the Spirit for his church. The Spirit descends. The Spirit is in fact spoken of as the "the Spirit of glory" who rests on the suffering believer (1 Pet 4:14), and his ministry is to regenerate, incorporate, sanctify, and ultimately impart glory to the church.

As already noted, Jonathan Edwards expressed a distinct desire to honor the Holy Spirit with glory in the economy of salvation, a glory that in fact was the end goal of the depths of the suffering of the Son on earth. Of the unfathomable riches contained within what the atonement accomplished, the gift of the person of the Holy Spirit was surely the center and zenith. In speaking of the Spirit as "Gift," Edwards is in fact echoing a deep tradition going all the way back to Irenaeus and Augustine.[4] In more recent theology, Tom Smail develops this further by speaking of the Spirit not merely as Gift but, acknowledging the deity of the Spirit, as the Giving Gift, the fully divine person who endows gifts that only God can give.[5] These include regeneration, sanctification, and glory, such that the glory of the Son is seen in the lives of believers personally ("one degree of glory to another," 2 Cor 3:18 ESV) and in the church corporately ("glory in the church," Eph 3:21).

The doctrine of the believer's participation in Christ through participation in the Spirit is an important focus of ascension theology. It is grounded in the assumption that because Christ became one with humanity in his incarnation, all that he does in his

---

[4]This is documented in Raniero Cantalamessa, *Come Creator Spirit: Meditations on the Veni Creator* (Collegeville, MN: Liturgical Press, 2003).

[5]Thomas Smail, *The Giving Gift: The Holy Spirit in Person* (Eugene, OR: Wipf & Stock, 2004), passim.

first advent, each aspect of his history, including the ascension, is accomplished vicariously for humanity. The order of our salvation corresponds to the order of his history, including his ascension. He always stood in our place: he was born for us, lived for us, died for us, rose again for us, and ascended for us. His hypostatic union is the grounding for accomplishing our atonement, objectively speaking. This may be called participation de jure; salvation has been accomplished for humanity in Christ.[6] This is in keeping with the eternal benevolence of God toward humanity in his election of the Son to become human.[7] However, there is a second dimension of participation. Those who have faith in Christ, those who receive the regenerating work of the Spirit, come into acknowledgment and appropriation of objective atonement. They are those who subjectively participate de facto in the salvation Christ has accomplished. The possibility of this by the Spirit is grounded in the actuality of the salvation accomplished in the history of the Son. They are made alive, are raised up, and are seated with Christ in the heavenlies (Eph 2:5-6). We will now trace the theme of the Christian's participation in the ascended Christ and his glory by the work of the Spirit in the New Testament.

THE ASCENDED SON AND THE SPIRIT: BIBLICAL REFLECTION

Peter and participation in the ascension and salvation. Peter implies that the resurrection of Jesus and his ascension and session are salvific. Referring to the waters of baptism, Peter says, "It saves you by the resurrection of Jesus Christ, who has gone into heaven and is at God's right hand—with angels, authorities and powers in submission to him" (1 Pet 3:21-22). As the preceding baptismal

---

[6] Adam Neder employs the de jure, de facto terminology with reference to Barth's doctrine of participation in Christ. See Neder, *Participation in Christ: An Entry into Karl Barth's Church Dogmatics* (Louisville, KY: Westminster John Knox, 2008), 26, 72, 84.

[7] "God's voluntary inclination towards humanity" is how Thomas Erskine (1750–1823) puts it.

context reveals, the theme of participation is implicit in these statements. The sacrament of baptism is the outward sign of an inward reality, that of the union of persons being baptized by the Spirit into Christ in his death and resurrection, and here also in his ascent and session above all heavenly powers, which are in submission to Christ and therefore his people.

Peter speaks more directly to the theme of the believer's participation in Christ in 2 Peter 1:1-9. Before embarking on this discussion, however, Peter places an explanatory caption over the topic that suggests that our participation in Christ depends on his ascended state in glory. The endowment of the power for participation and its outworking into virtue formation is a consequence of the calling of Christ "by his own glory and goodness" (2 Pet 1:3). What does "his own glory" mean in this Petrine context? The mention of both power and glory recurs later in this same chapter and refers to the transfiguration, which, as I noted in chapter two, is figural of the ascension. There Peter reminds his hearers that he had spoken to them concerning "the coming of our Lord Jesus Christ in *power*," something he was sure about because he and his fellow disciples "were eyewitnesses of his *majesty*" (2 Pet 1:16), a term referring to his transcendent glory.[8] Here Peter is referring to the transfiguration on "the sacred mountain" (2 Pet 1:18). Peter says, on that mountain, "[Jesus] received honor and glory from God the Father when the voice came to him from the Majestic Glory, saying, 'This is my Son, whom I love; with him, I am well pleased'" (2 Pet 1:17). This honor, glory, and power Peter saw in the transfiguration informs his understanding of the ascended Christ, who called his hearers "by his own glory." The transfiguration event anticipated what occurred at Christ's ascension

---

[8] It seems most likely that by "the coming of our Lord Jesus Christ in *power*," Peter is referring to the first coming of Christ here, although two chapters later, in 2 Pet 3:3, there is a reference to those who scoffed at the idea of Christ's second coming: "'They will say, 'Where is this "coming" he promised?'" (2 Pet 3:4). If the certitude of the second coming is in mind in 2 Pet 1:16, it was still based on what Peter had seen in Christ's first advent at the transfiguration.

and anticipates his second coming in glory. The "divine power" in 2 Peter 1:3, which gives us "everything we need for a godly life through our knowledge of him," finds its source in the power seen in Christ on this transfiguration mountain. We participate in the power of the transfigured and ascended Christ. Peter does not mention the Spirit, but the Spirit's work in cultivating glory in the saints may be inferred from other texts.

With reverberations of the ascension in mind, Peter then discusses the reality and consequences of the participation of believers in the ascended, glorious Christ. Here in this passage (2 Pet 1:3-9), he speaks specifically of the reality that believers in Christ "participate [*koinōnoi*] in the divine nature" (2 Pet 1:4). Peter fills out the meaning of the term by referring to the knowledge of God three times over in this paragraph: participation (2 Pet 1:4) is equated with or explained by the believer's knowledge of God/Christ (2 Pet 1:2-3, 8). One might say, therefore, that participation is grounded in relational, experiential union with Christ and is thus expressed in communion with Christ. Peter in fact represents participation in the ascended, glorious Christ as the very core reality of salvation. In consequence of this union, there logically flows our righteousness in his righteousness (2 Pet 1:1) and the pursuit of virtue (2 Pet 1:5-9) in his virtue. That is, union with Christ produces the twin graces of justification and sanctification. Peter first describes the people of God as "those who through the righteousness of our God and Savior Jesus Christ have received a faith as precious as ours" (2 Pet 1:1), in which the believer's justification is expressed as a consequence of the righteousness of Christ for us in a way that emphasizes the first dimension of the doctrine of participation, the union of the Son with humanity, and his vicarious life and death for us. However, the second half of this verse indicates that this act of Christ is also how faith appropriates salvation. This refers to the second—the human—part of participation. Peter says they "have *received* a faith as precious as ours" (2 Pet 1:1).

Thus, even the human aspect of participation in salvation is a *gift*. Even the capacity for faith is a consequence of the righteous offering up of Christ for us objectively and our subjective appropriation of it by the Spirit. This is not to say there is no human agency in our coming into union with Christ by the Spirit. It simply means that our agency is responsive to, and participates in, his agency. Philippians 2:12-13 refers to this: "Work out your own salvation . . . for it is God who works in you." Thus, our participation in Christ and his salvation is one of *asymmetric concursus*, the idea that in our coming to faith and in our growth in holiness, God acts (hence the asymmetry) *and* that we act responsively in his working. His working in us does not mean the loss of our agency. It is a noncompetitive, mysterious operation of the Spirit in us, creating our dependent responsive faith in us, leading to all the virtues, climaxing in love.

Peter moves to what participation in the divine nature empowers: sanctification, expressed here as godly character or virtue. The glorious character of Christ anticipates the present and final aim of the believer's pursuit of sanctification since the believer is in union with the person who imparts that glory. His is an inherent radiance; ours is a reflected glory. Ours is the glory that combines all the virtues in balance that Peter mentions here. However, every one of those virtues is found first in the Christ with whom we are in union, and he imparts them to us by the Spirit.

Having reminded the believers of these great evangelical realities, Peter then commands them in a manner that emphasizes that participation is not passive. It is a relationship in which God in the ascended Christ by the Spirit is active in our transformation, but we are active too: "For this very reason, *make every effort* to add to your faith goodness; and to goodness, knowledge; and to knowledge, self-control; and to self-control, perseverance; and to perseverance, godliness; and to godliness, mutual affection; and to mutual affection, love" (2 Pet 1:5-7). We should not separate these virtues from union, participation with Christ, or knowledge of Christ. Failure to progress in these virtues is a failure, an ineffectiveness in the knowing of "our Lord Jesus Christ" (2 Pet 1:8). Virtue spirituality and ethics are all good, but if they can lack at their center the dynamic of participation in the life and love of God, they will promote an inward and even vainglorious spirituality—which is to say, Pharisaism. Christian sanctification and ethics must be grounded in the gospel. They are evangelical, not legal. They are an outflow of the knowledge that God is for us and in us.

The primary virtue of love caps this list of virtues. The context for these virtues is relationality or love. Love, as the chief of all the virtues, agrees with Jesus' teaching on the two greatest commandments. Love is also the first of the characteristics or fruit of the Spirit in Paul's list of graces in Galatians 5:22-23. All the characteristics that follow love in that list are a description of love. Among the few mentions of the Spirit in his epistles, Peter says in his first epistle, "If you are insulted because of the name of Christ, you are blessed, for the *Spirit of glory* and of God rests on you" (1 Pet 4:14). The believers' pursuit of the virtues, the sum of which may be called glory, must be effort empowered by the Spirit. Peter indicates this in the opening of his first epistle, where he speaks of "the sanctifying work of the Spirit" (1 Pet 1:2). Furthermore, returning to 2 Peter 1, the Spirit's title, "the Spirit of glory" (1 Pet 4:14), is a reminder of his deity and also of his intimate role in beatifying the people of God, encouraging them in transformation through contemplation of the glory of the Lord by faith now, and so preparing them in the *now* for seeing the glory that would transform them *then* when they see the ascended Lord of glory.

Shortly after he finishes this list of virtues, Peter repeats the phrase "make every effort," suggesting that the cultivation of virtue in believers will provide a sense of assurance of their divine calling and election. Assurance of our salvation is best arrived at by a contemplative looking away from ourselves to the ascended Christ, who has accomplished our atonement and sat down at the right hand of God for us. Some assurance can also be gained from awareness of a hunger for the sanctifying influence of the Spirit within ourselves, revealed in service to humanity. It is one dimension of our assurance to recognize our own spiritual growth, virtues, and holy and glorious acts. This spurs us on toward the ultimate purpose of our transformation in participation with Christ, which is outlined in 2 Peter 1:11: "You will receive a rich welcome into the eternal kingdom of our Lord and Savior Jesus Christ." This welcome reminds us of the reality that our participation in Christ includes the event by which Christ entered into his "eternal kingdom." He has gone home, and he will bring us home. He has ascended, and we are destined for ascent.

In the next paragraph of 2 Peter 1, exhortations towards holiness and glory in participation with Christ continue. Then Peter reminds the readers of this calling home. This reminder's effect is heightened by the statement of his imminent "departure" to be with Christ. Here he uses the phrase "make every effort" for a third time in this short passage, which he addresses to himself. He makes every effort to make sure "that after [his] departure," his readers "will always be able to remember these things" (2 Pet 1:15). The assurance he demonstrates regarding the destiny of his departure is based on what he has seen of the regal glory of Christ in his transfiguration. Peter's own departure reminds Peter of the departure that Jesus discussed with those on the Mount of Transfiguration, "They spoke about his departure [Greek *exodos*], which he was about to bring to fulfillment at Jerusalem" (Lk 9:31), and of the specific reference in Luke 9:51 to Christ's being taken up (*analēpsis*) to heaven. Most importantly, according to Luke's account, Peter, with the others, "saw his glory" (Lk 9:32). This memory would no doubt fuel Peter's desire to see it again in perpetual fullness.

The association of *glory* with the transfiguration is echoed when Luke describes the ascension as Christ's entry into glory (Acts 3:13;

7:55; 22:11). These references to the ascension in Acts confirm the idea of glory as the central idea of the ascension:

> The God of Abraham, Isaac and Jacob, the God of our fathers, has *glorified* his servant Jesus. (Acts 3:13)
>
> But Stephen, full of the Holy Spirit, looked up to heaven and saw the *glory of God*, and Jesus standing at the right hand of God. (Acts 7:55)
>
> My companions led me by the hand into Damascus, because the *brilliance* [lit. "the glory"] *of the light* had blinded me. (Acts 22:11)

This blinding glory of Jesus' face is already anticipated on the Mount of Transfiguration: "As he was praying, the appearance of his face changed, and his clothes became as bright as a flash of lightning" (Lk 9:29). J. G. Davies thus points out that the synoptic writers understood the transfiguration to "be a foreshadowing of the *Parousia*."[9] However, Acts 1:11 affirms that the ascension foreshadows the parousia. Thus, "If . . . the transfiguration was a prefigurement of the *Parousia*, it must logically be a prefigurement of the Ascension too, and as such, it is presented in the third Gospel."[10] How marvelous it is, then, that we, as God's people, participate in the glory of the ascended Son and one day will participate in the parousia? Paul states that this will happen in its fullest sense "on the day he comes to be *glorified* in his holy people and to be marveled at among all those who have believed" (2 Thess 1:10). Though not a Petrine emphasis, the role of the Spirit in seeing the face of Christ, and the glorification of the saints in participation with Christ, is the work of the Spirit. Pauline theology is more emphatic in this regard.

Paul and participation in the ascension and salvation. Paul tends to employ the word *union* rather than *participation*, though they are overlapping concepts. The believer's union with Christ is inherent in the phrase "in Christ." Paul's soteriology is wrapped up in the concept

---

[9]John G. Davies, *He Ascended into Heaven: A Study in the History of Doctrine*, Bampton Lectures (London: Lutterworth, 1958), 40.
[10]Davies, *He Ascended into Heaven*, 41.

of the union of the Son with humanity (Rom 8:3) at the incarnation and the corresponding union of believing persons and the church (Eph 5:32) with him enabled by the Spirit. Believers participate in his saving history, especially in his death and resurrection but also in his ascension and glorification. Union with Christ is thus the basis for the justification, sanctification, vocation, and glorification of the people of God. Paul sums up the gospel with the following words: "For those God foreknew, he also *predestined to be conformed to the image of his Son*, that he might be the firstborn among many brothers and sisters. And those he predestined, he also called; those he called, he also justified; those he justified, he also *glorified*" (Rom 8:29-30).

The surprising absence of the word *sanctified* in this text does not infer that Paul neglects this in his corpus. It is absent here because Paul is stressing the telos of the eternal councils of God as a fait accompli. At the core of Paul's understanding of the process of sanctification when he does speak of it is the idea that persons in Christ can already in this life begin to share the glory of the ascended Christ, and that by the work of the Spirit. In 2 Corinthians 3, for example, he describes sanctification as a process of Spirit-empowered transformation through contemplation of the glory of Christ: "Now the Lord is the Spirit, and where the Spirit of the Lord is, there is freedom. And we all, who with unveiled faces contemplate the Lord's glory, are being transformed into his image with ever-increasing glory, which comes from the Lord, who is the Spirit" (2 Cor 3:17-18). This assumes the ascension into the glory of Christ, for it is his state as glorified in heaven that is the object of the believer's gaze. The work of the Spirit—who descended on the day of Pentecost in response to the ascension of the Son—accompanies this act of contemplation of the ascended Christ, and so we notice again the two hands of the Father at work here in the sanctification and the gradual glorification of the believer. Upon ascending, Christ received the gift of the Spirit from the Father and poured out the Spirit on his people to constitute them the church and to work in the world through them, in a coinherent manner with Christ's work in heaven as Head of the church and Lord of creation and King-Priest for his people.

In another passage, Paul speaks again of how Christ's people can be in the process of transformation, on the road to being glorified, in the present age with a specific reference to the ascension. In Ephesians 2, Paul uses three verbs to describe how Jesus' history (*ordo historia*) becomes his people's salvation (*ordo salutis*). In Christ, the people of God have been made alive, raised up, and seated with him in the heavenly realms. He thereby includes the concept of union with Christ in the ascension as the basis for transformation. The saving history of Jesus is described first in Ephesians 1:20-21: God "raised Christ from the dead and *seated him at his right hand* in the heavenly realms, far above all rule and authority, power and dominion, and every name that is invoked, not only in the present age but also in the one to come." The italicized words indicate that the ascension is in Paul's mind here. However, flowing from the immeasurable love and mercy of God, his people, who once were spiritually dead (Eph 2:1), have been made alive with Christ. Then the participation of God's people in the ascension becomes irreducibly clear: "And God raised us up with Christ and seated us with him in the heavenly realms in Christ Jesus, in order that in the coming ages he might show the incomparable riches of his grace, expressed in his kindness to us in Christ Jesus" (Eph 2:6-7).

This is the glorious epitome of the doctrine of union with Christ: his people have ascended in his ascent. In that elevated place of nearness to Christ, best accessed by prayer, we contemplate his glory and are transformed. The Spirit is active in this process—the awakening and regeneration of believers (Titus 3:5-6), their sanctification (Gal 5:16, 22-23, 25), and their glorification (2 Cor 3:18). Glorification is a confident hope for those who are justified: "And we boast in the hope of the glory of God" (Rom 5:2). This hope is accessed by the

Spirit, who pours out the love of God into our hearts (Rom 5:4). Acts 7 gives a living example of the involvement of the Spirit in Stephen's seeing the glory of the ascended Christ as he was being glorified: "But Stephen, full of the Holy Spirit, looked up to heaven and saw the glory of God, and Jesus standing at the right hand of God" (Acts 7:55).

The Protestant tradition, following Calvin, emphasizes the believer's union with Christ at conversion and the twin gifts of justification and sanctification leading toward glorification. Justification is usually associated with the history of Christ for us, whereas sanctification and onward with the work of the Spirit in us. Nevertheless, the work of the Spirit is operative in all the works of the ascended Son. By the Spirit, the Son became incarnate, lived a holy and vicarious life for us, offered himself up to God in his atoning death, and rose again. His atoning life and death was by the Spirit. As a result of this objective history, we are justified. God has pronounced us justified in Christ before we were even born. The Spirit enables our subjective appropriation of this. The same Spirit, operative in preparing our *objective* salvation in his full engagement in the saving incarnation, life, death, resurrection, and ascension of Jesus, is at work in the *subjective* application of it. Thus, Paul teaches a theology of the union of God's people with Christ, which in the future brings to fruition the work of glorifying the saints to be like the ascended Christ.

John and participation in the ascension and salvation. John's record of Jesus' high-priestly prayer indicates that Jesus longed that his people might one day see him in his ascended glory and that they would be glorified. Jesus prays, "Father, I want those you have given me to be with me where I am, and to see my *glory*, the *glory* you have given me because you loved me before the creation of the world" (Jn 17:24). John spells this out explicitly in 1 John 3:2: "Dear friends, now we are children of God, and what we will be has not yet been made known. But we know that when Christ appears, we shall be like him, for we shall see him as he is." This description of the beatific vision affects our present from the future: "All who have this hope in him purify themselves, just as he is pure" (1 Jn 3:3). John elsewhere acknowledges the ministry of the Holy Spirit in this purification or sanctification. He affirms that a sanctified life, which is a life of obedience to the commands of God, is an outflow union with Christ, but that the source, assurance, and power for this union and communion are by means of "the Spirit he gave us" (1 Jn 3:24). John repeats this in 1 John 4:13, "This is how we know that we live in him and he in us: He has given us of his Spirit." The indwelling of the descended Spirit enables union with the ascended Son.

In anticipation of the *visio Dei*, the vision of the ascended and glorified Son, the Spirit imparts hope and empowers change gradually until that day. That neither John nor Peter speaks much of the Spirit in their respective epistles does not mean he is not implicit in their assertions about the pursuit of virtue or holiness. Their reticence to speak of the Spirit may be in keeping with the self-effacing nature of this person of the Trinity, as Jesus taught them (Jn 16:13-14). Honorable as the work of Edwards, Smail, and third article theologians is in seeking to confirm the deity and personhood of the Spirit and to honor his function in redemption, these sentiments must be in tension with the fact that the chief orientation of the Spirit is to speak about Christ, and in perfect perichoretic communion with Christ to glorify Christ.[11] That is to honor him whom we may guardedly call the shy person of the Trinity (John 16:13-14).

The writer of Hebrews and participation in the ascension and salvation. The citations of Psalm 110:1 in Hebrews are crucial in reinforcing the exaltation of the Son in his session and kingly glory

---

[11] "Third article theologians" refers to a movement of some theologians toward honoring the deity and personhood of the Spirit, who is referenced in the third article of the Nicene Creed, but especially to take a fresh look at theology through pneumatological lenses. Some theologians in this movement are Amos Yong, Eugene Rogers, Veli-Matti Kärkkäinen, Joel Green, Marc Cortez, Frank Macchia, and Myk Habets.

after the completion of his atoning work. This may be seen in Hebrews 1:3 and Hebrews 10:12-13. In this latter passage, the sitting-down phrase of Psalm 110:1 follows the statement of the completeness of the atonement of the Son as Priest to his people. In Hebrews 10:14 comes the link to the *people* of the King-Priest: "For by one sacrifice he has *made perfect forever* those who *are being made holy*." What is the link? In the immediate context, it refers to the enemies being made his footstool. Those enemies include the sin with which Christians battle all their lives. So what God has done in exalting Jesus at the ascension and his session works its way into the lives of believers in their "being made holy," that is, their sanctification. As he has been set apart, so are they set apart. His ascension and victory over their enemies has become theirs. Being made holy is effected by participation in the Son, but in other New Testament sentiments, it is the Spirit who makes participation and holiness de facto.

Hebrews 10 also speaks of the new covenant (Heb 10:15-18) and how, by that covenant, not only are sins forgiven (the Pauline equivalent might be *justification*) but God's laws are transplanted into hearts and minds (the Pauline equivalent of *sanctification*). The core of the new covenant, implicit in this context, is the belonging, the union of the Lord with his people: "I will be their God, and they will be my people" (see Heb 8:10; Jer 31:33). The union between the Son and the covenant people he has mediated on their behalf links the ascension and session of Jesus with the transformation of his people. Interestingly, in Hebrews 10:15, prior to speaking of the new covenant, which entails the union of God and his people, there is a reference to the Spirit's role in this: "The Holy Spirit also testifies to us about this. First he says . . ." The Spirit is the person in the Godhead who alongside the Son confirms and internalizes the covenant. This is already anticipated when Ezekiel announces the new covenant: "And I will put my Spirit in you and move you to follow my decrees and be careful to keep my laws" (Ezek 36:27). Union with Christ ascended and communion with the Spirit descended enables the transformation of the community of grace.

This theme is also implicit in the wider context of Hebrews. Though the words *union* and *participation* are not found, from the beginning of the writer's argument for the efficacy of the priesthood of Christ, the Son and his people have become one (Heb 2). He has become one with them by the incarnation; he has been made "lower than the angels," and he has tasted "death for everyone" (Heb 2:9). In his history (*ordo historia*)—by his incarnation, death, and ascension—he has been crowned with glory and honor. Because they are one with him, he has likewise brought "many sons and daughters to glory" (Heb 2:10; *ordo salutis*). In Hebrews 2 the writer says, "Both the one who makes people holy and those who are made holy are *of the same family*. So Jesus is not ashamed to call them brothers and sisters" (Heb 2:11). The writer adds, "Since the children have flesh and blood, he too shared in their humanity so that by his death he might break the power of him who holds the power of death—that is, the devil" (Heb 2:14). Their salvation, their transformation, means that "he had to be made like them" (Heb 2:17). The language is different from that in Paul or Peter, but the content is the same. By the ascension of Jesus, his union with us, and our corresponding union with him, we are empowered for characteral and moral transformation.

As a consequence of the participation of every believer in Christ, it becomes apparent that Christ's people share in his ascension and his session at the Father's right hand. But equally emphatic in the New Testament is that believers must appropriate and access this. The frequency of the citation of Psalm 110:1 by the New Testament writers emphasizes the glory of the one who has sat down at the right hand of God. However, as Seamands suggests, the writers also "believed that not only was Jesus seated on the throne at God's right hand, but since they were now joined to him, they too were destined and invited to sit with him on the throne (cf. Rev 3:21)."[12] Seamands emphasizes the importance of this reality to the Christian life:

> Unfortunately, many Christians have little or no awareness of this. Consequently, they never learn to live in Christ from the seated-on-the-throne position that's theirs. No doubt we can be "so heavenly minded were no earthly good." But if we are going to be any earthly good, according to the New Testament, we must be heavenly minded. That's why focusing on the fact and the significance of Christ's ascension is so essential.[13]

Andrew Murray writes similarly concerning the first citation of Psalm 110:1 in Hebrews 1:3. He states:

> The knowledge of Jesus as having entered heaven for us, and taken us in union with Himself into a heavenly life, is what will deliver the Christian from all that is low and feeble, and lift him [her] to a life of joy and strength. To gaze upon the heavenly Christ in the Father's presence, to whom all things are subject, will transform us into heavenly Christians, dwelling all the day in God's presence, and overcoming every enemy. Yes, my Redeemer, seated at God's right hand—if I only know Him aright and trust Him as able to save completely—He will make me more than conqueror.[14]

What Murray sees in Hebrews 1 is reinforced in the pivotal passage of Hebrews 10. It is one thing to have access to the throne of God. It is another to access our access. This is evident when the writer says, "Therefore, brothers and sisters, since we have confidence to enter the Most Holy Place by the blood of Jesus, by a new and living way opened for us through the curtain, that is, his body, and since we have a great priest over the house of God, *let us draw near to God*" (Heb 10:19-22). This is the tour de force of the whole epistle. The sacrificial blood of Jesus

---

[12]Stephen A. Seamands, *Give Them Christ: Preaching His Incarnation, Crucifixion, Resurrection, Ascension, and Return* (Downers Grove, IL: InterVarsity Press, 2012), 142.
[13]Seamands, *Give Them Christ*, 142.
[14]Andrew Murray, *The Holiest of All: An Exposition of the Epistle to the Hebrews* (London: Nisbet, 1949), 65.

(note his earthly title here) has provided access; his body, which functioned as the curtain between God and humanity, has provided access, an access celebrated every time the Eucharist is celebrated, and a "great priest" over God's house ensures our continued access. We can be bold to enter because of an efficacious sacrifice and an interceding great High Priest. But we must access the access: "Let us draw near to God."

Several exhortations follow, but the first and key to the rest is accessing the presence of God in prayer. Living into the ascension, in which we have the privilege to participate, is no chore, but it does require our agency. It is we who pray, even if it is in his praying that we pray. We are engraced in order to pray by the Holy Spirit, as Paul suggests in Romans 8:26, but grace empowers our agency.[15] Our High Priest intercedes for us as we pray, but human agency is not diminished. It is actually enhanced by that. The form grace takes is our action in God's actions in our lives. Everything about this is evangelical, not legal. Living into the ascension means a life of prayer. The high priesthood of Jesus assures us that we are always heard. It is at his discretion how he may answer. Praying to the one who is the King-Priest over all the cosmos invites expectant prayers. Realizing the kingdom has not yet fully come means that we do not pray demandingly, with a triumphalist spirit. Albert B. Simpson states, "The ascension of Christ, therefore, has given us the right to expect his interposition, even to the utmost extent of the miraculous and supernatural, when the interests of his kingdom truly require it; and yet his power may be no less mighty when it is working along lines of perfect simplicity and naturalness."[16]

The intertwining role of the ascended Son and the Spirit in trinitarian salvation, which is the doctrine of participation of the saints in God, has been an exploding theme in the last thirty years.[17] The role

---

[15]For more on the trinitarian concept of prayer, see Graham Redding, *Prayer and the Priesthood of Christ in the Reformed Tradition* (London: T&T Clark, 2003), 281-300.

[16]Albert B. Simpson, *The Christ of the Forty Days* (New York: Christian Alliance, 1868), 302-3.

[17]The doctrine of participation has been summarized recently by Andrew Davison, *Participation in God: A Study in Christian Doctrine and Metaphysics* (Cambridge: Cambridge University Press, 2020). See also Paul L. Gavrilyuk, "The Retrieval of Deification: How a

of the ascension is not much considered in this. The work of John Calvin is one exception.

CALVIN AND PARTICIPATION IN THE ASCENSION

Theologian Julie Canlis convincingly shows Calvin to be an advocate of participation and declares, "It is impossible to deny that the concept (and praxis) of participation is at the center of the Christian faith."[18] She clarifies that while this is a relationship of "sharing and mutual indwelling," it should not be understood as a pantheistic or essentialist sharing. She insists it is to take its meaning from the New Testament word *koinōnia* and not from a prior philosophical, Platonic notion of *methexis*.[19] Semantics aside, the core of the biblical notion of participation is this: in light of the incarnation by which the Son of God participated in our humanity, we can participate in the life of Christ. Since Christ fully shared in our humanity, human persons can share in all of the historical acts of Christ and benefit from them vicariously. Bringing this to bear on the act of ascension, Canlis summarizes Calvin's view: "For Calvin, ascent was more than a metaphor: it was the decisive and final action of Jesus Christ, into which we are included, and, as such, is the foundation of his doctrine of participation. Ascent not only represents the moment when the *human* Jesus was taken up to his Father, but also when all of humanity is opened to this relationship as well."[20] Second Peter 1:4 is a key text for Calvin in this regard. He writes:

Once-Despised Archaism Became an Ecumenical Desideratum," *Modern Theology* 25, no. 4 (2009): 647-59; Norman Russell, *The Doctrine of Deification in the Greek Patristic Tradition*, Oxford Early Christian Studies (Oxford: Oxford University Press, 2004).

[18]Julie Canlis, *Calvin's Ladder: A Spiritual Theology of Ascent and Ascension* (Grand Rapids, MI: Eerdmans, 2010), 5.

[19]In this she dissembles from the radical orthodox view. This issue becomes complicated when one knows that Maximus uses the term *methexis* and disavows any essentialist or pantheistic sharing.

[20]Canlis, *Calvin's Ladder*, 2.

> Peter declares that believers are called in this to become partakers of the divine nature. How is this? It is because "he will be . . . glorified, in all his saints, and will be marveled at in all who have believed." If the Lord will share his glory, power, and righteousness, with the elect—nay, will give himself to be enjoyed by them and, what is more excellent, will somehow make them to become one with himself, let us remember that every sort of happiness is included under this benefit.[21]

The text Calvin refers to here is 2 Thessalonians 1:10. The glorification of Christ in his people, who reflect his radiant glory, catches the very essence of the ascension and our participation in it. Calvin does not doubt that the ascension was distinct from the resurrection, that our participation in ascension was crucial to our salvation, and that our own ascent one day will be fulfilled: "Ascension follows resurrection: hence if we are members of Christ we must ascend into Heaven, because He, on being raised up from the dead was received up into Heaven that He might draw us with Him."[22]

Calvin captures the essence of the doctrine of participation in its twofold dimensions: the Son's participation in humanity and humanity's participation in the Son by the Spirit by faith. Calvin carefully points out that even in the human-participation dimension, which involves faith, God is active in our engraced response. The Son empowers our prayers, our worship, and our best acts of service, and that through the Spirit. This full-orbed description given by Calvin actually captures the whole tradition well:

> Thus when he said to the apostles, "It is expedient that I go up to the Father," "because the Father is greater than I," he does not attribute to himself merely a secondary deity so that he is inferior to the Father with respect to eternal essence; but because endowed with heavenly glory *he gathers believers into participation in the Father.* . . . And certainly for this reason Christ, descended to us, to bear us up to the

---

[21] Calvin, *Institutes* 3.25.10, cited in Canlis, *Calvin's Ladder*, 4.
[22] Calvin's comments on Col 3:1, cited in Canlis, *Calvin's Ladder*, 5.

Father, and at the same time to bear us up to himself, inasmuch as he is one with the Father.[23]

Participation does not have to do with philosophical ideas but is a question of Christ drawing us into full participation in all of his works and indeed into the very life of the Trinity and the community of the church. How Calvin accordingly articulates his theology of the Eucharist using the language of exchange and participation will unfold in the chapter on ecclesiology.

---

[23]Calvin, *Institutes* 1.13.26, italics added, cited in Canlis, *Calvin's Ladder*, 5.

10

GLORY IN THE CHURCH

IN THIS CHAPTER, we ask what the identity of Christ as revealed by the ascension means for the church's identity, given that it is in mystical union with the ascended Christ. The *synaxis* or communion that characterizes the Trinity and the two natures of Christ also characterizes the relationship between Christ and his church (and the marriage union). This is the grounding for ecclesiology. Furthermore, the recapitulation of humanity in the ascended Christ means that the new humanity is a corporate, ecclesial humanity. The popular notion that Christians need not be part of a church community runs profoundly contrary to the identity of the Christian *person* as a *person in ecclesial communion*. If the local church is a microcosm of the universal body of Christ, and Paul's use of the Head-body metaphor for both the universal and the local church suggests it is so, then the concept of an unchurched Christian is an oxymoron of note. When we are unchurched, we experience something less than the shalom God invites us into as persons in relation to the ascended Christ and his church. We are not fully human apart from the church, for the church makes us human because we are made human by being in union with the ascended Head of the church. If the ascended Jesus is the new Head of the human race by recapitulation, the new Israel fulfilling its prophetic, kingly, and priestly anointings, the one who has become one with humanity to cleanse and constitute it the new humanity, he is all of those things as one with his church. He constitutes us the body of which he is the Head, the temple of which he is the chief cornerstone, the bride to whom he is the Bridegroom, the branches to the Vine, the new humanity of the *eschatos* Adam.

In keeping with the theme of this book, this means that as the human community in Christ, the church shares in his ascended *glory*. Jesus anticipates that his church will bring him glory in John 17:10—"All I have is yours, and all you have is mine. And glory has come to me through them." Yet it is clear that this is a reflected glory arising from the church's oneness with Jesus as the all-glorious, radiant Son. Jesus asserts this in his prayer: "I have given them the glory that you gave me, that they may be one as we are one—I in them and you in me—so that they may be brought to complete unity" (Jn 17:22-23). Furthermore, this glory connection becomes apparent in Paul's profoundly trinitarian second prayer in Ephesians 3, a prayer for the church to appropriate the life and love of God, which ends with these words: "to him be *glory in the church* and *in Christ Jesus* throughout all generations, for ever and ever! Amen" (Eph 3:21). For all the weaknesses of the church, which is both a divine and a profoundly human community, it brings glory to God, a glory it receives from its union with the ascended one, a glory received in the Eucharist. In his earlier prayer in Ephesians 1, Paul makes the organic connection between Christ as ascended in power and the availability of that same power for his church, experienced as a result of its union with him, a theme established throughout that chapter, prior to the prayer. The "incomparably great power for us who believe" is found in the communion of the church with the "mighty strength [God] exerted when he raised Christ from the dead and *seated him at his right hand in the heavenly realms*, far above all rule and authority, power and dominion, and every name that is invoked, not only in the present age but also in the one to come" (Eph 1:19-21). This powerful and majestic act of God in the ascension of Jesus, by which "God placed all things under his feet and appointed him to be head over everything," is precisely "for the church," because it is

"[Christ's] body, the fullness of him who fills everything in every way" (Eph 1:22-23).

This nature of the church, as conjoined to its risen Head and a reflector of his glory, brings a great sense of dignity to the church and inspires awe and reverence. It invites the church to engage in doxological worship with a profound sense of being led by and participating in Christ's glorious high-priestly leadership. This encourages the church to offer in its liturgy signs of the glory of God and means of grace that facilitate connectedness to the ascended Lord—liturgies that invite both intimacy and reverence, epicletic prayers, expositional preaching by preachers who are profoundly conscious that they speak the very words of the living Christ (1 Pet 4:11), around the centrality of the practice of the Lord's Supper or Eucharist.

This sacrament is profound and mysterious, evoking much debate in the church's history. This has partly been around the questions of the absence/presence dynamic: the obvious absence of the ascended Lord and his presence in or around or alongside the elements.[1] This is not the place for this debate.[2] It seems that all the traditions, even the memorialist, value in some sense the reality that Christ is present, even if not actually in the elements. In my own early experience of the memorialist tradition, I valued the profound meditation on the suffering and glory of Christ that is countercultural and would often sense the intimate presence of the Savior. In this tradition, we sang words such as these: "If now with eyes defiled and dim, we see the

---

[1] It is interesting to note that a presence/absence dynamic is not new for the people of God, being present in the lament literature in the Old Testament. Similarly Eucharist is celebrated with some awareness of the presence of Christ, by the Spirt, accompanied by longings for his presence "til he come." See Brittany N. Melton, *Where Is God in the Megilloth? A Dialogue on the Ambiguity of Divine Presence and Absence*, Oudtestamentische Studiën 73 (Leiden: Brill, 2018), 2-6, 179-89.

[2] See, e.g., the work of Farrow. For a recent, nuanced summation of the positions of Reformation theologians on the Lord's Supper, including Calvin, Martin Luther, Philipp Melanchthon, Johannes Brenz, Peter Martyr Vermigli, Ulrich Zwingli, and Heinrich Bullinger, among others, see Jacob Samuel Raju, "The Word Became Flesh and Dwelt Among Us: An Investigation into the Lutheran-Reformed Christological Debates on the Extra Calvinisticum" (ThM thesis, Regent College, 2022).

signs but see not Him, Oh may his love the scales displace and bid us see him face to face."³ Though not articulated, the assumption was that Christ was present to the church by the Spirit. Christ's presence made real to us by the Spirit alongside the elements was an aspect of the eucharistic theology of John Calvin.

Rather than offer debate regarding the real presence/transubstantiation view or the Lutheran consubstantiation view, views that, along with memorialism, have strengths and weakness, here I present the real-presence-by-the-Spirit view of Calvin. This is not because it has no weaknesses but primarily for its obvious relevance to the ascension of Christ, to the descent of the Spirit, and to the understanding that in the Eucharist, the uniting of the church with Christ results in the realization of the church's being caught up afresh into the heavenly glory of Christ. This involves something more than cerebral recalling by memory of the suffering and glory of Christ, though it must not neglect this. It is both memorial and visceral. It leads Christ's people to feed on him spiritually.

First, I believe that Calvin's view gets the Christology right, with the *communicatio idiomatum* properly understood.⁴ In the *extra Calvinisticum*, the eternal Son in his deity maintained his existence beyond his human flesh during his earthly ministry and perpetually. Likewise, the divine Son is present beyond his humanity in his ascension, as he was in his incarnate state on earth, but as in his time here on earth, his humanity per se remains located in heaven. That is contra Martin Luther, for whom all the attributes of the deity of the Son in heaven are communicated to his humanity, making his

---

³Charles H. Spurgeon, "Amidst Us Our Beloved Stands," Hymnary.org, accessed July 18, 2024, https://hymnary.org/text/amidst_us_our_beloved_stands.
⁴Bruce McCormack comments that the absence of a statement on *communicatio idiomatum* at Chalcedon left the door open for Luther to invoke it to account for the ubiquity of the human nature of the ascended Christ and therefore to justify the bodily presence of Jesus at the Eucharist, despite the fact that the tradition, expressed through Cyril of Alexandria, did not justify this. Bruce L. McCormack, "The Ontological Presuppositions of Barth's Doctrine of Atonement," in *The Glory of the Atonement: Biblical, Theological and Practical Perspectives*, ed. Charles E. Hill and Frank A. James (Downers Grove, IL: InterVarsity Press, 2004), 351.

humanity ubiquitous and thus enabling a consubstantiation view of the Eucharist feasible. According to Calvin, the humanity of the Son is located in heaven, and he does not come down physically every time and in every place where there is a Eucharist in his churches. Calvin communicates this with a certain amount of wit: "To them, Christ does not seem present unless he comes down to us. As though, if he should lift us to himself, we should not just as much enjoy his presence! The question is, therefore, only of the manner, for they place Christ in the bread, while we do not think it lawful for us to drag him from heaven."[5]

Second, Calvin assumes that at the Eucharist, the Son becomes present to us alongside the elements, not in them, through the coinherent presence of the Holy Spirit. Every service mirrors what happened, historically, when Jesus went up at the ascension and when the Spirit came down at Pentecost. This reality is invoked by the prayer of epiclesis, which the priest or pastor prays after the words of institution. As Laura Smit expresses, this work of the Spirit is "the 'turn' between the downward movement of revelation or proclamation and the upward movement of the sacrament." In this moment, "the Holy Spirit is the agent uniting us to Christ," just as "the Holy Spirit is the agent opening the Scriptures to us."[6]

The most attractive aspect of Calvin's view of the Eucharist is how he perceives in the movements the outworking of the union of believers with Christ, especially in the upward movement of the mystical body into the ascended glory of Christ. There is no downward movement of Christ in a physical sense for Calvin. Rather, as Smit points out, "Calvin thinks that the dialogue between God and humanity is initiated by the revelation of God's Word, both the incarnate Word . . . but also by the inspired word of Scripture and its

---

[5] John Calvin, *Institutes* 4.17.31.
[6] Laura Smit, "'The Depth Behind Things': Toward a Calvinist Sacramental Theology," in *Radical Orthodoxy and the Reformed Tradition: Creation, Covenant, and Participation*, ed. James K. A. Smith and James H. Olthuis (Grand Rapids, MI: Baker Academic, 2005), 218-19.

proclamation." Thus, she perceives that "the first downward movement from God to us . . . is the movement of revelation, not of sacrament."[7] The living Word comes to us in the written Word, read and expounded. This highlights the necessity of the Word as well as sacrament in the worship of the church. Thus, Calvin sees the Eucharist as predominantly an upward movement, as we are caught up by the Spirit and lifted to him. George Hunsinger calls Calvin's idea an "upward vector."[8] Smit explains that Calvin teaches that "Christ is ascended in the body and, through the sacrament, draws all believers into union with him and thus into communion with the inner life of the Trinity, suggesting the movement of convergence."[9] In this way, the church "becomes the body of Christ, a symbol exhibiting the ascended body of our sovereign Lord. Through our participation in the Lord's Supper, we as the Church become the body that is 'lifted up' in order to draw all people to Christ." Smit adds: "In Christ's ascension, humanity is ushered into the presence of the Godhead. Through our union with him, the body of Christ that is the Church expands, not because the physical body of Christ is distributed throughout the world, but rather because we are lifted into heaven with him."[10]

This is the very rehearsal of the gospel, for Calvin refers to what transpires in the rite of the Eucharist as "the wonderful exchange" God has made with us:

> that, becoming Son of man with us, he has made us sons of God with him; that, by his descent to earth, he has prepared an ascent to heaven for us; that, by taking on our mortality, he has conferred his immortality upon us; that, accepting our weakness, he has strengthened us by his power; that, receiving our poverty unto himself, he has transferred his

---

[7] Smit, "Depth Behind Things," 215.
[8] George Hunsinger, "The Bread That We Break: Toward a Chalcedonian Resolution of the Eucharistic Controversies," *Princeton Seminary Bulletin* 24, no. 2 (2003): 251.
[9] Smit, "Depth Behind Things," 215.
[10] Smit, "Depth Behind Things," 215-16.

wealth to us; that, taking the weight of our iniquity upon himself (which oppressed us), he has clothed us with righteousness.[11]

Calvin adds, "Through the sacrament, *we participate in the ascension of Christ. We are united to his ascended body and pulled upward to where he is.*"[12] Clearly, Calvin believes that something happens in the Eucharist. This is emphasized in the Belgic Confession, which states that the sacraments "are not empty or meaningless, so as to deceive us. For Jesus Christ is the true object presented by them, without whom they would be of no moment."[13]

Twentieth-century American theologian John Nevin expounds a similar view of the Eucharist. He writes:

> It is not simply an occasion, by which the soul of the believer may be excited to pious feelings and desires; but it embodies the actual presence of the grace it represents in its own constitution; and this grace is not simply the promise of God on which we are encouraged to rely, but the very life of the Lord Jesus Christ himself. We communicate—in the Lord's Supper—not with the divine promise merely, not with the thought of Christ only, not with the recollection simply of what he has done and suffered for us, not with the lively present sense alone of his all-sufficient, all-glorious salvation; but with the living Savior himself, in the fullness of his glorified person, made present to us for the purpose by the power of the Holy Spirit. into God's presence through uniting us with Christ.[14]

This Calvinist view of the Eucharist is not transubstantiation but rather might be called trans-participation. In his commentary on 1 Corinthians 11:24, Calvin speaks of participation and clarifies in short order his view of the Eucharist:

---

[11] Calvin, *Institutes* 4.17.2.
[12] Calvin, *Institutes* 4.17.2, emphasis added.
[13] Article 33. See James T. Dennison, ed., *Reformed Confessions of the Sixteenth and Seventeenth Centuries in English Translation* (Grand Rapids, MI: Reformation Heritage, 2008), 2:444.
[14] John Williamson Nevin, *The Mystical Presence, and Other Writings on the Eucharist*, Lancaster Series on the Mercersburg Theology 4 (Philadelphia: United Church, 1966), 33-34.

> But that participation in the body of Christ, which, I affirm, is presented to us in the Supper, does not require a local presence, nor the descent of Christ, nor infinite extension, nor anything of that nature, for the Supper being a heavenly action, there is no absurdity in saying, that Christ, while remaining in heaven, is received by us. For as to his communicating himself to us, that is effected through the secret virtue of his Holy Spirit, which cannot merely bring together, but join in one, things that are separated by distance of place, and far remote. But, in order that we may be capable of this *participation, we must rise heavenward.*[15]

There is no loss to the symbolism and sacramentality of all creation and its beauty in Calvin's way of seeing the sacrament in this real-presence-by-the-Spirit mode. Calvin is of the tradition in that he followed Augustine with respect to his understanding of signs and symbols, following a symbolic theology (not to be confused with memorialism) rather than an allegorical one.[16] In light of the symbols of bread and wine that pointed to the more real reality of the body and blood of Christ, Calvin extrapolated this to interpret the world as a "set of symbols that pointed to God."[17] Calvin states, "For instance, if in baptism, the figure of water were to deceive our eyes, we would have no sure pledge of our washing; indeed, that false show would give us occasion to hesitate. The nature of the Sacrament is therefore cancelled, unless, in the mode of signifying, the earthly sign corresponds to the heavenly thing."[18] In his commentary on 1 Corinthians, Calvin clarifies further:

> Hence, if there must be a correspondence between the sign and its reality, it is necessary that the bread be real—not imaginary—to

---

[15] John Calvin, *The Epistle of Paul the Apostle to the Corinthians*, trans. John Pringle, Calvin's Commentaries 20 (Grand Rapids, MI: Baker, 2003), 380, emphases added.

[16] For this distinction, see C. S. Lewis in *Allegory of Love*, where he explains that allegory begins with something in the sensible world and invents something fictional, which is less real than the sensible thing, whereas symbolism, or symbolic theology, tries to look past the sensible world to something that is more real beyond it to which it points.

[17] Smit, "Depth Behind Things," 222.

[18] Calvin *Institutes* 4.17.14.

represent Christ's real body. Besides, Christ's body is here given us not simply, but as food. Now it is not by any means the color of the bread that nourishes us, but the substance. In fine, if we would have reality in the thing itself, there must be no deception in the sign.[19]

Similarly, for the Lord's Supper, regarding the phrase "This is my body," Calvin comments that this expression "is a metonymy, a figure of speech commonly used in Scripture when mysteries are under discussion," and he understands it to be a symbol "that 'truly exhibits' the thing it represents," in this case the body of Christ.[20] Smit sums up Calvin's eucharistic theology as something that "is both a supremely analogical and a supremely eschatological understanding of the sacrament." This is so because for Calvin "the bread is genuinely exhibiting the body of Christ, without being univocal with the body; and the whole of the sacrament points forward to the wedding feast we will someday enjoy, giving us already now an actual foretaste both of the feast and (more importantly) of our union with Christ."[21]

Whereas Karl Barth chose to revert to a memorialist view of the Lord's Supper and a nonsacramental understanding of baptism, T. F. Torrance is the inheritor of Calvin's sacramental views, though he developed them. This had a great deal to do with his theology of the ascension. David Fergusson comments that, for Torrance, "the ministry of Christ continues in *ascended mode*, particularly in the set of relations that are established in church, sacraments, and ministry."[22] He adds:

> Torrance's treatment of the ascension is replete with doxological and sacramental references. Indeed, a theology of church, sacraments, and ministry emerges from this rendition of the ascension that might fairly be described as both Reformed and catholic, affirming a sacramental

---

[19] Calvin, *Epistle of Paul the Apostle to the Corinthians*, 378.
[20] Calvin, *Institutes* 4.17.21.
[21] Smit, "Depth Behind Things," 222.
[22] David Fergusson, "The Ascension of Christ: Its Significance in the Theology of T. F. Torrance," *Participatio* 3 (2012): 102, emphases added.

relation between the church as the body of Christ and Christ as the head of that body.²³

Torrance further observes that "as king and head of the church, Christ has instituted the ministry of word and sacrament within history, whereby he continually nourishes, sustains, orders and governs his people on earth." For Torrance, it is by "the fusion of resurrection with the ascension in one indivisible exaltation that we are to understand the continuing ministry of Christ in presenting his 'many brethren' along with himself, amidst the sanctities of the new creation and in eternal glorification of the Father."²⁴

The ongoing ministry never loses sight of the historical, once-for-all event, however. Hunsinger discerns that Torrance's understanding of the Eucharist consists of "one priestly sacrifice of Christ in two temporal forms."²⁵ These are the historical/incarnational and the eucharistic forms. Hunsinger states that the "Eucharistic form here and now participates in, manifests, and attests the incarnational form of the sacrifice there and then."²⁶ Fergusson judges that for Torrance, the Eucharist and what takes place in it is "neither a repetition nor a wholly different type of activity, but something that must be understood in terms of participation, manifestation, and witness to that upon which it is dependent and to which it constantly returns."²⁷ Torrance sees worship as a participation in the action of the ascended Christ, so that he is both its object and its subject. Torrance notes that this notion and the theme of the ascended Christ as the leader of his church's worship was present in the Scottish Reformation tradition from John Knox on. Torrance comments:

---

²³Fergusson, "Ascension of Christ," 102.
²⁴T. F. Torrance, *Space, Time, and Resurrection* (Grand Rapids, MI: Eerdmans, 1976), 279, 111.
²⁵Cited in Fergusson, "Ascension of Christ," 104.
²⁶George Hunsinger, *The Eucharist and Ecumenism: Let Us Keep the Feast*, Current Issues in Theology (Cambridge: Cambridge University Press, 2008), 151-52.
²⁷Fergusson, "Ascension of Christ," 104.

> Ascension introduced the "distance" between the symbols of bread and wine on earth and the ascended Christ, but nevertheless, a "distance" bridged by the real presence of the risen and ascended Christ through the Spirit. Hence, the place of the *sursum corda* in the heart of the Reformed Eucharistic Rite—the ascension with Christ became of primary importance again: we are made to sit with Christ in the heavenly places.[28]

This high sacramental theology in Torrance is very much related to his theology of the ascension. However, it must be noted that Torrance does not employ a Platonic worldview to understand the Eucharist in this way. For him, the eucharistic sacrifice must be seen

> not only as a *correspondence* or *reflection* on earth of what Christ does in his vicarious self-offering to the Father in the heavenlies, but as such a *participation* through the Spirit in Christ that he with his vicarious self-offering is the real Agent and Content of our worship as we through prayers and thanksgivings in the Eucharist offer Christ to the Father.[29]

For Torrance, as John Witvleit makes clear, earthly worship is not to be seen in some Neoplatonic manner as a "mere shadow or pale reflection of heavenly worship."[30] Rather, Torrance "uses the metaphor 'stereoscopic' to describe this relationship, a view of the sacraments which sees in the sacraments 'a dimension of depth,' . . . in which we are directed to look for its meaning not in itself as such, but in the paschal mystery of Christ itself. The rite always points beyond itself 'to its constitutive reality in Jesus Christ.'"[31]

The dimension of depth in Torrance's view of the Eucharist arises from its grounding in the paschal history of Christ's work but also

---

[28]Thomas F. Torrance, *Scottish Theology: From John Knox to John Mcleod Campbell* (Edinburgh: T&T Clark, 1996), 40.

[29]Thomas F. Torrance, *Theology in Reconciliation: Essays Towards Evangelical and Catholic Unity in East and West* (Eugene, OR: Wipf & Stock, 1996), 136, emphases added.

[30]John D. Witvliet, "The Doctrine of the Trinity and the Theology and Practice of Christian Worship in the Reformed Tradition" (PhD diss., University of Notre Dame, 1997), 214, referencing Torrance's *Theology in Reconciliation*, 93, 108.

[31]Witvleit, "Doctrine of the Trinity," 108.

from an awareness of his ongoing, saving presence in heaven since the ascension. A dimension of depth is also found in Hunsinger's ecumenically driven presentation of the concept of transelementation (in which one object is saturated with another's reality and power) as opposed to transubstantiation (one substance changes into another). Hunsinger finds this in Peter Martyr Vermigli, Martin Bucer, and Thomas Cranmer and the Fathers, but its basis is in the ascended Christ, who acts by the Spirit in this way for those who take the Eucharist in faith.[32]

---

[32]Hunsinger, *Eucharist and Ecumenism*, 50-52.

11

THE GLORY OF THE KINGDOM COME, HIS COMING AGAIN IN GLORY

Inaugurated and Future Eschatology

THE ASCENSION IS CONNECTED to *future eschatology* since at the ascension, the angels promised Jesus' disciples that he would come again in the "same way" they had "seen him go" (Acts 1:11). Gregory Nazianzen long ago understood that "the logic of the ascension, must respond to the logic of the *Parousia*."[1] *Inaugurated eschatology* also has a profound connection to the ascension. At the ascension, the Lord Jesus is enthroned as King at the right hand of God, and the kingdom is spread throughout the world through the church's mission, by the Spirit, throughout this "now but not yet" season of the kingdom. The place of the ascension within eschatology, both inaugurated and future, therefore brings strong hope for the people of God in turbulent times. Each in turn will be considered in this chapter.

THE ASCENSION AND INAUGURATED ESCHATOLOGY

The King reigns now in heaven, but his reign is not visible until the parousia. Psalm 110:1, along with Psalm 110:4, is the primary passage on which the writer of Hebrews meditates and riffs: "The LORD says to my Lord: 'Sit at my right hand *until* I make your enemies a footstool

---

[1] Douglas Farrow, "Confessing Christ Coming," in *Nicene Christianity: The Future for a New Ecumenism*, ed. Christopher R. Seitz (Grand Rapids, MI: Brazos, 2001), 137.

for your feet.'" Although the crucial battle over all Christ's enemies has been won at the cross and the resurrection, this is not yet apparent, and his Father promises to subjugate them while he reigns in heaven until the day of his second coming, when they will be the "footstool for [his] feet." Therefore, the Son's ascension has introduced a period of "eschatological reserve" in human history.[2] That is, "the ascension creates a pause in the *Parousia*, creating time for the gospel before the final coming of Jesus."[3] The ascension led to the ascended King's hiddenness in a way that placed the parousia, or the full revelation of the King, on reserve. On the other hand, that ascension inaugurated or continued the kingdom on earth already come, which is expressed through the church's mission and God's work in the world. There are expressions of glory attributed to the church and to the kingdom that reflect the glory of the ascended Head of the church and the King of the kingdom. Paul, for example, writes: "*To him be glory in the church* and *in Christ Jesus* throughout all generations, forever and ever! Amen" (Eph 3:21). Whatever may be the failings of the church on earth, it reflects the glory of God in its Head in heaven.

Oliver O'Donovan expresses the eschatological tension aptly. The New Testament generally and Hebrews in particular reflect the reality that

> the Christ-event is the last thing in God's plan for the world, and that with its completion the end of time has, in effect, already come. We are seen to have our existence, as it were, in the middle of the end, in between the last things and the last things. Still to come is the universal manifestation of Christ's glory, but the time-lapse which separates that from the accomplishment of that glory in the ascension is of no significance. . . . The triumph is already achieved; it only remains for that triumph to be manifested universally.[4]

---

[2] T. F. Torrance, "Universalism or Election?," *SJT* 2, no. 3 (September 1949): 311.
[3] T. F. Torrance, *Atonement: The Person and Work of Christ* (Downers Grove, IL: IVP Academic, 2009), x. It also invites reserve concerning judgments about matters that are mysterious, including how to reconcile limited atonement with its ontological nature.
[4] Oliver O'Donovan, *On the Thirty Nine Articles: A Conversation with Tudor Christianity*, Latimer Monograph (Exeter, UK: Paternoster, 1986), 33.

In this inaugurated time, the kingdom and the church operate in a coinherent fashion, with much overlap, though there is a distinction. At minimum, the church is the seat of the kingdom and the primary means by which the ascended Son carries out his mission through the agency of the Holy Spirit. The image of the king seated in glory does not mean he is idle. The temporal closeness of the ascension of the Son (Acts 1) and the outpouring of the Spirit are not accidental. The ascension transformed the mindset of the apostles cognitively, no doubt, for as they watched him go into heaven, his identity as God and man must have dawned on them. The Spirit's empowerment also transformed them subjectively. The kingdom and trinitarian participatory impulses in the mission of the church in the Acts are what accounts for that church's remarkable growth then, which continues until Christ returns in glory.

HIS COMING AGAIN IN GLORY: THE ASCENSION AND FUTURE ESCHATOLOGY

If the resurrection of Jesus was the harbinger of the resurrection of his people at the second coming, the ascension likewise signals not just an eschatological reserve now but the ascending of Christ's people when he returns. Then his glory will be revealed to his people in heaven, and when heaven comes to earth, the whole cosmos will resound with his praises and reflect his glory. Beyond all the controversy that surrounds eschatology, we may safely say that the glory of Christ, endowed at the ascension and hidden in the interval, will be the great theme of the eschaton in its consummation.

There are some possible conclusions about the ascent-descent trajectory of the people of God in Christ for possible schemes in future eschatology. One possibility is that Christ will cause his people to ascend to heaven away from judgment at the second coming. I do not wish to speculate whether this is a pretribulational rapture, a posttribulational rapture, a simple amillennial ascent when Christ comes, or an event following a postmillennial revival. But in all these schemata, it does seem that a second coming takes the people alive at the time of its occurrence to join the church triumphant who are already there (1 Thess 4:13-18). That church then descends to reign with its Bridegroom on earth forever (Rev 21).

Revelation 5 envisions that this is not just the reality that Christ will inhabit his people on that day but rather that they will specifically *reign* together. This co-dominion is a future reality: "They *will* reign on the earth" (Rev 5:10). In keeping with this, Revelation 3:21 makes promises to the overcomers related to their future co-dominion with Christ: "To the one who is victorious, I will give the right *to sit with me on my throne*, just as I was victorious and sat down with my Father on his throne." Similarly, in Revelation 20:4, the writer sees "thrones on which were seated those who had been given authority to judge." This depiction of the church's involvement in the administration of justice in the future eschaton is an incentive for believers in the present phase not to be passive regarding the pursuit of justice within the church now (1 Cor 5:9-13).

The ascension event as described by Luke has some categoric things to say regarding *future* eschatology. When the angels speak to the apostles, they say, "This same Jesus, who has been taken from you into heaven, will come back in the same way you have seen him go into heaven" (Acts 1:11). The nature of his return will be personal ("This same Jesus") and visible ("in the same way you have seen him go into heaven"). The glory revealed in the ascension event, though not explicit here as elsewhere (Ps 24), is implicit in two ways. First, Christ ascends in a "cloud" that recalls the Shekinah glory that fell on the tabernacle. The glory the Son receives as he ascends and is crowned king and priest is the iridescent glory he will radiate at his second coming. The veiling or hiddenness of his ascended ministry as Prophet, Priest, and King will give way to an unprecedented unveiling of the glory of God in Christ. Luke in his Gospel also refers to the second coming with a corresponding allusion to a "cloud" and a resounding reference to glory: "At that time they will see the Son of Man coming in a cloud with power and *great glory*" (Lk 21:27). Thus, in addition to being personal and visible, the second coming will be theophanic, an all-glorious revelation of God in the triumphant Christ. It will be a revelation of grace and judgment. Grace in the transformation of those who see his face (1 Jn 3:2); judgment on all who are unrepentant.

Three aspects of this coming are mentioned in Douglas Farrow's summation of the eschatology of the schoolmen: "The schoolmen used to say of the *Parousia* that it would be *personalis, visibilis, beatificus, terribilis, et gloriosus*; and so it shall be if Christ has indeed ascended in the flesh."[5] The *terribilis* dimension is the judgment aspect of his coming, mentioned by Paul: "They will be punished with everlasting destruction and shut out from the presence of the Lord and from the *glory of his might* on the day he comes to be glorified in his holy people and to be marveled at among all those who have believed" (2 Thess 1:9-10). This is a stark contrast between his redeemed people, who participate in his glory, and the unbelieving people, who must fear that consuming glory, the "glory of his might" expressed in divine judgment. Jesus himself speaks about it: "For the Son of Man is going to come in his Father's glory with his angels, and then he will reward each person according to what they have done" (Mt 16:27). Here the judgment appears to be remunerative, as is the case in 2 Corinthians 5, where Paul speaks about the "judgment seat [the *bēma*] of Christ" (2 Cor 5:10), where believers (those who in the context are now "at home with the Lord," 2 Cor 5:8) "may receive what is due us for the things done while in the body, whether good or bad" (2 Cor 5:10). This involves the evaluation of the work of each believer: "Their work will be shown for what it is because the Day will bring it to light. It will be revealed with fire, and the fire will test the quality of each person's work" (1 Cor 3:13).

---

[5]Douglas Farrow, *Ascension Theology* (London: T&T Clark, 2011), 141.

This remunerative rather than retributive judgment may be what Peter is referring to: "For it is time for judgment to begin with God's household; and if it begins with us, what will the outcome be for those who do not obey the gospel of God?" (1 Pet 4:17). Peter speaks of the "fiery" ordeals Christians go through in this life, which are an opportunity to "participate in the sufferings of Christ" and even rejoice because they are a harbinger of his glory: "so that you may be overjoyed when his *glory* is revealed" (1 Pet 4:13). Peter then returns to the sharp edge of the double-edged nature of Christ's glory: "And, 'If it is hard for the righteous to be saved, what will become of the ungodly and the sinner?'" (1 Pet 4:18). There can be no relishing of judgment on those who do not believe, even if they are the perpetrators of the persecution referred to here. However, there can be no grace without judgment in the righteous character of God, no revelation of glory without responsibility for its reception.

Many of the questions arising within the study of future eschatology, such as who will be saved, for example, await resolve until the parousia. This is implicit from the eschatological reserve the ascension brought. For example, both Barth and T. F. Torrance hold hope that all will be saved in light of the scope of the atoning work of Christ but denied universalism, the latter consistently adhering to the consistent voice of the church catholic throughout the ages, that universalism is "a heresy for faith and a menace to the Gospel."[6] Similarly, the emphasis of future eschatology is not on amillennial, postmillennial, and premillennial persuasions but to focus on what the parousia means for the completion of the salvation of redeemed humanity, for the judgment of the living and the dead, for the coming of the kingdom in its fullness, and for the completion of the new creation. One particular example of eschatological speculation is the scientific perspective of Kathryn Tanner, which seems to preclude a new creation based on the

---

[6]Cited in Paul D. Molnar, "Thomas F. Torrance and the Problem of Universalism," *SJT* 68, no. 2 (2015): 164.

coalescing of the earth into the sun. Her eschatology and her science are suspect. The promise of a new creation is evident in Romans 8:21-24, and astrophysics predicts a universe that will cause all life on earth to freeze if it continues to expand, not burn up.[7]

Two theologians who have contributed richly to a possible understanding of the relationship between the form of the kingdom now, where Jesus reigns in ascended glory, and the kingdom to come, when he appears, are Jürgen Moltmann and Wolfhart Pannenberg. A full account of the similarities of the eschatologies of these theologians and their undergirding ontologies is not possible here. Suffice it to say that eschatology becomes for each a dominant category in theology, and that for both Christ is the center, pulling the church and creation toward its future in him. For example, with respect to Pannenberg, E. F. Tupper notes, "The *eschaton* is finally the transformation of the whole of reality, but Christ is the *prolepsis* of the End of history."[8] Similarly, Moltmann asserts, "Christian eschatology does not speak of the future as such. It sets out from a definite reality in history and announces the future of that reality, its future possibilities and its power over the future. Christian eschatology speaks of Jesus Christ and his future."[9]

Thus we may safely say that the glory of Christ that he received at his ascension will be the central theme of the eschaton in its fullness. At his second coming, the glory of the ascended one in his glorified humanity will be manifested in his church and in all creation. Jesus speaks of his coming "in clouds with great power and glory" (Mk 13:26), that his coming will be "in his glory and in the glory of the Father and of the holy angels" (Lk 9:26). Peter, who witnessed his majesty on Tabor, speaks of "the glory to be revealed" (1 Pet 5:1) and of "eternal

---

[7]Andrew R. Liddle and David H. Lyth, *Cosmological Inflation and Large-Scale Structure* (Cambridge: Cambridge University Press, 2000).
[8]E. F. Tupper, *The Theology of Wolfhart Pannenberg* (London: SCM Press, 1974), 257.
[9]Jürgen Moltmann, *Theology of Hope: On the Ground and the Implications of a Christian Eschatology* (Philadelphia: Fortress, 1993), 17.

glory in Christ," to which his people are called (1 Pet 5:10). And the songs of Revelation that describe his ascension and anticipate his coming are laced with glory. One of those songs will suffice: "In a loud voice they were saying: 'Worthy is the Lamb, who was slain, to receive power and wealth and wisdom and strength and honor and glory and praise!'" (Rev 5:12).

How does one practice ascension in light of these outcomes? It is to anticipate and watch for that coming. If in the now we ascend in our hearts and minds to take our place as those seated in the heavenlies with our ascended Lord, the imperfections of our experience of that seatedness can create within us a longing for the day when faith gives way to sight, the day when there will be no more loss or pain or sorrow. Above all that day is when, upon seeing his glorious face, "the knowledge of God's glory displayed in the face of Christ" (2 Cor 4:6), we shall be transformed and beatified and glorified. Farrow says poignantly, "The church that celebrates the ascension . . . can no more fail to watch for his *parousia* than the congregation of Israel could fail to watch for Aaron . . . to return from the inner sanctuary on *Yom Kippur*."[10] It is necessary to add that "watching" in the New Testament does not mean idleness or speculative obsession with times and seasons (Acts 1:7) but vigilance regarding the moral quality of one's life and service, an orientation toward his present presence, and anticipation that when suffering for Christ has come to an end, the fullness of his presence will give way to being "overjoyed when his glory is revealed" (1 Pet 4:13).

---

[10] Farrow, *Ascension Theology*, 140.

12

THE SHARED GLORY OF THE COSMIC CHRIST

THE GLORY OF THE ASCENDED CHRIST has repercussions for both humanity and the whole cosmos. They are, however, connected. Paul witnesses to this in Ephesians 1:22-23, which makes the connection between Christ's exaltation, "God placed all things under his feet," and his union with his mystical body, the church, which shares in that reign, "and appointed him to be head over *everything* for the church, his body," through which Christ's fullness "fills *everything* in every way." Similarly, Paul ends his sublime christological passage in Colossians 1:17-20 with staggering cosmological assertions. He writes there of the exalted nature of Christ as a consequence of his resurrection and ascension: "so that in *everything* he might have the supremacy" (Col 1:18). But this is grounded in his divine nature as the incarnate Son: "God was pleased to have all his fullness dwell in him" (Col 1:19). This leads Paul to speak of the scope of a reconciling work that corresponds to who he is in the depths of his being: "and through him to reconcile to himself *all things*, whether things on earth or things in heaven, by making peace through his blood, shed on the cross" (Col 1:20).

These realities are cause for doxology. They also impart security in troubled times, since they indicate that God is not finished with his creation but has destined it for the glory that is a reflection the glory of the ascended Son. However, it must be admitted that how the cosmological aspects of the ascension and its glorious consequences are to be understood is not a trivial matter.

New Testament scholars note the role cosmology plays in the ascension of Jesus. Steve Walton, for example, observes,

> In Luke's story, both heaven and earth are transformed through Jesus and by the Spirit. This process of transformation affects even how God is to be seen and understood, for there is now a human being in heaven at God's right hand—and he pours out the Spirit upon God's people to equip them to reclaim creation for its Creator.... By contrast with angels, who come from heaven and return there, Jesus is a human being who enters heaven. Jesus both shares the rule of God over the universe and continues to intervene in the story of his followers, both in his own person and by the Spirit. In piercing the barrier between earth and heaven, Jesus restructures how reality is understood, both now and in the days to come.[1]

The nature of these cosmological changes raises some challenging questions. John Stroman expresses this well: "How is it that 2000 years ago a group of men and women on a hilltop in Palestine watched one of their number take off vertically from the ground and disappear into a cloud, proceeding nonstop until he arrived at a precise location in space called heaven? There is no *up* and *down* in space. So where did Jesus go?" These baffling questions may be one reason for the paucity of preaching on this topic in the church. And why would we not stay away from this subject, wonders Stroman: "How can we celebrate the absence of the presence?" Stroman's own partial answer is to point to Jesus' words when he "spoke directly about his going," in John 16:7. There he specifically says, "It is for your good that I am going away. Unless I go away, the Advocate will not come to you." There Jesus speaks of being not just "*with* his people but *within* them (John 14:17)."[2] This answers the question concerning the presence of Jesus in the church and the world despite his absence, that it is through the Spirit, who mediates his presence.

---

[1] Steve Walton, "'The Heavens Opened': Cosmological and Theological Transformation in Luke and Acts," in *Cosmology and New Testament Theology*, ed. Jonathan T. Pennington and Sean M. McDonough, LNTS 355 (London: T&T Clark, 2008), 60.

[2] John Stroman, *Ashes to Ascension*, Cycle B ed. (Lima, OH: CSS, 1999), 95.

Another positive result of his ascent is the goodness of his exaltation in glory, his kingly and high-priestly intercession, the church's global mission, and his coming again in glory. The historical Jesus gave way to the cosmic Christ, though not by leaving the embodied, historical Jesus behind. Even though he was taken up, the living presence of Christ "was not limited to the first century, but is for all centuries, all times and all places. . . . It has eternal dimensions. . . . What God did in Jesus' day in Palestine, God continues to do through the Holy Spirit today."[3]

Not to minimize these remarkable pneumatological compensations due to the coinherence of trinitarian persons (Jn 14:18, 20), but we are still left with the question, Where did Jesus go, or where is heaven?

One author has suggested that, given the genre of the text in Acts 1, and the reality that "historical presentation *interprets*" and has *theological* meaning, the presence of the "cloud" at Jesus' ascension is a "theological image" teaching us that we cannot penetrate these questions. Just as the cloud hid the ascending Jesus from the disciples' eyes (Acts 1:9), it marks out "a boundary beyond which all our ideas about Christ's elevation must fail." It is as impenetrable as the Shekinah cloud that accompanied the tabernacle. Whatever the actual elevation of Jesus meant from the perspective of his watching disciples, it was not intended to depict "a trip in a balloon."[4] The focus should be on what the ascension means theologically, without denying its literal, historical nature. The event represents the coronation of the King. It declares that he is Lord of all, that his enemies are being subjected under his feet; that we, his people, are reigning and will reign with and in his reign; that it leads to his high-priestly ministry for his people; and that the Spirit's ministry in this era of salvation history imparts the "reinforcing presence of Christ" so that we "can march on [on mission] without waiting or without fear."[5] However, we may be

---

[3]Stroman, *Ashes to Ascension*, 96.
[4]Gerhard Lohfink, *Between Heaven and Earth: New Explorations of Biblical Texts*, trans. Linda M. Maloney (Collegeville, MN: Liturgical Press, 2022), 160-62.
[5]Stroman, *Ashes to Ascension*, 98.

permitted a humble curiosity about why Jesus went up and where he went.

We must avoid two mistakes in this pursuit. The first is to suggest that there was no literal, historical ascension, thus removing any solid ground for theological reflection. The second is to become so focused on the literal that we thus neglect the *theological* meaning of a text that describes what the first-century disciples genuinely experienced. The cosmology of heaven as "up," assumed in Acts 1, is carried over into the epistle to the Hebrews, although there is much more detail there. I will say more about the location of heaven in chapter thirteen.

THEOLOGICAL REFLECTION ON THE COSMOLOGY OF THE ASCENSION

The most challenging issue regarding the ascension is somehow harmonizing the transcendence of the eternal divine Son with the human creature of space and time and his particular locatedness. We may say this is the obverse of the incarnation, not a divine person becoming human but a human-divine person returning to heaven. How can a transcendent Son still be a human being?

T. F. Torrance believed this could best be understood by drawing on a relational view of space and time based on relativity theory. That space and time are relative, that is, that they depend on the motion of the observer who measures them, is the basis of Einstein's theory of special relativity. Time and space are not to be considered "absolute containers, independent of the objects they happen to contain. Instead, they are to be viewed as functions of those principles or forces that by their actions define their form." The intention is not to say that space-time "in a four-dimensional continuum" determines "the identity and activity of God."[6] However, Torrance believes we can speak of "the 'place' and 'time' of God in terms of his own eternal life

---

[6]David Fergusson, "The Ascension of Christ: Its Significance in the Theology of T. F. Torrance," *Participatio* 3 (2012): 99-100.

and his eternal purpose in the divine love, where he wills his life and love to overflow to us whom he has made to share with him his life and love."[7] Thus, for Torrance, the time and space coordinates and framework that describe God's actions in eternity are provided within the divine life, and in an analogous manner, the space-time continuum of the created world provides "a framework relative to creaturely events and forces." Torrance suggests, therefore, that a historical date and place can be assigned for all other events within the life of Jesus on earth, whereas the place and actions of the ascended Christ come under the former case, that is within divine life.[8] This corresponds with the theology of time in both Barth and Torrance. They distinguish between divine or unfallen time and earthly, fallen time, the latter participating in the former.

Fergusson observes that "two important theological consequences" arise from Torrance's refusal to demythologize the ascension or detach it from history. First, Fergusson states, "We must think of there always being a place or *room for humanity in the life of God*." Thus, heaven should be considered to be "Christ-shaped, as ensuring a place in the eternal life of God for creatures."[9]

Second, Torrance's approach, as explained by Fergusson, suggests that we must view God's actions toward the world as those of the ascended Christ. While upholding Calvin's view that the human body of Christ is not ubiquitous, Torrance affirms the ubiquitous action of the ascended Son as a person utilizing his divine nature. In this way, the ascension results in "the withdrawal of one mode of presence for the enabling of another one. It is now a differentiated sign of absence and presence." The *absence* is the absence of his physical presence to the church; the *presence* is his presence through the Holy Spirit to the church in its gatherings, in its practice of the Eucharist and the preaching of the Word, in its mission to the world, and in the hearts

---

[7]T. F. Torrance, *Space, Time, and Resurrection* (Grand Rapids, MI: Eerdmans, 1976), 290.
[8]Fergusson, "Ascension of Christ," 99.
[9]Fergusson, "Ascension of Christ," 100, emphasis added.

of every believer. This role of the Spirit in making Christ present through coinherence does not mean immaterializing the ascension of Jesus. The incarnate Son continues in his heavenly offices in concrete ways discussed in earlier chapters. Those functions correspond with "his once-for-all historical work as the enactment of his identity and mission." In Torrance's view, "the Son of God is not now detached from a rootedness in the story of Jesus of Nazareth. On the contrary, the ongoing action of the ascended Christ carries a constant reference to the gospels."[10] As Torrance observes, "All contact with the majesty of God as of the glorified Lord is in and through the crucified one."[11] There is thus an inviolable relation between the history of Jesus on earth and his continuing work on earth: "His eternal humanity prevents any abstracting of his identity from that of the gospel record of his earthly life, death, and resurrection. We cannot think of God without reference to Jesus."[12]

Regarding *time*, Torrance, again as explained by Ferguson, speaks of the eschatological reference and framework created by the ascension of Jesus around his absence and future presence. The New Testament consistently portrays the resurrection of Jesus as an "eschatological sign, foretaste, and down payment of the general resurrection of the dead." His exaltation anticipates his final reign over the cosmos. These two events—resurrection and ascension—in the history of Jesus were not private; rather, Torrance affirms that they have "a corporate character that heralds a new age in which his kingship will be universally acknowledged and accomplished."[13] As Torrance says, the ascension generated "a kind of hiatus in which Christ's full reign is deferred for the time being." This hiatus means that the kingdom on earth will not come immediately and fully but gradually and partially until the second coming. Torrance calls this

---

[10]Fergusson, "Ascension of Christ," 100-101.
[11]Torrance, *Space, Time, and Resurrection*, 293.
[12]Fergusson, "Ascension of Christ," 101.
[13]Fergusson, "Ascension of Christ," 101.

"an eschatological pause," or a season of eschatological reserve.[14] However, the mission of Jesus' church under his kingship and Jesus' intercessory, priestly, and prophetic ministry continue during this season; the ascended Christ is not idle. The space caused by the ascension is not a vacuum, for Christ has not "emptied the world of his presence," as Fergusson puts it. He is at work in the church, in its ministry and sacraments, in its mission, and in the world, over which he reigns invisibly.[15]

Oliver O'Donovan also undertakes cosmological discussions surrounding the ascension. He asks whether the statement "he ascended into heaven" can stand alongside the statements "he was crucified, died and was buried" and "on the third day, he rose again." However problematic the statement of the resurrection may seem, the problems posed by the ascension, he thinks, are of a much more fundamental kind, for heaven, God's throne, and the right hand of the Father cannot be mapped topographically within space. The verb *ascended*, like the verb *came down* in the creed, can refer to "no spatial movement known to man."[16]

O'Donovan's solution to the times and places associated with the ascension and heaven is to speak in metaphysical terms. First, he challenges the "conventional modern metaphysic," popularized within modernity by Immanuel Kant, who proposed the existence of a *phenomenal* world, "the world of our experience," which is accessed by reason, and over against this, the *noumenal* world, "the world of things as they are apart from our experience," a realm assumed to be accessed purely by faith, being "subjectively deduced from the nature of reason itself."[17] The *noumenal* world exists, but Kant sees no way to know anything about that world, including God, objectively. A

---

[14]Torrance, *Space, Time, and Resurrection*, 303.
[15]Fergusson, "Ascension of Christ," 101.
[16]Oliver O'Donovan, *On the Thirty Nine Articles: A Conversation with Tudor Christianity*, Latimer Monograph (Exeter, UK: Paternoster, 1986), 30.
[17]Herman Bavinck, *Reformed Dogmatics*, vol. 2, *God and Creation*, ed. John Bolt, trans. John Vriend (Grand Rapids, MI: Baker, 2003), 42.

common assumption that has made its way into today's world is Kant's assertion that whereas the domain of science is the "sensuous world," which "*a priori* brings with it forms of space and time," the supernatural one consists of "transcendental ideas" of "the soul, the world, and God." Ideas in this noumenal realm have "objective reality, but none" that is "demonstrable."[18] This led to the subjective turn in theology. Theological ideas are subjectively deduced from the nature of reason (and, in Friedrich Schleiermacher, from *feeling*). The Kantian, or modern, metaphysic thus leads theology into the way of idealism, which O'Donovan suggests was "popular among twentieth-century theologians," whom he fears have "had in mind the conversion of the Christian faith into a species of humanism." It seeks to limit the faith to what the collective reason can conceive, which devolves merely into the limitations of the human mind. He points out that the human "thinking mind," which is "not susceptible to location within our universe of space and time," is thus eliminated.[19]

O'Donovan is quick to point out, "Classical Christianity knew of another possibility. Space and time are dimensions of our created universe, but God is not located within them, but beyond, as a craftsman is beyond the dimensions of what he has made." This classical approach was "not so ready to absolutize the experience of thinking. Even when it used it as an analogue, it understood that it must still point yet further 'beyond,' for the thinking mind, too, belonged in the here-and-now of creation." With this in mind, O'Donovan proposes that "the classical concept of transcendence was objective at points where the modern one is subjective." Following the classical view, O'Donovan points out that "when we use such terms in phrases of transcendence, 'outside space and time, before time began,' or 'above the highest heavens,' our context indicates clearly enough that it is not a spatial outside or a temporal 'before,' but a

---

[18]Bavinck, *Reformed Dogmatics*, 2:42, 46.
[19]O'Donovan, *On the Thirty Nine Articles*, 30.

metaphysical one." When we think of transcendence, we have no option but "to use these spatial and temporal analogues, because we are ourselves spatial and temporal creatures and cannot think apart from the dimensions in which we live. Our imaginations are visual." If we as human persons cannot even think of *time* without doing so spatially—we use "a line, a circle, a flowing stream"—much more so do we need spatial images to "help us think of what transcends space and time."[20]

The window for meaningful language about the ascension is a revelatory one. O'Donovan affirms that "Christians believe that God, in the person of his Son, has established communication between his being and our created space-time order." This is the only way we can articulate the incarnation and the ascension as directional: as a coming down and a going up. We thus "do not think of the incarnation and ascension as journeys through space from one location to another, like a journey between the earth and the moon."[21] Athanasius's witty quote, "When Christ sat on the right hand of the Father, he did not put the Father on his left," is an illustration of this.[22] Crucially, O'Donovan concludes that these events, like the incarnation and the ascension, are "transitions between the universe of space and time that God has made and his being which is (in a sense that we can apprehend, but not comprehend) beyond it. Yet these transitions are 'objective' in the sense that they cannot be reduced to states, or occurrences, of Mind." Thus, incarnation, ascension, and "the triumph of the cross" are not mythical portrayals of fellowship between humans and God, but "insofar as these transitions have one foot in our space and time, they are seen there as events—events which, however, have another end to them beyond the historical sequence of which, at this end, they form a part."[23]

---

[20] O'Donovan, *On the Thirty Nine Articles*, 30-31.
[21] O'Donovan, *On the Thirty Nine Articles*, 31.
[22] Athanasius, "Four Discourses Against the Arians" (*NPNF*² 4:341).
[23] O'Donovan, *On the Thirty Nine Articles*, 31.

We may think of the ascension as an event in time, one Luke mentions as the end of Christ's resurrection appearances. However, it is more than that. It "is not only a 'taking from,' it is a 'taking up.'" It is "a material event which involves the material body of Jesus; it leaves this spatio-temporal order to enter the immediate presence of the Creator." What does this mean? It means that just as "Jesus' ascension means the elevation of humanity beyond the limits of 'our' space, it also means the elevation beyond the limits of 'our' time."[24] It also means that the verbs used to describe what Jesus does in heaven, such as "he sits," "he intercedes," and "he will come again," must be taken to indicate that these are real events described in heavenly terms, understood by way of heavenly space and heavenly time.

BIBLICAL SCHOLARSHIP ON THE COSMOLOGY OF THE ASCENSION

Concerning creation. Biblical scholar Jon Laansma offers a careful exegetical treatment of cosmology in Hebrews.[25] His work follows the structure of Hebrews as outlined by George Guthrie.[26] This entails two main parts to the homily or "word of exhortation": Hebrews 1:5–4:13 (the dominant christological category is the sonship of Jesus, and creation or cosmos is uppermost) and Hebrews 4:14–10:25 (the dominant category is the high priesthood of Jesus, and earthly and heavenly tabernacle is uppermost), both of which alternate between exposition and exhortation, after which the sermon becomes largely exhortational in Hebrews 10:26 onward. The first section has a positive

---

[24]O'Donovan, *On the Thirty Nine Articles*, 31-32.
[25]Jon Laansma, "Hidden Stories in Hebrews: Cosmology and Theology," in *A Cloud of Witnesses: The Theology of Hebrews in Its Ancient Contexts*, ed. Richard Bauckham et al., LNTS 387 (London: T&T Clark, 2008), 9-18; Jon Laansma, "Hebrews," in Pennington and McDonough, *Cosmology and New Testament Theology*, 125-43. See also a recent detailed discussion of the cosmology of the ascension in Stephen C. Wunrow, "Passing Through the Heavens: Heavenly Space in Hebrews and Its Jewish and Christian Environment" (PhD diss., Wheaton College, 2023).
[26]George H. Guthrie, *The Structure of Hebrews: A Text-Linguistic Analysis*, Supplements to Novum Testamentum 73 (Leiden: Brill, 1994).

theology of the cosmos and its destiny, related to the Son as the divine-human ascended Lord. Through him, the cosmos was created; he sustains it and has "provided cleansing for it and is its heir" (Heb 1:1-3). Psalm 102:26-27, cited in Hebrews 1:12, is often associated with the idea of the new creation as found in Isaiah 65:17; 66:22. Psalm 8, cited in Hebrews 2, speaks also of the destiny of humanity and creation, and Laansma indicates that the writer of Hebrews develops this in Hebrews 2:5-9 "in such a way that the creative purposes of Genesis 1–2 are being brought to fulfillment precisely in the Son."[27]

Hebrews 2:10 also speaks of "everything" being "for God," thus "underscoring again that creation has a point, a goal," and along with this comes the ruling or stewarding role of humanity in the ascended, exalted human-divine person, Jesus. Therefore, the context of bringing "many sons and daughters to glory" in that verse is precisely the earthly creation. Psalm 8, quoted in the lead-up to this glorious destiny of Christ's congregation in Hebrews 2:10-13, clarifies that this co-dominion of the church with Christ in a renewed creation is God's design for humanity. As Laansma states, "God will act in such a way that his design for all things that he created will be achieved."[28] Although the Son has ascended into heaven, earth is never far from his concern, and its created destiny and glory are always in mind.

In the second section of Hebrews (Heb 4:14–10:25), creation is less prominent, not surprisingly, given that the high-priestly ministry of Christ in the heavenly sanctuary is the primary theme. Paul Ellingworth writes extensively on challenging combinations of this section's "latent [assumed, presupposed] cosmology and patent soteriology."[29] This includes the following cosmological allusions: Jesus is "made lower than the angels" (Heb 2:9); Jesus "has passed through the heavens" (Heb 4:14 ESV), perhaps referring to a sphere

---

[27]Laansma, "Hidden Stories in Hebrews," 10-11.
[28]Laansma, "Hidden Stories in Hebrews," 11, emphasis original.
[29]Paul Ellingworth, "Jesus and the Universe in Hebrews," *Evangelical Quarterly* 58, no. 4 (January 1986): 337-50.

populated by angels or the atmospheric or even stellar heavens, as if this were a stage on his way to heaven, the abode of God; Jesus is exalted "above the heavens" (Heb 7:26); and he enters heaven (Heb 9:24). In addition to these vertical movements of Jesus in his exaltation, Hebrews speaks of horizontal movements of Christ that relate to heaven in a way that is depicted in the typology of the tabernacle or temple in the Old Testament. The heavenly tabernacle was the basis for the making of the earthly one (Heb 8:5; see Heb 9:24; 10:19). As noted earlier, the location of the heavenly sanctuary and what transpired in Jesus' death on earth merges, for example, in Hebrews 1:3: "After he had provided purification for sins, he sat down at the right hand of the Majesty in heaven."

In summary, Ellingworth suggests, "The author thinks synthetically, not analytically: for him, what Jesus did, who he was, and how the universe is framed, belong together, though the last is least important for him." Ellingworth adds that the "author's terminology is fluid, imprecise, and sometimes confusing; yet it is *not incoherent*."[30]

In the exhortational final section, Hebrews 12:25-29 is the most important cosmologically relevant passage. Whereas some interpreters see here the annihilation of the visible universe, Laansma puts forward a different view, influenced by the work of William L. Lane.[31] This view, guided by the context (Haggai; Ps 96; the context of Heb 12 itself), deduces that this passage does not envision a creation that has been annihilated but one that has been cleansed and, as Laansma indicates, is "reconstituted as God's temple, city, fatherland, world, and kingdom." All that is left is the city of the living God, the heavenly Jerusalem. This is not the end of the cosmos, in other words, but rather the creation "being reclaimed as God's temple." Laansma indicates that this is in keeping with the "promising things said of the cosmos in chapters 1–4," and rather than the removal of creation, this

---

[30]Ellingworth, "Jesus and the Universe," 340, 349-50.
[31]William L. Lane, *Hebrews 9–13*, Word Biblical Commentary 47B (Dallas: Word, 1991), 435-91.

passage is about "God's judgment, of cleansing (1:3), of removal of that which opposes God, and then of entrance into the place of salvation which goes under the name of the heavenly tabernacle, city, κατάπαυσις, and so forth."[32]

Thus, the writer of Hebrews aligns with Paul, who insists that "the creation itself will be set free from its bondage to decay, and will obtain the freedom of the glory of the children of God" (Rom 8:21). But this is also in keeping with the bookends of the narrative of God with his creation. The creation that began under the co-dominion of God and humanity in Genesis consummates—as a result of the atonement and ascension of the last Adam, in a human body, for humanity—under the co-dominion of the *eschatos* Adam and his church. The witness of the whole biblical narrative is that creation is the subject of redemption, and redemption is the redemption *of* creation, not its annihilation. In sum, the Son's perpetual assumption of material existence, signaled by the ascension, implies that the incarnation is not just a doctrine but a way of seeing the world, a metaphysic that invites the integration of theology and science.

Concerning redemption. Cosmology also plays a significant and even gloriously mind-stretching role in the accomplishment of redemption by the incarnate, crucified, risen, and ascended Lord. In Hebrews, there is a fluidity to how heaven and earth are viewed. Jesus clearly ascends through the heavens and above the heavens and then enters heaven itself, even when he is here on earth, especially as he goes to the cross. Heaven and earth seem to merge, though without losing the distinction. We have noted the theological juxtaposition in Hebrews 1:3 of his purgative act on the cross and his sitting at the right hand of God as if they were adjacent. This reflects the writer's cryptic style and focus on theology rather than locality. The earthly tabernacle was constructed after the pattern of the heavenly sanctuary, and Christ's sacrifice, answering to the typology of the earthly cultus,

---

[32]Laansma, "Hidden Stories in Hebrews," 14-15.

is being offered in heaven even as he is on the cross on earth. As Laansma states,

> This bears on the problem of how to relate the earthly cross to the idea of the heavenly offering (cf. 9:11-14). The writer's conception has shifted the altar geographically from the tabernacle and temple to the cross on Golgotha (13:10-13), while continuing to think of it as the intersection of heaven and earth, as in the temple ideas of the [ancient Near East] and Old Testament.[33]

There is, however, a *limited* dualism in the writer's thought in the sense that there is a boundary between the earthy and heavenly: the earthly sacrifice is offered on earth with earthly or cosmic redemptive effect, even if it is also offered in heaven. However, the ascension is definitely into heaven with an ongoing intercessory ministry that is heavenly but touches his people on earth. The limits to this dualism suggested by Laansma make the idea that atonement may have been effected in heaven at the ascension moment somewhat problematic. This discussion naturally invites the question, What and where is heaven? This is the subject of the next chapter.

---

[33]Laansma, "Hidden Stories in Hebrews," 17.

13

THE GLORY OF HEAVEN

WHY IS IT THAT ASCENSION TO HEAVEN is considered "up" from the perspective of the disciples of Jesus? Where does Jesus go at his ascension, given that there is no up and down in space? For several reasons, it happened as an "up" event for the disciples. First, the ascension had an intelligible purpose—it was not to show that Jesus was the first astronaut (!). He could have vanished as he did on other occasions; he could have gone to the Father secretly and invisibly. Second, he wanted his disciples to know that this time, his disappearance was for good. They were not to wait for his next resurrection appearance but for the Holy Spirit to come. It had its desired effect—they returned to Jerusalem. Third, the physical, literal event fittingly conveys the theological reality that Christ was being exalted. Real though it was, the event was nevertheless intended to symbolize exaltation to heaven and his occupation of a throne. He was entering into his reign, his kingdom. Fourth, the literal ascension graphically depicted another invisible, symbolic reality—the glorification and coronation that happened in heaven as he ascended. Peter says:

> God has raised this Jesus to life, and we are all witnesses of the fact. *Exalted to the right hand of God,* he has received from the Father the promised Holy Spirit and has poured out what you now see and hear. For David did not ascend to heaven, and yet he said,
>
> > "The Lord said to my Lord:
> >   'Sit at my right hand
> >   until I make your enemies
> >   a footstool for your feet.'"

Therefore let all Israel be assured of this: God has made this Jesus, whom you crucified, both Lord and Christ. (Acts 2:32-36)

However, what was Jesus' destination in this elevation, and what is heaven? Is it possible that the event accommodated the cosmology of the day? Did he keep rising through the air and then space, or did Jesus rise before the disciples' eyes and stay long enough in this upward trajectory to satisfy their understanding that he was returning to heaven but then disappear into another invisible realm? Being the Son of God, he could have traversed the atmospheric heavens and even the stellar heavens to what is beyond both in some spatial sense. He could even have done that instantaneously but chose not to in order to accommodate his disciples' sense of his exaltation and to influence their understanding that he was not coming back, at least not just then, and to prepare them for the descent of the Holy Spirit as Pentecost.

WHAT IS THE CHARACTER OF HEAVEN?

It is transcendent and immanent. The theory that heaven is another parallel universe, "a reality outside this created time-space order" characterized by the immediate presence of God and invisible to earthlings, rather than a place "high up" past the galaxies, has been expressed by theologians such as Oliver O'Donovan.[1] Noting the common understanding of both John Calvin and Karl Barth that the ascension should not be considered "merely in terms of space and time," Patrick Schreiner also notes, "When Christ ascended, he sat on the right hand of God, but that place is also everywhere—for God is everywhere," and concludes that "the reality of the ascension goes beyond our human comprehension."[2] He cites T. F. Torrance in support: "The ascension must be thought of as an ascension

---

[1] Oliver O'Donovan, *On the Thirty Nine Articles: A Conversation with Tudor Christianity*, Latimer Monograph (Exeter, UK: Paternoster, 1986), 34.
[2] Patrick Schreiner, *The Ascension of Christ: Recovering a Neglected Doctrine* (Bellingham, WA: Lexham, 2020), 32.

beyond all our notions of space and time, and therefore as something that cannot ultimately be expressed in categories of space and time."[3] On the other hand, N. T. Wright suggests that, in biblical cosmology, heaven and earth "are not two locations within the same spatial continuum" but are "two different dimensions of God's creation. . . . First, heaven relates to earth tangentially, so that the one who is in heaven can be present everywhere at once on earth." He adds, "The ascension, therefore, means that Jesus is available, accessible, without people having to travel to a particular spot on earth to find him."[4]

These ideas of heaven seem difficult to reconcile with the assertion of Hebrews that Jesus, the *Man* who is God, has ascended as a finite man and is seated at the right hand of God. Some insights from theology proper may be helpful. A reality of the doctrine of the triune God revealed in Scripture is that he is transcendent and therefore cannot be bound by a place at all, and yet, mysteriously, he is also immanently present in the place designated as heaven in Scripture, and even immanent to humans on earth in their suffering. Rather than saying heaven is another parallel realm where transcendence operates (whatever that means), perhaps it is the place where the transcendent God is immanent to his creation, including angels and redeemed humans in Christ. This is difficult but not impossible to conceive. Regarding God's ability to be present to suffering humans, Brad Gregory states, "God as traditionally conceived is not spatial in any sense, which is precisely how and why, if such a God is real, he could be present to all moments of space-time and to every bit of matter-energy." This therefore implies that "with the Christian conception of God as transcendent creator of the universe, it is precisely and only *because*

---

[3] T. F. Torrance, *Atonement: The Person and Work of Christ* (Downers Grove, IL: IVP Academic, 2009), 286.

[4] N. T. Wright, *Surprised by Hope: Rethinking Heaven, the Resurrection, and the Mission of the Church* (New York: HarperOne, 2008), 110-11.

of his radical difference from creation that God *can* be present to and through it."[5]

As Tyler Loewen wisely says, God must "remain transcendent in order to save, but . . . given classical metaphysics, such a total transcendence is what actually *makes it possible* for him to be immanent to human suffering at all."[6] We may then extrapolate this to refer to God's capacity to occupy a place called heaven beyond our space and time. In accordance with classical trinitarian metaphysics, which speaks of God as Being *in se* and not a being among beings, the transcendent God can also be completely immanent. David Bentley Hart confirms this, speaking of the "great discovery" of the Christian metaphysical tradition, which was "the true nature of transcendence, transcendence understood not as mere dialectical supremacy, and not as ontic absence, but as the truly transcendent and therefore utterly immediate act of God, in his own infinity, giving being to beings."[7] Loewen argues, "This is possible, not least because the Christian God is Trinitarian. For it is the Trinitarian God, three personal hypostases in completely mutual union in their divine being, yet irreducibly differentiated and defined by their relations and economic roles, 'which frees God from being fundamentally substance.'" This is because the understanding of God as three divine hypostases in union, "defined and differentiated by their relationships, allowed for *relational hypostasis* to become the Ground of Being."[8]

Therefore, because this trinitarian God is not located anywhere *within* creation, God is not restrained by the rules and mechanisms of creation and is also "transcendently present in all beings, the ever

---

[5] Brad S. Gregory, *The Unintended Reformation: How a Religious Revolution Secularized Society* (Cambridge, MA: Harvard University Press, 2012), 71, 56.
[6] Tyler Loewen, "Bringing God Down: The Influence and Effects of the Metaphysical Concept of Univocal Being in Jürgen Moltmann's Staurocentric Theology" (MA thesis, Regent College, 2024), 98.
[7] David Bentley Hart, "The Hidden and the Manifest," in *Orthodox Readings of Augustine*, ed. George E. Demacopoulos and Aristotle Papanikolaou (Crestwood, NY: St. Vladimir's Seminary Press, 2008), 204.
[8] Loewen, "Bringing God Down," 90-91.

more inward act within each finite act." Since God is situated outside any "ontic continuum with creation," he cannot be determined in any way *by* creation.[9] As Loewen writes, this "frees him to be immanently present *in* creation; and frees him to be the sovereign ontological source *of* creation."[10] This leads Hart to conclude, "True divine transcendence, it turns out, transcends even the traditional metaphysical divisions between the transcendent and the immanent."[11] The idea of a heaven where God dwells, where the Son occupies a throne, is consonant with such transcendence and immanence.

That there is a location called heaven, distinct from earth, irrespective of where heaven may be, is beyond question if we take the Bible seriously. Hebrews makes it clear that after Jesus had finished the work of atonement, he applied that work when he ascended, including the purification of "heavenly things" (Heb 9:23). The writer adds, "For Christ did not enter a sanctuary made with human hands that was only a copy of the true one; he *entered heaven itself*, now to appear for us in God's presence" (Heb 9:24). So not only does he purify it upon his ascent, or perhaps even before that, on the cross, which in Hebrews is enacted in the heavenly sanctuary even though it is on earth (Heb 9:14, 25-26), but he is also present in that heavenly locale to continually appear and intercede for his people.

Why would the heavenly sanctuary, which was the pattern according to which the Old Testament sanctuary was built, need to be cleansed? In Hebrews 9, the writer reminds his readers that this had a figural precedent: "In the same way, he sprinkled with the blood both the tabernacle and everything used in its ceremonies. In fact, the law requires that nearly everything be cleansed with blood, and without the shedding of blood there is no forgiveness" (Heb 9:21-22). Though not explicitly stated, the priests under the Levitical order needed cleaning, for they were sinful mortals characterized by

---

[9] Hart, "Hidden and the Manifest," 204-5.
[10] Loewen, "Bringing God Down," 99, emphases original.
[11] Hart, "Hidden and the Manifest," 205.

"weakness" (Heb 7:28). This is not the case for the high priest Jesus functioning in the heavenly sanctuary, for as Hebrews 7 affirms, he is "holy, blameless, pure, set apart from sinners, exalted above the heavens" (Heb 7:26). He did not need to offer "sacrifices day after day, first for his own sins, and then for the sins of the people" (Heb 7:27). Rather, he "sacrificed for their sins once for all when he offered himself" (Heb 7:27).

The answer seems clear here that the cleansing of the heavenly sanctuary relates to the access to it of the priestly people of God, who do come with their fallenness and sinfulness to offer imperfect worship. Whether those who have died and are now "with the Lord" (2 Cor 5:8), or those who are living and access the throne of grace in prayer (Heb 4:16), or even the rare cases such as Enoch and Elijah, who were taken up without dying, they are characterized by imperfection and require purification, or in the case of the departed dead or the embodied living, beatification or glorification. Farrow sums up the reasons why cleansing in heaven is necessary:

> It is necessary, because heaven has been the place of traffic between God and the fallen world. For the same reason that Isaiah's lips require to be purged with a coal taken from the heavenly altar, in that they are an avenue of the word of God to sinners, the altar itself and the sanctuary and the ministers in the sanctuary require purification. And there is nothing that can purify them, except Jesus Christ, "the Man who sinless came and sinless went." He is the only one who can traffic with sinners and effect atonement, rather than need atonement.[12]

He adds that there is a further reason for the need for purification in heaven that relates to the angelic rebellion that preceded that on earth. Thus, not just hell or Hades was harrowed by Jesus by his descent to earth and ascent to heaven. There is a cosmic dimension to the effects of his reconciling and purifying work commanded "from the place from which the world is ruled." Farrow states that

---

[12] Douglas Farrow, *Ascension Theology* (London: T&T Clark, 2011), 124.

"though he does not forgive the sins of angels, he does purge the heavens of every trace of angelic sin, and shred every banner of the one whom Dante astutely called 'the Emperor of the kingdom of despair.'"[13] The decisive battle in the defeat of Satan and his forces occurred in the death and resurrection Jesus, and the mopping-up operations continue in a war in which the risen Lord will surely prevail, for his enemies will be made the footstool of his feet. Whereas the self-offering of Jesus leads to two possibilities in humanity on earth, forgiveness or the inciting of sin and the man of lawlessness, Farrow comments that from a heavenly perspective it "puts an end to sin, and comes to *glory, unadulterated glory*. It restores paradise as the seed to the new creation. It generates the church and sends it forth into the world."[14] This naturally comes under the *Christus Victor* motif of the atonement.

The atonement and the ascension involved cosmic structures and powers, leading Andrew Lincoln to say that even heaven had to be reinterpreted. He states that for Paul, "what God has done in Christ has given a special content to the concept of heaven, for it has become involved in a new way in that act of the drama of redemption, inaugurated by Christ's resurrection and ascension."[15] Farrow counters suspicions of some scholars of Hellenization concerning Paul's cosmological discussions of Christ's conquest over Satan, his subjugation of the elementary principles of the cosmos (*stoicheia*), and his understanding of the fullness of God (*plēroma*), suggesting instead that the building blocks of his theology were rather the Jewish Scriptures. However, he goes on to say that the exaltation of Jesus precipitated the discovery of new dimensions in Paul's understanding that transcended these roots without violating them. This involved his

---

[13] Farrow, *Ascension Theology*, 125. The Dante reference is to *Inferno* 34.28.
[14] Farrow, *Ascension Theology*, 125, emphasis added.
[15] Andrew T. Lincoln, *Paradise Now and Not Yet: Studies in the Role of the Heavenly Dimension in Paul's Thought with Special Reference to His Eschatology* (Cambridge: Cambridge University Press, 1981), 184.

understanding of heaven and the whole creation around the descent-ascent history of the Son.[16]

It is the case, Farrow suggests, that "reflection on the ascension appears to have contributed to important breakthroughs in biblical thought about God, man, and the universe, and to have shaped ecclesiology, in a quite fundamental way." A "quite new reality had been forged out of the old," says Farrow, since the Christ who had met Paul on the Damascus road had demanded to be understood "as nothing less than the Lord of creation. To him, all things have been made subject; and him all things were seen to cohere; by him all things would reach their goal. Even the highly paradoxical conclusion that through him all things derive their being forced itself upon Paul."[17] This is reflected in Pauline texts such as 1 Corinthians 8:6, "Yet for us there is but one God, the Father, from whom all things came and for whom we live; and there is but one Lord, Jesus Christ, through whom all things came and through whom we live," and Ephesians 4:10, "He who descended is the very one who ascended higher than all the heavens, in order to fill the whole universe."

Farrow asserts that a "new ontology and a new Christocentric cosmology were being conceived." Central to this cosmology is the church, which according to Paul is constituted in and with the ascension of Christ in that by his heavenly session he is given to the church as "head over everything" (Eph 1:22). As Farrow states, "The ecclesial communion as such is the prophetic sign to the world that God has organized all things around the one whom he has enthroned at his right hand. The church has cosmic significance, precisely in its anticipation of the appearance of that order. It is the community of the *recapitulation*."[18] The role of the church as precisely the humanity in union with Christ, destined for co-dominion with

---

[16]Douglas Farrow, *Ascension and Ecclesia: On the Significance of the Doctrine of the Ascension for Ecclesiology and Christian Cosmology* (Grand Rapids, MI: Eerdmans, 1999), 30-31.
[17]Farrow, *Ascension and Ecclesia*, 30-31.
[18]Farrow, *Ascension and Ecclesia*, 32, emphasis original.

him in the fullness of the new creation and already coreigning with him now, explains Farrow's use here of *recapitulation*, capturing Irenaeus's understanding of this soteriological motif.

It is appropriate to use quotation marks for "location" and "place" in this discussion of heaven because these descriptors fall woefully short of describing the abode of a transcendent God who is omnipresent, transcendent, yet somehow immanent. The whole cosmos cannot contain him. This has led to speculation that perhaps the word *heaven* in Hebrews, for example, is used for the "place from which God's rule over the world is effected through the angels, the place where God's presence to and for creation is manifested and known, the place around which all creation is therefore ordered and arranged."[19] Yet the conceptual difficulty in assigning a realm to an infinite God should not cloud what Jesus or the apostles reveal about it, even if he is accommodating human understanding.

Hebrews reveals not so much heaven as the world of love. The balancing reality is that the God defined by love is also the God described by "unapproachable light" and glory. The emphasis also shifts from the church, which will indwell heaven, to the enduring purpose of creation. Heaven, at least in Hebrews, is, according to Farrow, not "God's own place"—that is, the abode of God—since God cannot be contained in any place, and no place could ever be larger than God, as if to house him. At any rate, he "dwells in unapproachable light." The Son "never left" that place, "even as incarnate and crucified," since he eternally has his being in the Father. Rather, we think of heaven as "where God's presence to and for creation is manifested and known, the place around which all creation is therefore ordered and arranged." It is not of this creation, as Hebrews 9:11 indicates, but it is the venue through which God communicates with humanity and creation. Farrow thinks that "this is the heaven that Jesus enters through his ascension, and he enters it to prepare the new creation by

---

[19] Farrow, *Ascension Theology*, 124.

conforming that place to himself, we might almost say, by revealing himself—his incarnate self—*as* that place."[20]

We might consider this to be the heavenly tabernacle, the original tabernacle, "the greater and more perfect tabernacle that is not made with human hands," that is to say, is not a part of this creation (Heb 9:11). This prototype in heaven was what the earthly tabernacle of the Old Testament was patterned after (Heb 9:8). The writer refers to the features of the old tabernacle as "copies of the heavenly things" (Heb 9:23), already extant in heaven. It was then fully fulfilled in the person of the Son, who tabernacled among us (Jn 1:14) on earth, in the New Testament. This resonates with the writer's speaking of what is behind the veil as the place Jesus enters for us as our High Priest (Heb 6:19-20), and of the Son's body as the *curtain* (Heb 10:20), the veil into the divine presence. Again, in Hebrews 9:24, the writer states, "For Christ did not enter a sanctuary made with human hands that was only a copy of the true one; he entered *heaven itself*, now to appear for us in God's presence." Here Christ functions not so much as a fulfiller of the figural tabernacle but as the priest within it, facilitating the spiritual ascension of the people of God in this phase of the kingdom and their holistic ascent at the parousia.

The idea that heaven in Hebrews is not the immediate presence of God but a mediating place, one manifestation of heaven in the form of a heavenly tabernacle, has appeal, especially as it seems to overcome the challenge raised by a place called heaven that outsizes an infinitely immense God. However, two notes of caution are in order. The first is that passages such as Hebrews 9:24 just cited make little sense if this is the case. The phrasing "heaven itself" seems rather emphatic. And what is the point of a high priest if he is not actually in the very presence of God for us so he might mediate our prayers and one day draw us into the presence of God, as Hebrews 6 seems to anticipate? Speaking of the ultimate "hope set before us" at the second coming,

---

[20]Farrow, *Ascension Theology*, 124.

the writer states: "We have this hope as an anchor for the soul, firm and secure. It enters the inner sanctuary behind the curtain, where our forerunner, Jesus, has entered on our behalf. He has become a high priest forever, in the order of Melchizedek" (Heb 6:19-20).

Furthermore, Revelation 22 envisions a heaven occupied by the people of God in which God is clearly present and where his light illumines rather than consumes them: "The throne of God and of the Lamb will be in the city, and his servants will serve him. They will see his face, and his name will be on their foreheads. There will be no more night. They will not need the light of a lamp or the light of the sun, for the Lord God will give them light. And they will reign for ever and ever" (Rev 22:3-5). In the previous chapter, John hears the divine voice, which says, "Look! God's dwelling place is now among the people, and he will dwell with them. They will be his people, and God himself will be with them and be their God" (Rev 21:3). Heaven comes to earth, and it is spoken of as God's dwelling place. If "the glory of the LORD filled the tabernacle" (Ex 40:34), and if the Shekinah glory of the Lord filled the old covenant temple (1 Kings 8:11), then unsurprisingly, Revelation depicts the final dwelling place of God with humans in this way: "it shone with the glory of God" (Rev 21:11). Isaiah anticipated this in glory language: "The moon will be dismayed, the sun ashamed; for the LORD Almighty will reign on Mount Zion and in Jerusalem, and before its elders—with great glory" (Is 24:23; see Is 40:5).

The meaning of Revelation 21:3 anticipates the second comment. The idea that there is a heaven apart from the real heaven seems to rule out what the epistle of Hebrews conveys regarding the ultimate coming together of heaven and earth in a way that is already anticipated by how the writer speaks cryptically of Christ being in heaven as he is accomplishing the atonement on the cross on earth (Heb 1:3; 10:12). If the objection is that God lives in light unapproachable, isn't that what the glorification or beatification of the saints prepares them for? The philosophical problem of heaven as the home of God that seems to imply a place bigger than God must be shaded by the clarity of revealed Scripture in the totality of its references to heaven. There is much about heaven that by far exceeds our understanding, including this conundrum. Hence, *apophaticism* seems fitting in this regard. Heaven is a glory far exceeding our capacity to understand, for it is the locale, somehow, of the glory that is the triune God of glory.

So, if heaven is in Hebrews what it is everywhere else, canonically speaking, what are we to make of the tabernacle in heaven spoken of in that epistle, a tabernacle that both speaks of Christ's body and is the locale for his priestly functioning? If the Son in heaven is ubiquitous concerning his deity while limited to his real humanity, then we may need to rest in this regard also in apophatic territory. But we can do so without denying that all of what he does is really in heaven, while all of what he does is accessible by his people on earth, and all that he does in heaven will one day bring us to heaven, and then from heaven to earth: "The earth will be filled with the knowledge of the glory of the Lord as the waters cover the sea" (Hab 2:14). Rather than seeking to unscrew the inscrutable regarding the destiny of the ascension, it is more edifying to consider the character or characteristics that Scripture reveals about it, with greater certainty. Cosmological understanding of the nature of heaven is all very well. There is some wisdom in drawing a veil where Scripture is silent. However, Scripture is not totally silent. Various biblical authors provide some clues.

It has the character of the Father and his love. Heaven's character is determined by who is there: it is the "Father's house." The apostle John provides a very warm picture of heaven when he recalls how Jesus speaks of it as the "Father's house," actually even more endearingly as "my Father's house" (Jn 14:2). The disciples are to anticipate heaven as participants in the intimacy between the Father and the Son. Similarly, Jesus asks Mary Magdalene to share with his disciples, "I am ascending to my Father and your Father, to my God and your God"

(Jn 20:17). His ascent to heaven was a return to the Father's intimate presence in heaven ("to my Father"), and, grounded in his union with humanity, in his atonement on their behalf, and in their union with Christ, his people would know him as their Father and one day ascend to him also. That he is "our Father" is evident in the opening phrase of the prayer Jesus taught his disciples, which he expected we would continue to say: "Our Father who art in heaven" (Mt 6:9 KJV).

So, what gives character to heaven? Heaven is a place of intimacy between the Father and the Son, an intimacy that is hospitable to humanity in the Son. It is a place of infinite and inexpressible love between the Father and the Son in the communion and love of the Holy Spirit. The direction of heaven is also signaled in Jesus' high-priestly prayer for his disciples in John 17. Addressing his "Holy Father," he indicates their complete mutuality and then the impartation of glory that emanates from that mutuality: "I have made you known to them, and will continue to make you known in order that the love you have for me may be in them and that I myself may be in them" (Jn 17:26). The multiple appeals in this prayer that his people may be one are grounded in the unity of the Father and the Son, in which the church participates in the now and will fully realize in heaven.

The notion of home relates to this theme of heaven as the Father's house. In the context immediately following the reference to the Father's house in John 14, Jesus speaks of he and his Father making their home in his people, a notion repeated in Paul's prayer in Ephesians 3:17, referring immediately to the indwelling of the Spirit but anticipating when we shall be "at home with the Lord." Paul gives further evidence of the fatherly heart of the Father in Ephesians 3:14-15, praying, "For this reason I kneel before the Father, from whom every family in heaven and on earth derives its name." This prayer to the Father stimulates the work of the Spirit for the formation of Christ in his people, leading to an unparalleled revelation of the triune love of

God, one the believer may begin to experience now but that can be fulfilled only in heaven (Eph 3:17-18).

Jonathan Edwards expresses these thoughts well in his exposition of 1 Corinthians 13:8-10, which focuses on the love of God that may be experienced to some degree now but will be discovered more fully in heaven. Grounded in the notion that the very essence of God is love (1 Jn 4:8), Edwards extols the love of God that characterizes heaven. Heaven is the location where the triune God dwells in perfect union, a union open for human relations in Christ and by the Spirit. This is how Edwards expresses it:

> There in heaven this fountain of love, this eternal three in one, is set open without any obstacle to hinder access to it. There this glorious God is manifested and shines forth in full glory, in beams of love; there the fountain overflows in streams and rivers of love and delight, enough for all to drink at, and to swim in, yea, so as to overflow the world as it were with a deluge of love.[21]

Heaven is a place where the Trinity is open for particular relationships with particular human persons in Christ. It is a hospitable, welcoming place where everyone seems to have a place. All this has been opened up for us precisely by Christ's ascension. This assures the identity of the people of the Father as his sons and daughters. The consequence of his going up to heaven by way of the cross, leading to the outpouring of the Spirit, is "the proclamation of the Father's open house, a mission that hails the advent of ecclesial man, whose being is in communion." By this, Farrow means that the opening up of heaven by Christ's ascension, precipitating the outpouring of the Spirit, leads not just to the opening of the Father's house but to the constitution of true human being through the Spirit—the perichoretic and communal form of existence that leads to the "*co*-existence of the faithful with

---

[21]Jonathan Edwards, "Heaven Is a World of Love," in *The Sermons of Jonathan Edwards: A Reader*, ed. Wilson H. Kimnach, Kenneth P. Minkema, and Douglas A. Sweeney (New Haven, CT: Yale University Press, 1999), 245.

Jesus and his Father."[22] The perichoretic communion of God in heaven has, in Christ ascended and the Spirit descended, created a corresponding filial human community, the church, in Christ. It is destined for entry into the full communion of God in heaven where Christ has gone but called until then to faithful mission on earth as a community that already manifests true human being for the world, and is itself also hospitable and inviting.

These insights lead to a way of seeing the world, a "coherent Christian worldview" with broad cosmological significance, as Farrow puts it. This worldview is based first on "the mediation of Christ as [of] the ground of our existence," and it is "backed by a relational ontology based in the perichoretic power of the Spirit so that in his ascension, he does indeed fill and fulfill all things, as Ephesians teaches." This is a "doxological worldview," one that "traces out the trinitarian lines of Christian worship to form an image of the finished creation in which there is no higher category than communion."[23] Influenced here by Irenaeus, Farrow cites again his famous statement in *Against Heresies*: "For the glory of God is a living man, and the life of man consists in beholding God," adding that this is "in the Spirit, and through the Son, who is the visible of the Father."[24]

It has the character of glory. If heaven is the dwelling place for the Father, as John 14 indicates, this makes heaven a place of love and glory. This is who the Father is, the one who possesses infinite riches of glory (Eph 3:16), the one whose glory is revealed by the outcome of the Son's exaltation after his mission in humility to the world ("to the glory of God the Father," Phil 2:11). The Father shares this fullness of glory with the Son ("when he comes in his glory and in the glory of the Father," Lk 9:26). And according to the high-priestly prayer of Jesus, the wonder of the gospel means that the people of God share in this glory. Jesus speaks of the glory with the Father "before the world

---

[22] Farrow, *Ascension and Ecclesia*, 36.
[23] Farrow, *Ascension and Ecclesia*, 66.
[24] Irenaeus, *Against Heresies* 4.20.7 (ANF 1:490); Farrow, *Ascension and Ecclesia*, 66.

began" and his desire to enter that glory again after finishing the work the Father had given him to do (Jn 17:5). This glorification corresponds to his own glorifying of the Father in that work (Jn 17:4). But the consuming desire of this prayer and the Savior's heart is expressed in John 17:24: "Father, I want those you have given me to be with me where I am, and to see my glory, the glory you have given me because you loved me before the creation of the world." This is a reference to heaven, and it is undoubtedly a place of glory iridescent and glory imparted to the saints by participation in Christ. Earlier in the prayer, referring to his people given to him by the Father in his lifetime on earth, Jesus even states that "glory has come to me through them" (Jn 17:10). Their glory, and ours today and in the future when we see Christ, will be a derived glory gained by participating in the glory of the triune God. The glorifying of the Son in his ascension in the glory he had eternally prior to its veiling in his time on earth, as requested in his prayer, is how his human people, in union with him, will also be glorified. Christ must remain the center of God's purposes and his people's praises.

The glorifying of the Son in his ascension and the passion for his praises is reminiscent of Psalm 132, which recalls David's desire for a dwelling place for God on earth. I will not rest, he says, "till I find a place for the Lord, a dwelling for the Mighty One of Jacob" (Ps 132:5). In response, God assures him that one of his descendants will sit on his throne (Ps 132:11) in no other place but "Zion" (Ps 132:13), and that this future Davidic king, the Messiah king, "will be adorned with a radiant crown" (Ps 132:18). This anticipates three occasions when the ascended King of glory is described as wearing a crown or crowns in his heavenly reign. In Revelation 6:2, John describes the Son in ascended glory riding "a white horse," and he is "given a crown, and he rode out as a conqueror bent on conquest." This passage sounds like the coronation of Jesus described in the Hebrews "sit down" passages and suggests that his session by the Father until his enemies are defeated does not mean the ascended King is passive. He sits on a throne to reign from heaven, to exercise grace and judgment on earth.

In Revelation 14:14, a passage that recalls the ascension in a cloud and seems to depict his descent in the clouds, John says, "I looked, and there before me was a white cloud, and seated on the cloud was one like a son of man with a crown of gold on his head and a sharp sickle in his hand." In Revelation 19:12, John again describes the ascended Son in glory, exercising judgment, as having eyes "like blazing fire, and on his head are many crowns."[25] Utterly remarkable is that on several occasions in Revelation, the people of Christ also share, by sheer grace, in the Son's glory, as reflected in his crowns, by having crowns of their own (Rev 2:10; 3:11; 4:4, 10). The casting of the crowns of the twenty-four elders before the throne in Revelation 4:10 appropriately brings the focus to the ascended Christ and evokes worship for his creative work and lordship over creation: They lay their crowns before the throne and say, "You are worthy, our Lord and God, to receive glory and honor and power, for you created all things, and by your will they were created and have their being" (Rev 4:11).

It has the character of beauty. Akin to the notion that heaven, to which Jesus ascended and to which he will bring his people, is a place of glory is the idea that heaven is a place of exquisite beauty that defies description and emanates from the King of beauty. The idea that beauty is a descriptor for the Son, and indeed the triune God, and that he confers his beauty on his people conjoined to him and the whole creation, may be found in Scripture and the theological tradition. For example, beginning in the Old Testament, the psalmist's consuming desire is to "dwell in the house of the LORD all the days of my life, to gaze on the beauty of the LORD and to seek him in his temple" (Ps 27:4). Zion is described in Psalm 50:2 as "perfect in beauty," since this is the realm in which "God shines forth." An exquisite description of the

---

[25]That he "has a name written on him that no one knows but he himself" (Rev 19:12) recalls Phil 2:9's referenced to the "name that is above every name."

king's majesty in Psalm 45:1-9, referenced by the writer of Hebrews as referring to the Son in his session and his forever throne, leads to an equally exquisite description of the bride (Ps 45:10-15). The instructions to the bride make it abundantly clear that the bride's beauty is derived from the Bridegroom: "Let the king be enthralled by your beauty; honor him, for he is your lord" (Ps 45:11).

In sum, "Zion," the heaven to which the people of God aspire, is called in Psalm 50:2 "perfect in beauty," from which "God shines forth" in revelation (Ps 50:2). Texts such as Psalm 96:9, in which we are exhorted to worship Yahweh in his sanctuary in the "splendor of his holiness," remind us that beauty and holiness are not to be separated. The character of heaven is thus also that of God's holiness. The three aspects of the holiness of God—his *majestic holiness* ("I saw the Lord, high and exalted, seated on a throne"), his *moral holiness* ("Woe to me!" I cried. "I am ruined! For I am a man of unclean lips, and I live among a people of unclean lips, and my eyes have seen the King, the LORD Almighty"), and his *aesthetic holiness* ("the train of his robe filled the temple" . . . "Holy, holy, holy is the LORD Almighty; the whole earth is full of his glory")—are vividly conveyed in Isaiah's encounter with heaven in Isaiah 6:1, 3, 5.

If holiness adorns God's house, Peter speaks explicitly of his righteousness being a characteristic of heaven: "We are looking forward to a new heaven and a new earth, where righteousness dwells" (2 Pet 3:13). Heaven is a world *full* of righteousness. Whereas the prophet Isaiah describes the human appearance of the Messiah as having no particular "beauty or majesty to attract us to him" (Is 53:2), Revelation describes what he has imparted in ascended glory to his church as a beauty that defies description (Rev 21:2, 9-11). We are left in no doubt where that beauty of the saints in heaven comes from: "I did not see a temple in the city, because the Lord God Almighty and the Lamb are its temple. The city does not need the sun or the moon to shine on it, for the glory of God gives it light, and the Lamb is its lamp" (Rev 21:22-23).

Consistent with Jonathan Edwards's thought on beauty, Junius Johnson writes, "God is beautiful and the source of beauty; God is its source because God is the cause of God's own beauty and because God is the cause of all beauty that is not divine."[26] Beauty is not a category assigned to the Trinity; rather beauty is original and intrinsic to what the Trinity is, and heaven takes its character from this trinitarian beauty. The beauty of the ascended Son also corresponds to and is compatible with the beauty of the Trinity and the place where he ascends. Heaven is exquisitely beautiful because Jesus gives it that beauty. Other writers in the Catholic tradition, such as J. R. R. Tolkien and Hans Urs von Balthasar, also expound on the theme of the beauty of God.[27] The latter equates beauty with divine love. If heaven is a world of love, it is a place of beauty.

The description of heaven's coming to earth in Revelation 21 is one of both love and beauty. Its gates are never shut (Rev 21:25), and the "great street of the city [is] of gold, as pure as transparent glass" (Rev 21:21). The character of heaven is more beautiful and wonderful than we can imagine: "'What no eye has seen, what no ear has heard, and what no human mind has conceived'—the things God has prepared for those who love him" (1 Cor 2:9). But its center, surprisingly, is a nail-pierced Man, the crucified "Lord of glory" (1 Cor 2:8). The throne scene in Revelation 5 describes the Lamb in this way: "looking as if it had been slain" (Rev 5:6), the inference being it looked as if it was "freshly slain." It was at the center of the throne, surrounded by incense, with the voices of angelic and redeemed humans joining in the song, "Worthy is the Lamb, who was slain, to receive power and wealth and wisdom and strength and honor and *glory* and praise!" (Rev 5:12). In the words of the hymn writer:

---

[26]Junius Johnson, *The Father of Lights: A Theology of Beauty* (Grand Rapids, MI: Baker Academic, 2020), 2.

[27]See Lisa Coutras, *Tolkien's Theology of Beauty: Majesty, Splendor, and Transcendence in Middle-Earth* (New York: Palgrave Macmillan, 2016), for an exposition of the narrative theology of beauty in Tolkien in conversation with the well-known theology of glory in Hans Urs von Balthasar, *The Glory of the Lord: A Theological Aesthetics*, ed. Joseph Fessio and John Riches, trans. Erasmo Leiva-Merikakis, 7 vols. (San Francisco: Ignatius, 1962).

Majestic sweetness sits enthroned upon the Saviour's brow.
His head with *radiant glories crowned*, his lips with grace o'erflow.
No mortal can with Him compare, among the sons of men;
Fairer is He than all the fair who fill the heav'nly train, who fill the heav'nly train.[28]

The fairness of the Savior is what constitutes the fairness of heaven.

Its character is that it is pain-free. One of the reasons heaven is beautiful is that there is no more pain or death in it. Based on the finished work of the ascended one, bearing our sins, healing our disease, and conquering death by death, heaven is free of all the ugliness of disease and pain of every kind, and the last enemy, death, will have been destroyed (1 Cor 15:26). Paul in Romans 8:18 says, "The sufferings of this present time are not worthy to be compared with the glory which shall be revealed in us" (KJV). And in 2 Corinthians 4:17, he contrasts his life now and in the future: "This light and momentary affliction is preparing for us an eternal weight of glory far beyond all comparison" (ESV). The "eternal weight of glory" answers to the weight of the glory of the ascended King.

This heaven free of pain, loss, and grief is undoubtedly essential to a theodicy. That God has, in Christ, entered our human suffering, pain, and death is the principal theodicy, but heaven is a close second. C. S. Lewis certainly thought there was no theodicy without heaven: "A book on suffering which says nothing of heaven, is leaving out almost the whole of one side of the account. Scripture and tradition habitually put the joys of heaven into the scale against the sufferings of earth, and no solution of the problem of pain which does not do so can be called a Christian one." He leaves his readers in no doubt that the person who initiates the dance of healing, which makes pain bearable now and will compensate it beyond all proportion, is Jesus: "All pains and pleasures we have known on earth are early initiations

---

[28]Samuel Stennett, "Majestic Sweetness Sits Enthroned," Hymnary.org, accessed July 19, 2024, https://hymnary.org/text/majestic_sweetness_sits_enthroned.

in the movements of that dance: but the dance itself is strictly incomparable with the sufferings of this present time." And a few paragraphs later, Lewis adds that "the eternal dance 'makes heaven drowsy with the harmony,'" a harmony effected by Christ in his costly reconciliation of all things and his ascension in glorious triumph.[29]

Its character is of heaven-come-to-earth. The assertion of Revelation 21 that heaven is coming to earth, a strong emphasis within current eschatology, is unsurprising given the incarnation of the Son. The earthly nature of heaven is not just a bookend in the biblical story. It is a consequence of the nature of its Lord. It makes good sense that if the Son became truly human, and if that was God's eternal decree, he would finally reign on a heavenly earth with his earthly people. His perpetual existence in an earthly body, albeit fitted for a heavenly ethos, makes God's commitment to his creation (Rom 8:19-22) an understandable commitment. The "Word became flesh [Greek *sarx*]" (Jn 1:14) is not just a statement about his becoming human but about his participation in creation.[30] Furthermore, since his resurrection signaled the reaffirmation of creation, it is unsurprising that God is committed to the renewal of his creation, not its annihilation, in future eschaton.[31] The ascended divine-human Son derives both the future of the earth and its heavenly character.

This christological focus helps us understand why entering heaven and coming from heaven to earth makes us not less human but more. C. S. Lewis comments, "To enter heaven is to become more human than you ever succeeded in being on earth; to enter hell is to be banished from humanity."[32] This is not to minimize the glorified nature or heavenly state of earthy humans, for when they see Jesus,

---

[29]C. S. Lewis, *The Problem of Pain* (San Francisco: HarperSanFrancisco, 2000), 149, 159, here citing Shakespeare, *Love's Labor's Lost*, act 4, scene 3.

[30]David Clough, *On Animals* (London: T&T Clark, 2014), 85.

[31]That Jesus' resurrection signaled the reaffirmation of creation is a notion proposed and defended by Oliver O'Donovan throughout *Resurrection and Moral Order: An Outline for Evangelical Ethics*, 2nd ed. (Grand Rapids, MI: Eerdmans, 1994).

[32]Lewis, *Problem of Pain*, 112.

"[they] shall be like him" (1 Jn 3:2). This must be a reference at minimum to being like him in his moral holiness and to sharing in his visible glory, that is, in his aesthetic holiness. Predestined, called, and justified saints will be glorified (Rom 8:30). First will be those in the intermediate heaven where departed believers in Christ have gone at their death, in what is an anomalous, intermediate, temporary, disembodied state (2 Cor 5:1-10) until the resurrection, when the inner and outer aspects of their being will be reunited. Paul states with assurance in 2 Corinthians 4:14, "We know that the one who raised the Lord Jesus from the dead will also raise us with Jesus and present us with you to himself." This is the heaven where believers still alive at the second coming will also be transported, will see Christ, and will be made like their ascended Lord in his glorified body. All will then occupy the permanent heaven-come-to-earth.

How can the transcendent God dwell forever in this heaven on earth among glorified human persons in Christ? The answer lies in seeing the incarnation of Christ not just as a historical event but as in fact the metaphysical logic of all reality imparted by its Creator. Maximus the Confessor expounds this concept well.[33] For Maximus, all metaphysical concepts are under the umbrella of God's revelation of himself. Maximus insists, "The Word of God, very God, wills that the mystery of his incarnation be actualized always and in all things."[34] This means that the incarnation unveils the *metaphysical logic* of reality and, in particular, the relationship of created and uncreated natures: "Of each being and the whole cosmos, then, the [Logos] disclose[s] the

---

[33]There is a similar pattern of thought in the twentieth-century thought of T. F. Torrance, for whom the incarnation was also a way of seeing, a metaphysic. The relationship between coinherence in the two natures of Christ, then to the persons of the Trinity, and then on to concepts in creation and in science (modern particle theory and quantum theory), as well as the relationship between the theology and science as disciplines, is implicit in Thomas F. Torrance, *The Ground and Grammar of Theology*, The Richard Lectures (Charlottesville: University Press of Virginia, 1980), 174-78, and Torrance, *The Christian Frame of Mind: Reason, Order, and Openness in Theology and Natural Science* (Eugene, OR: Wipf & Stock, 1989), xl.

[34]Maximus, *The Ambigua* 7.22.

beginning and end of God's creative act."[35] Creation participates reciprocally in Christ the Logos because *all* creation is *incarnate* creation.[36] This metaphysical logic is sourced in the *hypostasis* of the Son, in whom two seemingly opposing natures (created and divine) coexist. Since the hypostasis of the Son is *eternally composed* of created nature in union with divine nature—the very definition of the Son's hypostasis—then creation is inevitable; creation is thus the manifestation of what the Son's hypostasis itself is.[37] The concept of the participation of creation and humans in Christ explains the metaphysics and the ability of God to dwell among humans in heaven-come-to-earth.[38]

In recent years, Danish theologian Niels Gregersen has made an emphatic contribution to this notion of the differentiated, unconfused but real union of God and creation (and therefore, by analogy, heaven and earth) through the concept of *deep incarnation*. This makes sense of the future union of heaven and earth. Gregersen expresses his debt to church fathers Athanasius and Gregory of Nyssa for this concept of deep incarnation. He bemoans the fact that the church has, since these thinkers, focused largely on the mechanics of the union of the divine and human natures of Christ, thereby "unintentionally minimizing the connection between Christ and the cosmos."[39] This has led to an "anthropocentric view of God," which he hopes to replace with a more inclusive cosmic perspective.

---

[35] Jordan D. Wood, *The Whole Mystery of Christ: Creation as Incarnation in Maximus Confessor* (Notre Dame, IN: University of Notre Dame Press, 2022), 55. In this section I am indebted to the work of Loewen, "Bringing God Down," 92-95.

[36] Demetrios Harper, *The Analogy of Love: St. Maximus the Confessor and the Foundations of Ethics*, Scholarly Monographs Series 3 (Yonkers, NY: St. Vladimir's Seminary Press, 2019), 61.

[37] See Wood, *Whole Mystery of Christ*, 27-38. As Loewen ("Bringing God Down," 94n18) indicates, Wood speaks to "how hypostasis makes possible the union of two entirely different natures without mixture—this is a problem Neoplatonist participation never fully resolved."

[38] See Wood, *Whole Mystery of Christ*, 34. Maximus's preponderant use of *methexis* for "participation" is interesting since for him, its meaning clearly avoids monism or the blurring of the divine and the human. *Koinōnia* might have been preferable.

[39] Niels H. Gregersen, "Deep Incarnation and the Cosmic Story of Christ," BioLogos, January 9, 2024, https://biologos.org/articles/deep-incarnation-and-the-cosmic-story-of-christ.

The concept of deep incarnation has at its core the idea that the eternal Son of God, the Second Person of the Trinity, who is both the Word (*Logos*) and the Wisdom (*sophia*) of God, was at the incarnation brought into union with ordinary flesh. However, like David Clough, Gregersen emphasizes the reality that the word *flesh* means something more than human flesh, though it includes it. Rather, it is a term that includes "the material conditions of all creaturely existence" so that Christ "ennobled the fate of all biological life forms ('grass' and 'lilies') and experienced the pains of sensitive creatures ('sparrows' and 'foxes') from within." In Gregersen's own words: "Deep Incarnation implies a radical embodiment of the Son of God that reaches into the depths of material and biological existence." The incarnation therefore represents more than just Jesus becoming a "male human person." It includes the fact that in Jesus, "God took part in the entire material universe—around us and within ourselves."[40]

The *depth* aspect relates to all the connections of the incarnate Word with nature. The close connection between the fully divine Christ, who was also fully human, and the material world is suggested, says Gregersen, by his "long genetic heritage" back to the first Adam; by the fact that even the word *Adam* is derived from the Hebrew term *adamah*, creature of the earth; by the fact that his birth is deeply ensconced within the world of the stars, shepherds, and sheep, with microbes from animal saliva as he lay in a manger frequented by cattle, to say nothing of the dusty air he breathed as a newborn. Gregersen affirms that Jesus was "what medical researchers today call a 'holobiont,' a body living in symbiosis and never-ending interaction with non-human micro-organisms such as archaea, bacteria, viruses and fungi." In the act of the incarnation, "God also took on the conditions of vulnerability and mortality of material existence." For in the Son sent "in the likeness of sinful flesh" (Rom 8:3), Gregersen asserts that "God became an earthling, moving from active omnipotence to a creaturely

---

[40]Gregersen, "Deep Incarnation and the Cosmic Story."

life in which he accepts suffering" and is susceptible to death just as "leaves of grass" or "any other animal." In that sense Jesus was "a microcosm of the cosmos at large and took upon himself all the sinful meshwork of social life."[41]

This entrance of the Son in "a deeply personal, biological and even cosmic way," in which "he was resurrected by the power of the Holy Spirit," infers also the continuance of the deep incarnation in the ascension of Jesus, and his bringing to fruition the reconciliation of all things in the age to come.[42]

CONSEQUENCES FOR THE CHRISTIAN

Cosmologically speaking, given that Hebrews seems to depict the notion that all is sacred space, what does Christ's ascension and high priesthood mean for heavenly and earthly existence and for the wellbeing and future of humanity? For one thing, our invitation to sit with Christ on his throne and Christ's sitting on the Father's throne are bound up together. There is an inseparable connection between the ascension for Jesus and its meaning for us, between where he goes and where we follow (now and when we die or are taken up). In this event of the ascension, as Orthodox theologian Patrick Reardon states, "Heaven and earth are joined forever. . . . The place on earth where heaven and earth meet is called the Church, which finds her identity in the exaltation of Christ. The mystery of the Ascension leads immediately to the mystery of the Church."[43]

In an earlier chapter on the atonement, when I considered the purification of heaven, which the atonement of Christ effects, the primary focus of that purification was on the priestly ministry of the people of God on earth, accessing heaven through prayer and worship. While Farrow includes this purification, he also speaks of the purification of the people of God as they access heaven when they die

---

[41] Gregersen, "Deep Incarnation and the Cosmic Story."
[42] Gregersen, "Deep Incarnation and the Cosmic Story."
[43] Patrick H. Reardon, *Christ in the Psalms* (Ben Lomond, CA: Conciliar, 2000), 91-92.

or are transported to heaven, including the purification of Enoch and Elijah. But he also includes the purification of the angelic host, among whom there had been rebellion before that on earth. Thus, he asserts that the harrowing of hell had an accompanying parallel in heaven. Not just the world but "the place from which the world is ruled" is "set to rights," he thinks.[44] Whereas the self-offering of Christ as he enters heaven has varied responses on earth, in heaven, "it puts an end to sin and comes to glory, *unadulterated glory*. It restores paradise as the seed of the new creation. It generates the church and sends it forth into the world."[45] Irrespective of what one makes of this (it does seem strange to think of heavenly angels as needing cleansing, since they were the angels who did not fall), Farrow's description of the close relationship between heaven and earth now as a result of the ascension, and his anticipation of the removal of that distinction at the parousia, is full of uplifting truth:

> Christ's appearance in heaven also makes heavenly things accessible on earth, even to the least of his brethren. . . . The churches . . . have access to the things of the Spirit. They have access to the heaven that orders earthly affairs. . . . All this may be partial and provisional, transitional, and hence sacramental, mysterious, and not altogether a trouble, but it is nonetheless real and effective.[46]

Farrow quotes the words of Jesus to Peter as evidence of the permeable nature of the boundary between heaven and earth: "Whatever you bind on earth will be bound in heaven, and whatever you loose on earth will be loosed in heaven" (Mt 16:19). His summation is a fitting end to this chapter:

> So if there remains until the *parousia* a profound distinction between earth and heaven, a distinction more wonderful and more terrifying than ever it was, that distinction is already redundant now that Christ

---

[44]Farrow, *Ascension Theology*, 124-25.
[45]Farrow, *Ascension Theology*, 125, emphasis added.
[46]Farrow, *Ascension Theology*, 126-27.

has entered heaven. To say, "heaven is not earth" is to speak of what was, not of what will be, which leads us to think also of the glorification of earthly things and of man himself.[47]

The third verse of Charles Wesley's hymn "Hail the Day That Sees Him Rise" seems appropriate:

> Highest heaven its Lord receives, alleluia!
> yet he loves the earth he leaves; alleluia!
> though returning to his throne, alleluia!
> *still he calls the world his own.* Alleluia![48]

---

[47] Farrow, *Ascension Theology*, 127.
[48] Charles Wesley, "Hail the Day That Sees Him Rise," Hymnary.org, accessed June 21, 2024, https://hymnary.org/hymn/CP1998/247, emphasis added.

CONCLUSION

In summing up this study, it seems appropriate to say that the ascension of Jesus the Son of God is fulfillment, fulfillment of glory. The significance of the ascension goes all the way *backward* to the eternal covenanting communion of God, in which it was decreed that the Son in the eternal three would become human and bring his representative humanity into the glorious being of God. The ascension was also in the history of Jesus the bookend to his incarnation, where he emptied himself of visible glory. After his suffering for us, at the ascension he recovered that glory and further glorified his Father, thereby receiving the glory of his redemptive accomplishments from his Father. And by that ascension was accomplished all of God's intent for his created image-bearers in the last Adam, who now reign with him as an ecclesial community of king-priests and seek to fulfill his mission to the world in the power of the Spirit of glory.

Prospectively, the ascension also led to the coronation of the King-Priest, the glorious celebration of the glory of his accomplished atonement and then the beginning of his unfinished intercessory ministry, bringing "many sons and daughters to glory" (Heb 2:10). *Prospectively*, looking even further ahead, the ascension signaled the fulfillment of the ages in the second coming of Christ (Acts 1:11), that is, his coming in glory. Then shall the whole cosmos be "filled with the knowledge of the glory of the Lord as the waters cover the sea" (Hab 2:14). God has glorified himself in the glory of the ascension of his Son, and all in the Son participate in that glory and are committed to sharing it.

In the words of this hymn written by Thomas Kelly (1769–1854):

GLORY, glory everlasting
Be to Him who bore the cross,
Who redeemed our souls by tasting
Death, the death deserved by us!
Spread His glory
Who redeemed His people thus.[1]

---

[1] Thomas Kelly, "Sing His Glory," Hymnary.org, accessed January 15, 2025, https://hymnary.org/text/glory_glory_everlasting_be_to_him.

ACKNOWLEDGMENTS

A NUMBER OF KIND AND COMPETENT PEOPLE have assisted me on this ascension journey. The first is my wife, Tammy, who is a constant and patient encourager to both my writing and to the diversions needed from the intensity of the writer's life. Grandchildren have also brought joy of a surprising nature in this season. I am also grateful to Regent College and the board of governors for the freedom to have a sabbatical during which this book has been written. Discussions on this subject with my theology colleague at Regent Jens Zimmermann have been enlightening and beneficial, and in particular his resonance with christological centeredness. Discussions with Brittany Melton on the presence/absence dynamic of the Eucharist have also been helpful. My former teaching assistant and friend, Jacob Raju, pursuing his PhD at Wheaton, has provided excellent editorial support as well as contributing to the discussion of the theology of the Eucharist. I am grateful to my present teaching assistant, Daniel Choi, for his editorial and bibliographical work. The work of the renowned St Andrews New Testament scholar, David Moffitt, has greatly stimulated and shaped my own work. Some slight differences of emphasis should not detract from the competence and insight of David's work and my great respect for him. Tyler Loewen's work on Maximus and Matt Crocker's on Bavinck have been helpful also. I am grateful also for the excellent editorial work of Zachary Gordon at IVP Academic, as well as the initial guidance of Jon Boyd and Colton Bernasol. I appreciate also the good work of the copyeditor at IVP, Claire Brubaker.

BIBLIOGRAPHY

Athanasius. "Four Discourses Against the Arians." *NPNF*² 4:301-447.

———. *The Incarnation of the Word*. Christian Classics Ethereal Library. www.ccel.org/ccel/athanasius/incarnation.iv.html.

Atkins, Peter. *Ascension Now: Implications of Christ's Ascension for Today's Church*. Collegeville, MN: Liturgical Press, 2001.

Augustine. *The City of God Against the Pagans*. Translated by Robert W. Dyson. Cambridge: Cambridge University Press, 1998.

———. *The Confessions and Letters of St. Augustin, with a Sketch of His Life and Work*. *NPNF*¹ 1.

Balthasar, Hans Urs von. *The Glory of the Lord: A Theological Aesthetics*. Edited by Joseph Fessio and John Riches. Translated by Erasmo Leiva-Merikakis. 7 vols. San Francisco: Ignatius, 1962.

Barron, Robert. *The Priority of Christ: Toward a Postliberal Catholicism*. Grand Rapids, MI: Baker, 2010.

Barth, Karl. *Church Dogmatics*. Edited by G. W. Bromiley and Thomas F. Torrance. Translated by G. W. Bromiley. 13 vols. in 4 parts. London: T&T Clark, 2009.

———. *The Doctrine of God*. Edited by Thomas F. Torrance and Geoffrey W. Bromiley. Translated by T. H. L. Parker, William B. Johnston, and J. L. M. Haire. Edinburgh: T&T Clark, 1957.

Bavinck, Herman. *Reformed Dogmatics*. Vol. 2, *God and Creation*. Edited by John Bolt. Translated by John Vriend. Grand Rapids, MI: Baker, 2003.

Berkhof, Louis. *Systematic Theology*. Louisville, KY: GLH, 2017.

Billings, J. Todd. *Calvin, Participation, and the Gift: The Activity of Believers in Union with Christ*. Changing Paradigms in Historical and Systematic Theology. Oxford: Oxford University Press, 2007.

Bliss, P. B. "'Man of Sorrows,' What a Name." Hymnary.org, accessed July 4, 2024. https://hymnary.org/text/man_of_sorrows_what_a_name.

Blowers, Paul M. "Maximus the Confessor, Gregory of Nyssa, and the Concept of 'Perpetual Progress.'" *Vigiliae Christianae* 46, no. 2 (June 1992): 151-71.

Bonhoeffer, Dietrich. *Sanctorum Communio: A Theological Study of the Sociology of the Church*. Dietrich Bonhoeffer Works 1. Minneapolis: Fortress, 1998.

Boobyer, G. H. *St. Mark and the Transfiguration Story*. Edinburgh: T&T Clark, 1942.
Brooks, David. *The Road to Character*. New York: Random House, 2015.
Bruce, Alexander B. *The Epistle to the Hebrews: The First Apology for Christianity*. Edinburgh: T&T Clark, 1899.
Bulgakov, Sergeï N. *The Comforter*. Grand Rapids, MI: Eerdmans, 2004.
Calvin, John. *Calvin's Commentaries*. Grand Rapids, MI: Baker, 1979.
———. *Commentary on the Gospel According to John*. Translated by William Pringle. Calvin's Commentaries 2. Grand Rapids, MI: Baker, 1979.
———. *The Epistle of Paul the Apostle to the Corinthians*. Translated by John Pringle. Calvin's Commentaries 20. Grand Rapids, MI: Baker, 2003.
———. *Institutes of the Christian Religion*. Edited by John T. McNeill. Translated by Ford L. Battles. 2 vols. Louisville, KY: Westminster John Knox, 2001.
Canlis, Julie. *Calvin's Ladder: A Spiritual Theology of Ascent and Ascension*. Grand Rapids, MI: Eerdmans, 2010.
Cantalamessa, Raniero. *Come Creator Spirit: Meditations on the Veni Creator*. Collegeville, MN: Liturgical Press, 2003.
Cary, Phillip. "Barth Wars." *First Things*, April 1, 2015. www.firstthings.com/article/2015/04/barth-wars.
Cerbus, Laura. "The Beauty of the Body and the Ascension: A Reclamation and Subversion of Physical Beauty." *SJT* 77 (2024): 1-11.
Chadwick, Henry. *Augustine of Hippo: A Life*. Oxford: Oxford University Press, 2009.
Clough, David. *On Animals*. London: T&T Clark, 2014.
Cohick, Lynn. *Philippians*. Story of God Bible Commentary. Grand Rapids, MI: Zondervan Academic, 2013.
Coutras, Lisa. *Tolkien's Theology of Beauty: Majesty, Splendor, and Transcendence in Middle-Earth*. New York: Palgrave Macmillan, 2016.
Dabney, Robert L. *Systematic Theology*. 2nd ed. Edinburgh: Banner of Truth, 1985.
Davidson, Richard M. "The Eschatological Hermeneutic of Biblical Typology." *TheoRhēma* 6, no. 2 (2011): 5-48.
Davies, John G. *He Ascended into Heaven: A Study in the History of Doctrine*. Bampton Lectures. London: Lutterworth, 1958.
Davis, Ellen F., and Richard B. Hays, eds. *The Art of Reading Scripture*. Grand Rapids, MI: Eerdmans, 2003.
Davison, Andrew. *Participation in God: A Study in Christian Doctrine and Metaphysics*. Cambridge: Cambridge University Press, 2020.
Dawson, Gerrit S. *Jesus Ascended: The Meaning of Christ's Continuing Incarnation*. Phillipsburg, NJ: P&R, 2004.
———. "Recovering the Ascension for the Transformation of the Church." *Theology Matters* 7, no. 2 (2001): 1-8.

Dennison, James T., ed. *Reformed Confessions of the Sixteenth and Seventeenth Centuries in English Translation*. Vol. 2. Grand Rapids, MI: Reformation Heritage, 2008.

Doughty, Thomas G. *Supralapsarian Christology and the Progressive Work of Christ: Christus Dominus*. Lanham, MD: Lexington, 2024.

Durand, Emmanuel. "The Trinitarian Being of God Revealed as Act and Event: Contrasting Interpretations of Karl Barth's Renewed Ontology." In *Les Réalisations du Renouveau Trinitaire au Xxe Siècle*, edited by Emmanuel Durand and Vincent Holzer, 31-55. Paris: Cerf, 2010.

Eberhart, Christian. *The Sacrifice of Jesus: Understanding Atonement Biblically*. Eugene, OR: Wipf & Stock, 2018.

Edwards, Jonathan. "Concerning the End for Which God Created the World." *WJE* 8:403-526.

———. "God Glorified in Man's Dependence." *WJE* 17:196-216.

———. "Heaven Is a World of Love." In *The Sermons of Jonathan Edwards: A Reader*, edited by Wilson H. Kimnach, Kenneth P. Minkema, and Douglas A. Sweeney, 242-72. New Haven, CT: Yale University Press, 1999.

———. "Miscellany 117." *WJE* 13:283.

———. "Observations." In *Treatise on Grace: And Other Posthumously Published Writings*, edited by Paul Helm, 77-98. Bristol: Lutterworth, 2022.

———. *The Philosophy of Jonathan Edwards from His Private Notebooks*. Eugene: University of Oregon Press, 1955.

———. "Treatise on Grace." In *Treatise on Grace: And Other Posthumously Published Writings*, edited by Paul Helm, 77-98. Bristol: Lutterworth, 2022.

Ellingworth, Paul. "Jesus and the Universe in Hebrews." *Evangelical Quarterly* 58, no. 4 (January 1986): 337-50.

Farrow, Douglas. *Ascension and Ecclesia: On the Significance of the Doctrine of the Ascension for Ecclesiology and Christian Cosmology*. Grand Rapids, MI: Eerdmans, 1999.

———. *Ascension Theology*. London: T&T Clark, 2011.

———. "Confessing Christ Coming." In *Nicene Christianity: The Future for a New Ecumenism*, edited by Christopher R. Seitz, 133-48. Grand Rapids, MI: Brazos, 2001.

Ferguson, Thomas C. K. "The Rule of Truth and Irenaean Rhetoric in Book 1 of Against Heresies." *Vigiliae Christianae* 55, no. 4 (2001): 356-75.

Fergusson, David. "The Ascension of Christ: Its Significance in the Theology of T. F. Torrance." *Participatio* 3 (2012): 92-107.

———. "He Ascended into Heaven: The Ascension and Agency of Christ in the Theology of T. F. Torrance." In *What Is Jesus Doing? God's Activity in the Life and Work of the Church*, 27-46. Downers Grove, IL: IVP Academic, 2020.

Ford, David S. *Self and Salvation*. Cambridge: Cambridge University Press, 1999.

Frei, Hans W. *The Eclipse of Biblical Narrative: A Study in Eighteenth and Nineteenth Century Hermeneutics*. New Haven, CT: Yale University Press, 1974.

Gavrilyuk, Paul L. "The Retrieval of Deification: How a Once-Despised Archaism Became an Ecumenical Desideratum." *Modern Theology* 25, no. 4 (2009): 647-59.

Gill, John. *Exposition of the Entire Bible: New Testament*. Springfield, MO: Particular Baptist Press, 2003.

Gorman, Michael J. "A 'Seamless Garment' Approach to Biblical Interpretation?" *JTI* 1, no. 1 (2007): 117-28.

Green, Joel B. "The (Re-)Turn to Theology." *JTI* 1, no. 1 (2007): 1-3.

Gregersen, Niels H. "Deep Incarnation and the Cosmic Story of Christ." BioLogos, January 9, 2024. https://biologos.org/articles/deep-incarnation-and-the-cosmic-story-of-christ.

Gregory of Nazianzus. *On God and Christ: The Five Theological Orations and Two Letters to Cledonius*. Popular Patristics Series. Crestwood, NY: St. Vladimir's Seminary Press, 2002.

Gregory, Brad S. *The Unintended Reformation: How a Religious Revolution Secularized Society*. Cambridge, MA: Harvard University Press, 2012.

Guthrie, George H. *The Structure of Hebrews: A Text-Linguistic Analysis*. Supplements to Novum Testamentum 73. Leiden: Brill, 1994.

Habets, Myk. *Theosis in the Theology of Thomas Torrance*. Farnham, UK: Ashgate, 2009.

Haenchen, Ernst. *The Acts of the Apostles: A Commentary*. Translated by Bernard Noble, Gerald H. Shinn, and Robert M. Wilson. Louisville, KY: Westminster John Knox, 1971.

Hallonsten, Gösta. "Theosis in Recent Research: A Renewal of Interest and a Need for Clarity." In *Partakers of the Divine Nature: The History and Development of Deification in the Christian Traditions*, edited by Michael J. Christensen and Jeffery A. Wittung, 281-93. Grand Rapids, MI: Baker Academic, 2008.

Harper, Demetrios. *The Analogy of Love: St. Maximus the Confessor and the Foundations of Ethics*. Scholarly Monographs Series 3. Yonkers, NY: St. Vladimir's Seminary Press, 2019.

Hart, David Bentley. *The Beauty of the Infinite: The Aesthetics of Christian Truth*. Grand Rapids, MI: Eerdmans, 2003.

———. "The Hidden and the Manifest." In *Orthodox Readings of Augustine*, edited by George E. Demacopoulos and Aristotle Papanikolaou, 191-226. Crestwood, NY: St. Vladimir's Seminary Press, 2008.

Hastings, W. Ross. *Echoes of Coinherence: Trinitarian Theology and Science Together*. Eugene, OR: Cascade, 2017.

———. "The Gospel Orientation of God in Karl Barth's Exposition of the Lord's Prayer." *Crux* 59, no. 1 (2023): 10-32.

———. *Jonathan Edwards and the Life of God: Toward an Evangelical Theology of Participation*. Minneapolis: Fortress, 2015.

———. *Pastoral Ethics: Moral Formation as Life in the Trinity*. Bellingham, WA: Lexham Academic, 2022.

———. *The Resurrection of Jesus Christ: Exploring Its Theological Significance and Ongoing Relevance*. Grand Rapids, MI: Baker Academic, 2022.

———. "Review of *Rethinking the Atonement: New Perspectives on Jesus's Death, Resurrection and Ascension*." *International Journal of Systematic Theology* 26, no. 1 (January 2024): 131-34.

———. *Theological Ethics: The Moral Life of the Gospel in Contemporary Context*. Grand Rapids, MI: Zondervan Academic, 2021.

———. *Total Atonement: Trinitarian Participation in the Reconciliation of Humanity and Creation*. Lanham, MD: Fortress Academic, 2019.

Hay, David M. *Glory at the Right Hand: Psalm 110 in Early Christianity*. Nashville: Abingdon, 1973.

Hays, Richard B. "Reading the Bible with Eyes of Faith: The Practice of Theological Exegesis." *JTI* 1, no. 1 (2007): 5-21.

Holmes, Frank. "A Selection of 'Choice Sayings' of Robert Cleaver Chapman." Plymouth Brethren Writings, accessed June 21, 2024. https://plymouthbrethren.org/article/6376.

Hunsinger, George. "The Bread That We Break: Toward a Chalcedonian Resolution of the Eucharistic Controversies." *The Princeton Seminary Bulletin* 24, no. 2 (2003): 241-58.

———. *The Eucharist and Ecumenism: Let Us Keep the Feast*. Current Issues in Theology. Cambridge: Cambridge University Press, 2008.

———. "The Mediator of Communion: Karl Barth's Doctrine of the Holy Spirit." In *The Cambridge Companion to Karl Barth*, edited by John Webster, 177-94. Cambridge: Cambridge University Press, 2000.

Ignatius. "The Epistle of Ignatius to the Philadelphians." *ANF* 1:79-85.

Irenaeus. *Against Heresies*. *ANF* 1:307-567.

———. *The Demonstration of the Apostolic Preaching*. Translated by J. Armitage Robinson and Iain M. MacKenzie. Burlington, VT: Ashgate, 2002.

Jenson, Robert W. *America's Theologian: A Recommendation of Jonathan Edwards*. New York: Oxford University Press, 1988.

Johnson, Adam, and Tessa Hayashida. "The Spirit of the Atonement: The Role of the Holy Spirit in Christ's Death and Resurrection." *Religions* 13, no. 10 (2022): 1-12.

Johnson, Junius. *The Father of Lights: A Theology of Beauty*. Grand Rapids, MI: Baker Academic, 2020.

Kaethler, Andrew T. J. *The Eschatological Person: Alexander Schmemann and Joseph Ratzinger in Dialogue*. Eugene, OR: Cascade, 2022.

Keating, Daniel A. "Typologies of Deification." *International Journal of Systematic Theology* 17, no. 3 (2015): 267-83.

Keil, C. F., and Franz Delitzsch. *Commentary on the Old Testament: Psalms*. Grand Rapids, MI: Eerdmans, 1971.

Kelly, J. N. D. *Early Christian Doctrines*. 5th ed. London: Adam & Charles Black, 1977.

Kelly, Thomas. "Sing His Glory." Hymnary.org, accessed January 15, 2025. https://hymnary.org/text/glory_glory_everlasting_be_to_him.

Kidner, Derek. *Psalms*. Tyndale Old Testament Commentaries 15. Downers Grove, IL: InterVarsity Press, 2014.

Kramer, Johanna. *Between Earth and Heaven: Liminality and the Ascension of Christ in Anglo-Saxon Literature*. Manchester Medieval Literature and Culture. Manchester: Manchester University Press, 2014.

Laansma, Jon. "Hebrews." In *Cosmology and New Testament Theology*, edited by Jonathan T. Pennington and Sean M. McDonough, 125-43. LNTS 355. London: T&T Clark, 2008.

———. "Hidden Stories in Hebrews: Cosmology and Theology." In *A Cloud of Witnesses: The Theology of Hebrews in Its Ancient Contexts*, edited by Richard Bauckham, Daniel R. Driver, Trevor Hart, and Nathan MacDonald, 9-18. LNTS 387. London: T&T Clark, 2008.

Lane, William L. *Hebrews 9–13*. Word Biblical Commentary 47B. Dallas: Word, 1991.

Lathbury, Mary A. "Break Thou the Bread of Life." Hymnary.org, accessed July 4, 2024. https://hymnary.org/text/break_thou_the_bread_of_life.

Lewis, C. S. *The Problem of Pain*. London: Centenary, 1940.

Liddle, Andrew R., and David H. Lyth. *Cosmological Inflation and Large-Scale Structure*. Cambridge: Cambridge University Press, 2000.

Lincoln, Andrew T. *Paradise Now and Not Yet: Studies in the Role of the Heavenly Dimension in Paul's Thought with Special Reference to His Eschatology*. Cambridge: Cambridge University Press, 1981.

Lindbeck, George A. *The Nature of Doctrine: Religion and Theology in a Postliberal Age*. Philadelphia: Westminster, 1984.

Loewen, Tyler. "Bringing God Down: The Influence and Effects of the Metaphysical Concept of Univocal Being in Jürgen Moltmann's Staurocentric Theology." MA thesis, Regent College, 2024.

Lohfink, Gerhard. *Between Heaven and Earth: New Explorations of Great Biblical Texts*. Translated by Linda M. Maloney. Collegeville, MN: Liturgical, 2022.

Lubac, Henri de. *Paradoxes of Faith*. San Francisco: Ignatius, 1987.

Mannermaa, Tuomo. *Christ Present in Faith: Luther's View of Justification*. Translated by Kirsi I. Stjerna. Minneapolis: Fortress, 2005.

Maximus. *On Difficulties in the Church Fathers: The Ambigua*. Edited and translated by Nicholas Constas. Dumbarton Oaks Medieval Library 28. Cambridge, MA: Harvard University Press, 2014.

McConville, J. Gordon. *Being Human in God's World: An Old Testament Theology of Humanity*. Grand Rapids, MI: Baker Academic, 2016.

McCormack, Bruce L., ed. "The Actuality of God: Karl Barth in Conversation with Open Theism." In *Engaging the Doctrine of God: Contemporary Protestant Perspectives*, 185-244. Grand Rapids, MI: Baker Academic, 2008.

———. "Grace and Being: The Role of God's Gracious Election in Karl Barth's Theological Ontology." In *The Cambridge Companion to Karl Barth*, edited by John Webster, 92-110. Cambridge Companions to Religion. Cambridge: Cambridge University Press, 2000.

———. "The Ontological Presuppositions of Barth's Doctrine of Atonement." In *The Glory of the Atonement: Biblical, Theological and Practical Perspectives*, edited by Charles E. Hill and Frank A. James, 346-66. Downers Grove, IL: InterVarsity Press, 2004.

———. "With Loud Cries and Tears: The Humanity of the Son in the Epistle to the Hebrews." In *The Epistle to the Hebrews and Christian Theology*, edited by Richard Bauckham, Daniel R. Driver, Trevor A. Hart, and Nathan MacDonald, 37-68. Grand Rapids, MI: Eerdmans, 2009.

McGrath, Alister E. *T. F. Torrance: An Intellectual Biography*. Edinburgh: T&T Clark, 2006.

McKirland, Christa L. "The Image of God and Intersex Persons." Paper presented at Logos Institute, St. Mary's College, University of St. Andrews, October 12, 2016.

Melton, Brittany N. *Where Is God in the Megilloth? A Dialogue on the Ambiguity of Divine Presence and Absence*. Oudtestamentische Studiën 73. Leiden: Brill, 2018.

Melton, Brittany N., and Megan D. Alsene-Parker. "Lamenting Placelessness: The Deconstruction of People and Place in Lamentations." Paper presented at Society of Biblical Literature annual meeting, San Diego, CA, November 26, 2024.

Milbank, John. "The Second Difference: For a Trinitarianism Without Reserve." *Modern Theology* 2, no. 3 (1986): 213-34.

Moberly, R. W. L. "What Is Theological Interpretation of Scripture?" *JTI* 3, no. 2 (2009): 161-78.

Moffitt, David M. *Atonement and the Logic of Resurrection in the Epistle to the Hebrews*. Leiden: Brill, 2011.

———. "Hebrews and the Atonement." In *The Oxford Handbook of Hebrews and the Catholic Epistles*, edited by P. Gray, 197-214. Oxford: Oxford University Press, 2024.

———. *Rethinking the Atonement: New Perspectives on Jesus's Death, Resurrection, and Ascension*. Grand Rapids, MI: Baker Academic, 2022.

Molnar, Paul D. "Resurrection and the Atonement in the Theology of Thomas F. Torrance." In *T&T Clark Companion to Atonement*, edited by Adam J. Johnson, 52-76. Bloomsbury Companions 5. London: T&T Clark, 2017.

———. "Thomas F. Torrance and the Problem of Universalism." *SJT* 68, no. 2 (2015): 164-86.

Moltmann, Jürgen. *Theology of Hope: On the Ground and the Implications of a Christian Eschatology*. Philadelphia: Fortress, 1993.

Morales, L. Michael. *Who Shall Ascend the Mountain of the Lord? A Biblical Theology of the Book of Leviticus*. Downers Grove, IL: IVP Academic, 2015.

Mowinckel, Sigmund. *Psalmenstudien III. Die Kultprophetie und Prophetische Psalmen*. Kristiania: Jacob Dybwad, 1923.

Muller, Richard A. *Calvin and the Reformed Tradition: On the Work of Christ and the Order of Salvation*. Grand Rapids, MI: Baker Academic, 2012.

Murray, Andrew. *The Holiest of All: An Exposition of the Epistle to the Hebrews*. London: Nisbet, 1949.

Neder, Adam. *Participation in Christ: An Entry into Karl Barth's Church Dogmatics*. Louisville, KY: Westminster John Knox, 2009.

Nee, Watchman. *The Christian*. Collected Works 1/6. Anaheim, CA: Living Stream Ministries, 1975.

Nevin, John Williamson. *The Mystical Presence, and Other Writings on the Eucharist*. Lancaster Series on the Mercersburg Theology 4. Philadelphia: United Church, 1966.

"O Lord Most High, Eternal King." Hymn 245 in *Common Praise*. Toronto: Anglican Church of Canada, 1998.

O'Collins, Gerald. *Jesus Our Priest: A Christian Approach to the Priesthood of Christ*. New York: Oxford University Press, 2010.

O'Donovan, Oliver. *On the Thirty Nine Articles: A Conversation with Tudor Christianity*. A Latimer Monograph. Exeter, UK: Paternoster, 1986.

———. *Resurrection and Moral Order: An Outline for Evangelical Ethics*. 2nd ed. Grand Rapids, MI: Eerdmans, 1994.

———. *The Ways of Judgment*. Grand Rapids, MI: Eerdmans, 2005.

Oduyoye, Mercy A. *Hearing and Knowing: Theological Reflections on Christianity in Africa*. Ossining, NY: Orbis, 1986.

Parker, Brent E. "The Differences Between Typology and Allegory." *Christ over All* (blog), September 7, 2023. https://christoverall.com/article/concise/the-differences-between-typology-and-allegory/.

Parry, Robin A. *Worshipping Trinity: Coming Back to the Heart of Worship*. Carlisle, UK: Paternoster, 2005.

Pickstock, Catherine. "Duns Scotus: His Historical and Contemporary Significance." In *The Radical Orthodoxy Reader*, edited by Simon Oliver and John Milbank, 543-74. London: Routledge, 2009.

"The Prayer of St. John Chrysostom." In *The Book of Common Prayer*, by Anglican Church in North America, 26. Huntington Beach, CA, Anglican Liturgy Press, 2019.

Raju, Jacob Samuel. "The Word Became Flesh and Dwelt Among Us: An Investigation into the Lutheran-Reformed Christological Debates on The Extra Calvinisticum." ThM thesis, Regent College, 2022.

Rakestraw, Robert V. "Becoming Like God: An Evangelical Doctrine of Theosis." *Journal of the Evangelical Theological Society* 40, no. 2 (January 1997): 257-69.

Reardon, Patrick H. *Christ in the Psalms*. Ben Lomond, CA: Conciliar, 2000.

Redding, Graham. *Prayer and the Priesthood of Christ in the Reformed Tradition*. London: T&T Clark, 2003.

Robbins, Howard C. "Hymn 248: And Have the Bright Immensities Received." In *Common Praise*, 248. Toronto: Morehouse, 1998.

Robinson, J. Armitage. "Hymn 281: 'Tis Good Lord to Be Here." https://hymnary.org/hymn/AM2013/281.

Russell, Norman. *The Doctrine of Deification in the Greek Patristic Tradition*. Oxford Early Christian Studies. Oxford: Oxford University Press, 2004.

Schaff, Philip, and Henry Wace, eds. *The Seven Ecumenical Councils*. NPNF^2 14.

Schreiner, Patrick. *The Ascension of Christ: Recovering a Neglected Doctrine*. Bellingham, WA: Lexham, 2020.

Seamands, Stephen A. *Give Them Christ: Preaching His Incarnation, Crucifixion, Resurrection, Ascension, and Return*. Downers Grove, IL: InterVarsity Press, 2012.

Shedd, William G. T. *Dogmatic Theology*. 3rd ed. Edited by Alan W. Gomes. Phillipsburg, NJ: P&R, 2003.

Sherman, Robert. *King, Priest, and Prophet: A Trinitarian Theology of Atonement*. New York: T&T Clark, 2004.

Simpson, Albert B. *The Christ of the Forty Days*. New York: Christian Alliance, 1868.

Smail, Thomas. *The Giving Gift: The Holy Spirit in Person*. Eugene, OR: Wipf & Stock, 2004.

Smit, Laura. "'The Depth Behind Things': Toward a Calvinist Sacramental Theology." In *Radical Orthodoxy and the Reformed Tradition: Creation, Covenant, and Participation*, edited by James K. A. Smith and James H. Olthuis, 205-27. Grand Rapids, MI: Baker Academic, 2005.

Spurgeon, Charles H. "Amidst Us Our Beloved Stands." Hymnary.org, accessed July 18, 2024. https://hymnary.org/text/amidst_us_our_beloved_stands.

———. "The Only Atoning Priest." Sermon, February 4, 1872. www.spurgeon.org/resource-library/sermons/the-only-atoning-priest/#flipbook/.

Stennett, Samuel. "Majestic Sweetness Sits Enthroned." Hymnary.org, accessed July 19, 2024. https://hymnary.org/text/majestic_sweetness_sits_enthroned.

Stott, John R. W. *Acts: Seeing the Spirit at Work*. Downers Grove, IL: InterVarsity Press, 2008.

Strobel, Kyle. *Jonathan Edwards's Theology: A Reinterpretation*. T&T Clark Studies in Systematic Theology 19. London: Bloomsbury, 2013.

Stroman, John. *Ashes to Ascension*. Cycle B ed. Lima, OH: CSS, 1999.

Tanner, Kathryn. *Christ the Key*. Current Issues in Theology. Cambridge: Cambridge University Press, 2010.

Tertullian. *On the Resurrection of the Flesh*. Christian Classics Ethereal Library. https://www.ccel.org/ccel/schaff/anf03/anf03.i.html.

Thomasius, Gottfried. "Christ's Person and Work. Part II: The Person of the Mediator." In *God and Incarnation in Mid-nineteenth Century German Theology*, edited by Claude Welch, 31-101. A Library of Protestant Thought. New York: Oxford University Press, 1965.

Thompson, Centra. "Gazing on Thee, Lord, in Glory." Hymnary.org, accessed June 25, 2024. https://hymnary.org/hymn/CHoF1944/271.

Toon, Peter. *Heaven and Hell: A Biblical and Theological Overview*. Nelson Studies in Biblical Theology. Nashville: Nelson, 1986.

Torrance, Alan J. *Persons in Communion: An Essay on Trinitarian Description and Human Participation*. Edinburgh: T&T Clark, 1996.

Torrance, James. *Worship, Community and the Triune God of Grace*. Didsbury Lectures 1994. Downers Grove, IL: InterVarsity Press, 1996.

Torrance, Thomas F. "The Ascension and Parousia of Jesus Christ." In *Atonement: The Person and Work of Christ*, 265-314. Downers Grove, IL: IVP Academic, 2009.

———. *Atonement: The Person and Work of Christ*. Downers Grove, IL: IVP Academic, 2009.

———. *The Christian Frame of Mind: Reason, Order, and Openness in Theology and Natural Science*. Eugene, OR: Wipf & Stock, 1989.

———. *The Ground and Grammar of Theology*. The Richard Lectures. Charlottesville: University Press of Virginia, 1980.

———. "Karl Barth and the Latin Heresy." *SJT* 39, no. 4 (January 1986): 461-82.

———. *A Passion for Christ: The Vision That Ignites Ministry*. Lenoir: PLC, 1999.

———. *Royal Priesthood*. Edinburgh: Oliver & Boyd, 1955.

———. *Scottish Theology: From John Knox to John Mcleod Campbell*. Edinburgh: T&T Clark, 1996.

———. *Space, Time, and Resurrection*. Grand Rapids, MI: Eerdmans, 1976.

———. *Theology in Reconciliation: Essays Towards Evangelical and Catholic Unity in East and West*. Eugene, OR: Wipf & Stock, 1996.

———. "Universalism or Election?" *SJT* 2, no. 3 (September 1949): 310-18.

Treier, Daniel J. "Biblical Theology and/or Theological Interpretation of Scripture?" *SJT* 61, no. 1 (March 2008): 16-31.

Tupper, E. F. *The Theology of Wolfhart Pannenberg*. London: SCM Press, 1974.
Vanhoozer, Kevin J. "What Is Theological Interpretation of the Bible?" In *Dictionary for Theological Interpretation of the Bible*, edited by Kevin J. Vanhoozer, 19-25. Grand Rapids, MI: Baker Academic, 2005.
von Allmen, Jean-Jacques. *Worship: Its Theology and Practice*. New York: Oxford University Press, 1965.
Walton, Steve. "'The Heavens Opened': Cosmological and Theological Transformation in Luke and Acts." In *Cosmology and New Testament Theology*, edited by Jonathan T. Pennington and Sean M. McDonough, 60-73. LNTS 355. London: T&T Clark, 2008.
Watson, Francis. "Theological Hermeneutics." In *Text, Church, and World: Biblical Interpretation in Theological Perspective*, edited by Francis Watson, 223-40. Edinburgh: T&T Clark, 1994.
Webster, John B. "The Identity of the Holy Spirit: A Problem in Trinitarian Theology." *Themelios* 9, no. 1 (January 1983): 4-7.
Weinandy, Thomas G. *Does God Suffer?* Notre Dame, IN: University of Notre Dame Press, 2000.
Wesley, Charles. "Hail the Day That Sees Him Rise." Hymnary.org, accessed June 21, 2024. https://hymnary.org/hymn/CP1998/247.
———. "Hark! The Herald Angels Sing." Hymnary.org, accessed June 24, 2024. https://hymnary.org/text/hark_the_herald_angels_sing_glory_to.
Witvliet, John D. "The Doctrine of the Trinity and the Theology and Practice of Christian Worship in the Reformed Tradition." PhD diss., University of Notre Dame, 1997.
Wolterstorff, Nicholas. "A Discussion of Oliver O'Donovan's *The Desire of the Nations*." *SJT* 54, no. 1 (March 2001): 87-109.
Wood, Jordan D. *The Whole Mystery of Christ: Creation as Incarnation in Maximus Confessor*. Notre Dame, IN: University of Notre Dame Press, 2022.
Wright, N. T. *Surprised by Hope: Rethinking Heaven, the Resurrection, and the Mission of the Church*. New York: HarperOne, 2008.
Wunrow, Stephen C. "Passing Through the Heavens: Heavenly Space in Hebrews and Its Jewish and Christian Environment." PhD diss., Wheaton College, 2023.
Zimmermann, Jens. *Recovering Theological Hermeneutics: An Incarnational-Trinitarian Theory of Interpretation*. Grand Rapids, MI: Baker Academic, 2004.
Zinzendorf, Nikolaus Ludwig von. "Jesus, Thy Blood and Righteousness." Translated by John Wesley. Hymn 371, Lutheran Hymnal, St. Louis, Concordia, 1941. https://www.ccel.org/a/anonymous/luth_hymnal/tlh371.htm.
Zizioulas, John D. "The Doctrine of the Holy Trinity: The Significance of the Cappadocian Contribution." In *Trinitarian Theology Today: Essays on Divine Being and Act*, edited by Christoph Schwöbel, 44-59. Edinburgh: T&T Clark, 1995.

GENERAL INDEX

access to God, 6, 8, 9, 10, 11, 112, 120, 128, 166, 172, 183, 187, 188-89, 219, 232, 238, 240, 251, 252
Alsene-Parker, Megan, 139
Anderson, Jonathan, 33-34
Aquinas, Thomas, 35, 166
Anselm, 35, 166
assurance of salvation, 2, 10, 113, 115, 179-80, 185
Athanasius, 35, 66-67, 69, 155, 221, 249
Atkins, Peter, 16, 68
atonement, 1, 7, 8, 9, 28, 43, 92, 102-29, 152-92
baptism, 176
Barth, Karl, 14, 17, 20, 30, 35, 39, 68-70, 121, 123, 146-47, 156, 171, 175 196, 201, 210, 217, 228
Bavinck, Herman, 219-21
Baxter, R, 35
beatific vision, 12, 74, 141, 168, 185, 209, 232, 237
beauty, 21-25, 105, 143, 200, 243-45
Billings, J. Todd, 116
Blowers, Paul M., 143
Bonhoeffer, Dietrich, 35, 156
Bruce, Alexander B., 127-28
Bultmann, R, 17
Calvin, John, 8-9, 35, 62, 88, 112, 116-17, 139, 159, 170, 184, 190-92, 195-201, 217, 228
Campbell, John McLeod, 156, 203
Canlis, Julie, 116-17, 190-92
Cerbus, Laura, 23
Chalcedon, 9, 25, 196, 198
Chapman, R. C., 56
Chrysostom, John, 70
church, ecclesiology, 8, 21, 25, 26, 31, 44, 193-204
Clough, David, 247, 250
coinherence, 25, 31, 44, 62, 64, 86-87, 100, 135, 142, 168, 170-74, 183, 197, 207, 215, 218, 248
comfort of the High Priest, 1, 9, 26, 45, 55, 86, 122, 124-129, 172,
concursus, 178
confession of sin, 10-11, 45, 115-23, 159-60, 165, 167
communicatio idiomatum, 31, 196
cosmology, 13-16, 26, 27, 32, 44-45, 91-92, 214, 216, 222-25, 228-29, 234
creation, new creation, 6, 10, 13, 25, 27, 43, 45, 82-83, 85, 88-89, 91, 93-98, 111, 131, 133, 137-38, 142-44, 148, 153, 161, 163, 183, 200, 202, 210-11, 213-14, 220, 222-25, 229-31, 233-36, 241, 243, 247-49, 252
cross of Christ, crucifixion, 13, 18, 28, 42, 64, 66, 71-72, 76, 79, 81, 83-85, 91-92, 100, 106-8, 110-12, 126, 160, 218-19, 225, 235, 245
Davis, Ellen, 40
Davies, John G 8, 14, 15, 16, 22-3, 38, 40, 47-51, 54, 75, 77-78, 181
Dawson, G., 68, 70, 146
death of Christ, 8, 10, 18, 19, 27, 42, 45-46, 48, 66, 69, 71, 75, 77-78, 82, 84, 92, 100, 102-3, 105-6, 112, 116, 118, 123, 131, 141-42, 151, 155-57, 160-63, 169, 171, 177, 182, 184, 187, 218, 224, 233, 246,
deity of Christ, 24, 30, 44, 46-64, 65-68, 77, 87, 96, 109, 118, 126, 179, 191, 196, 238
Doughty, Thomas, 89, 153
earth, earthiness, 11, 13, 26-27, 29, 44-45, 52, 60, 63, 65-66, 85-86, 89-90, 92, 97-98, 102-3, 109, 110-11, 122, 126, 132, 138, 139, 140, 143, 146, 154, 161-62, 170-74, 188, 198, 200, 203, 206-8, 211, 214, 217-18, 221, 223-26, 228-29, 231-32
Edwards, Jonathan, 21-22, 35, 73-74, 143, 168, 174, 185, 240, 245
Ellingworth, Paul, 223-24
embodiment, 24, 130, 138, 250
eschatology, 26-27, 29-30, 31, 44, 205-26
eternal security, 113-115
eucharist, sacraments, 15, 21, 26, 62, 196-204
evangelism, 144-48

Farrow, Douglas, 14, 15, 16, 19, 25, 62, 63, 141-45, 147-48, 152, 161-64, 167-68, 195, 205, 209, 212, 232-36, 240, 241, 251-53
Fergusson, David, 16, 87-88, 99, 160, 218
finished work of Christ, 10
filioque/per filium, 173
Ford, David S., 119
formation, transformation, 115-19, 141-44
Gill, John, 61
Giotto, 33-34
glorification, 12, 144-48, 182
glory, 12, 17, 20-21, 22, 26-33, 37, 43-46, 49-50, 52-53, 55, 57-60, 62-63, 65-78, 80, 85, 89, 90, 92-95, 97, 102-6, 112, 118-19, 123-24, 126, 130, 132, 134-35, 141-43, 144-50, 151-52, 168, 170, 172-85, 187, 191, 193-97, 205-12, 213, 215, 223, 225, 227, 233, 235, 237-46, 248, 252, 255
gnosticism, 11, 29
Gorman, Michael, 41
Green, Joel, 40
Gregersen, Niels H., 249-51
Gregory Nazianzen, 25, 171
Gregory of Nyssa, 143, 249
Guthrie, George, 222
Haenchen, Ernst, 47
Handel, George Frideric, 52
Hart, David Bentley, 143
Hays, Richard, 40
heaven, 9, 11, 12, 13, 227-53
heavenly tabernacle, 9
hermeneutics, interpretation, 36-43
Holy Spirit, pneumatology, 24, 31, 44, 55, 62, 74, 85, 91, 101, 112, 124, 135, 141-42, 149, 161, 167-68, 171-72, 174, 181, 184-86, 189, 197, 199, 200, 207, 215, 217, 227-28, 239, 251
homoousion, 9, 24, 62
humanity of Christ, humans, anthropology, 12, 26, 43, 63, 64, 68, 130-50
Hunsinger, George, 171
image of God, 59, 130-31, 133, 144, 163
incarnation, 27, 30, 65, 162-63, 171, 174, 182, 184, 187, 190, 202, 216, 221, 225, 247-51, 255
Intercession of Christ, 8, 9, 30, 113-29
Ignatius, 42
Irenaeus, 11, 14, 27, 41, 42, 95, 131, 145
Isaacs, Marie, 158
Jenson, Robert, 17, 22
Johnson, Adam, 171
justification, 10, 45, 69, 72, 115-16, 134, 160, 165, 177, 182, 184, 186
Kant, Immanuel, 219-20

kenosis, 66-7
kingdom of God, 1, 12, 26, 44, 81, 83, 85, 90, 134, 136, 140, 142, 154, 172, 189, 205-7, 209, 210-11, 218, 224, 227, 236
Knox, John, 109
Kramer, Johanna, 16
Laansma, Jon, 222-24
Lane, William L., 224
Lewis, C. S. 247
Loewen, Tyler, 230-31, 249
Lubac, Henri de, 162
Luther, Martin, 35, 195-96
Maximus, 30, 31, 143, 152, 190, 248-49
McConville, J. Gordon, 139
McCormack, Bruce, 30
McGrath, Alister E., 66
McKirland, Krista, 131
Melchizedek, 7, 18, 25, 29, 84, 114
Melton, Brittany, 139
Milbank, John, 168-69
mission, 138-40
Moberley, R. W. C., 40
Moffitt, David M., 108-10, 152, 155-58
Moltmann, Jürgen, 35
Morales, Michael, 110
Mowinckel, Sigmund, 78
Murray, Andrew, 188-89
Nee, Watchman, 106
Nevin, John, 199
Nicea, Nicene, 9, 14-15, 36, 185
O'Collins, Gerald, 16
O'Donovan, Oliver, 131, 133-37, 219-22
Oduyoye, Mercy, 63
Owen, John, 35
Pannenberg, Wolfhart, 35
parousia, second coming, 7, 12, 19-20, 25, 30, 31, 32, 44, 60, 68, 75, 80, 85, 93, 144, 155, 181, 205-6, 209-10, 212, 236, 252
Parry, Robin A., 120
participation, 10, 174-92
perichoresis, 173, 185
personhood, 131-34
Pickstock, Catherine, 31
Platonism, 11, 30
political theology, 133-37
prayer, 10, 119-24
prophet, priest and king, *munus triplex*, 1, 6-7, 30, 44, 79-101
purging, purgation, 13
reconciliation, 13, 87-8, 110, 126, 133, 153, 161, 163, 167, 247

regeneration, 12, 24, 130, 169, 171, 174, 183
resurrection of Jesus, 1, 6, 8, 10, 13, 17, 19-20, 22, 27, 32, 35, 42, 45, 47-8, 69, 70, 72, 75, 81, 92, 103, 106, 116, 118, 131-32, 247
sacred space, 13, 44, 92, 111, 158, 160, 251
sanctification, 182, 186
Schreiner, Patrick, 16, 81, 99
science and theology, 25
Seamands, Stephen, 19, 103
sexuality, 138
Simpson, Albert B., 129
Smail, Tom, 174
Smit, Laura 197-98, 200-1
Stott, John, 47
Strobel, Kyle, 74
Stroman, John, 214-15
Tertullian, 70, 146
theosis, deification, divinisation, 12, 69, 132
third article theologians, 185
Thomasius, Gottfried, 66-67
Toon, Peter, 147
Torrance, James, 122
Torrance, T. F., 14, 16, 19, 20, 25, 53, 66, 70, 73, 80-83, 87, 89, 126, 146-47, 156, 201-3, 206, 210, 216-19, 228-29, 248
transfiguration, 22-23, 60, 75-76, 176
Treier, Daniel J., 41
Trinity, 22-24, 61, 74, 173, 192
union of believers with Christ, 31, 187-92
union of Christ, hypostatic union, 25, 171, 183-84
Vanhoozer, Kevin, 40
vicarious life of Christ, 27, 53, 175
virtue, 176-80
von Allmen, Jean-Jacques, 122
Watson, Francis, 40
Walton, Steve, 214
Wesley, Charles, 53
Wolterstorff, Nicholas, 137
Wood, Jordan D., 249
worship, 119-24

SCRIPTURE INDEX

OLD TESTAMENT

Genesis
1, *161*
1–2, *88, 154, 223*
5:22, *49*
5:24, *49, 50*
9:6, *133*
14, *84*
14:18, *7*
14:18-20, *18, 83*
22:9, *157*

Exodus
7:1, *98*
20:24, *157*
28:11, *129*
28:11-12, *129*
28:29, *129*
40:34, *237*

Leviticus
1–7, *159*
1:15, *157*
8:30, *167*
16, *152, 159, 165, 167*
16:16, *166*
16:33, *166*

Numbers
29, *165*

Deuteronomy
6:4, *57*
18:18, *94*
34:10, *98*

2 Samuel
6, *50*
7, *55*

1 Kings
8:11, *237*

2 Kings
1:11-13, *49*
2:11, *50*

Psalms
2, *81*
2:7, *51*
22:1, *108*
22:22, *112*
22:27-28, *113*
24, *50, 81, 208*
24:3-4, *53*
24:5, *53*
24:7, *53*
24:7-12, *53*
24:8, *53*
24:10, *53*
27:4, *243*
45:10-15, *244*
45:11, *244*
47, *50*
49:15, *50*
50:2, *244*
68, *50, 81*
68:16-18, *54*
68:18, *35*
73:24, *50*
89, *55*
96, *224*
110, *50*
110:1, *18, 83, 85*
110:4, *18*
132:5, *242*
132:11, *242*
132:13, *242*
132:18, *242*

Isaiah
6:1, *244*
6:3, *244*
6:5, *244*
9:6-7, *58*
24:23, *237*
40:5, *237*
45:23, *59*
53, *71, 72, 156*
53:2, *244*
53:5, *156*
53:10, *112*
53:10-11, *71*
53:12, *72*
61, *96*
65:17, *223*
66:19, *150*
66:22, *223*

Jeremiah
31:33, *186*

Ezekiel
36:27, *186*

Daniel
7, *28, 57, 58*
7:9, *56, 57*
7:13, *77*
7:13-14, *56*
7:14, *57*

Joel
2, *99*

Habakkuk
2:14, *27, 238, 255*

Zechariah
12:10, *57*

New Testament

Matthew
1:20, *171*
6:5-13, *123*
6:9, *239*
6:11, *123*
8:20, *139*
13:38, *42*
13:44, *42*
16:19, *252*
16:27, *209*
17:5, *60*
22:41-45, *18*
24:30, *104*
26:36-46, *108*
27:46, *108*
28:18-19, *85*
28:18-20, *149*
28:20, *85*

Mark
8:29-31, *78*
8:38, *77*
9:31, *77*
10:33, *77*
10:45, *77*
13:26, *20, 77, 211*
14, *57*
14:21, *77*
14:41, *77*
14:61-62, *78*
14:62, *57, 77*
16:15, *149*

Luke
1:35, *171*
2:14, *65*
3:22, *76*
4:18, *96*
9:26, *211, 241*
9:28-36, *75*
9:29, *181*
9:31, *76, 180*
9:32, *180*
9:35, *76*
9:51, *75, 84, 180*
21:27, *209*
23:34, *108*
23:46, *108*
24, *42*
24:26, *58*
24:26-27, *37*
24:51, *34, 76*

John
1:1-4, *95*
1:14, *60, 111, 236, 247*
2:23-25, *115*
3:14, *84*
5:16-19, *24*
7:39, *172*
8:28, *84, 96*
10:30, *108*
10:38, *13, 24, 108*
12, *71*
12:23, *28, 71*
12:24, *71*
12:27, *71*
12:28, *28, 71*
12:32-33, *84*
13, *115, 159, 167*
14, *239, 241*
14:2, *140, 238*
14:2-3, *154*
14:9, *61*
14:10, *61*
14:12, *61*
14:16, *112*
14:17, *62, 214*
14:18, *215*
14:20, *61, 215*
14:28, *61*
15:26, *112*
16:7, *214*
16:13-14, *185*
16:14-15, *173*
16:28, *61*
17, *239*
17:1, *59*
17:3, *28*
17:4, *242*
17:4-5, *74*
17:5, *65, 68, 242*
17:9, *116*
17:10, *194, 242*
17:22-23, *194*
17:24, *184, 242*
17:26, *239*
20:17, *47, 132, 239*
20:19-23, *47, 99, 149, 172*
20:26-27, *47*
21, *47*

Acts
1, *15, 46, 47, 81, 207, 215, 216*
1:1-3, *142*
1:1-11, *75*
1:2, *34*
1:4, *112, 172*
1:7, *212*
1:9, *34, 154, 215*
1:9-10, *34*
1:10, *21*
1:11, *12, 20, 30, 144, 181, 205, 208, 255*
2, *174*
2:17, *99*
2:17-18, *172*
2:23, *106*
2:32-36, *228*
2:33, *34, 112, 173*
2:36, *79, 149*
3:13, *180, 181*
5:31, *85*
7, *184*
7:55, *181, 184*
13:31, *48*
22:11, *181*

Romans
1:4, *19*
3:24-26, *72*
3:25-26, *116, 166*
5:1, *116*
5:2, *183*
5:4, *184*
6:1, *116*
6:1-11, *157*
6:10, *92*
8:3, *182, 250*
8:11, *142*
8:18, *104, 246*
8:19-21, *131, 143*
8:19-22, *247*
8:21, *225*
8:21-24, *211*
8:26, *189*
8:29-30, *182*
8:30, *30, 248*
13, *134*

1 Corinthians
1:29-31, *73*
1:30, *116*
2:8, *245*
2:9, *245*
3:13, *209*
5:9-13, *208*
8:6, *234*
10:16-17, *21*
11:24, *199*
11:26, *100*
12–14, *173*
12:1-11, *86*
12:3, *173*
12:13, *172*
13:8-10, *240*
15:21-22, *163*
15:26, *246*
15:43, *23*
15:44, *69, 138*
15:48, *69*

2 Corinthians
3, *118, 182*
3:7-18, *141*
3:10, *141*
3:17, *118*
3:17-18, *86, 142, 182*
3:18, *29, 104, 119, 141, 170, 174, 183*
4, *59*
4:4, *59*
4:6, *59, 212*
4:14, *248*
4:17, *246*
5, *209*
5:1-10, *155, 248*
5:8, *209, 232*
5:10, *209*
5:18, *91*
5:21, *163*
13:4, *18*

Galatians
3:28, *133*
5:16, *183*
5:22-23, *179, 183*
5:25, *183*

Ephesians
1, *194*
1:12-14, *171*
1:13-14, *142*
1:19-21, *19, 194*
1:20-21, *183*
1:22, *234*
1:22-23, *195, 213*
2:1, *183*
2:1-7, *142*
2:5-6, *175*
2:6, *9, 10, 20, 24, 26, 154*
2:6-7, *183*
3, *194*
3:14-15, *239*
3:14-21, *10*
3:16, *241*
3:17, *123, 140*
3:17-18, *240*
3:21, *21, 29, 174, 194, 206*
4:7-10, *54, 124*
4:8, *35, 54*
4:9, *52*
4:10, *234*
4:12, *124*
4:13, *124*
4:15, *124*
5:2, *108*
5:25, *8*
5:26, *8*
5:32, *182*

Philippians
1:21-25, *155*
2:6-8, *66*
2:9, *59, 71, 243*
2:9-11, *85*
2:10, *59*
2:10-11, *113*
2:11, *59, 241*
2:12-13, *178*

Colossians
1:17-20, *213*
1:18, *213*
1:19, *213*
1:20, *213*
1:24, *88*
1:27, *104*
2:20, *118*
2:20–3:4, *118*
3, *12, 59*
3:1, *59, 191*
3:1-2, *11, 157*
3:1-3, *97*
3:1-4, *103, 118*
3:3, *11*
3:4, *12, 25, 59*

1 Thessalonians
4, *154*
4:13-18, *208*
4:17, *154*

2 Thessalonians
1, *104*
1:8, *104*
1:9-10, *104, 209*
1:10, *104, 181, 191*

1 Timothy
3, *104*
3:16, *20, 21, 104, 112, 168*

2 Timothy
2:10, *105*

Titus
3:5-6, *183*
3:6, *171*

Hebrews
1, *55, 56, 59, 104, 125, 188*
1–2, *109*
1:1-2, *94*
1:1-3, *6, 80, 105, 223*
1:2, *6, 95, 105*
1:2-3, *94*
1:3, *6, 13, 26, 45, 55, 56, 60, 72, 76, 83, 93, 95, 104, 105, 109, 152, 158, 164, 188, 224, 225, 237*
1:4, *35*
1:5, *55*
1:5–4:13, *222*
1:6, *55*
1:8, *56*
1:12, *223*
1:13, *85, 107*
2, *45, 55, 97, 104, 125, 187, 223*
2:5-9, *223*
2:5-18, *97*
2:9, *82, 187, 223*

2:10, *29, 71, 97, 104, 187,*
  223, 255
2:10-13, *223*
2:11, *187*
2:14, *156, 187*
2:14-15, *8*
2:17, *187*
2:17-18, *26*
3, *97*
3:1, *97*
3:1-6, *80*
3:2, *98*
3:2-6, *98*
3:3, *98*
3:4, *98*
3:5, *98*
3:6, *98, 99*
4, *129*
4:14, *9, 18, 35, 223*
4:14-16, *26, 125, 127*
4:14–10:25, *222, 223*
4:16, *121, 128, 232*
5:10, *7*
6, *113, 114, 236*
6–7, *107*
6:17-18, *113*
6:18, *113*
6:19, *114*
6:19-20, *236, 237*
6:20, *7, 114*
7, *83, 84, 158, 232*
7–10, *80*
7:1-17, *7*
7:11-28, *26*
7:16, *7, 44, 45, 106, 114, 125*
7:16-25, *103*
7:21, *114*
7:22, *114*
7:24, *114*
7:24-25, *2, 8*
7:25, *97, 114, 158*
7:26, *224, 232*
7:27, *90, 232*
7:28, *232*
8:1, *8, 18, 26, 35, 93, 152, 173*
8:1-2, *106, 113*
8:1-3, *8*
8:2, *120, 160*
8:3, *18, 90*
8:5, *224*
8:7-13, *91*

8:10, *186*
9, *164, 165, 166, 231*
9–13, *224*
9:1-26, *110*
9:8, *236*
9:11, *111, 235, 236*
9:11-14, *18*
9:12, *90, 111*
9:14, *8, 45, 90, 91, 111, 120, 142,*
  157, 160, 166, 169, 173, 231
9:21, *167*
9:21-22, *231*
9:23, *231, 236*
9:23-24, *164, 165, 167*
9:24, *26, 45, 224, 231, 236*
9:25, *92*
9:25-26, *92, 231*
9:25-28, *164, 165*
9:26, *18, 26, 45, 91, 92, 111, 165*
9:28, *26, 158*
10, *7, 91, 116, 186, 188*
10:1-2, *91*
10:10, *8, 91, 112, 159*
10:10-14, *18, 45*
10:12, *10, 26, 93, 109, 152, 237*
10:12-13, *83, 186*
10:12-14, *107, 164*
10:13, *7, 85*
10:14, *8, 116, 159, 186*
10:15, *186*
10:15-18, *186*
10:16, *116*
10:17, *116*
10:18, *116*
10:19, *9, 224*
10:19-20, *18*
10:19-22, *10, 188*
10:19-23, *9*
10:19-25, *26*
10:20, *111, 236*
10:21, *18*
10:26, *222*
10:32, *129*
10:32-35, *129*
10:35, *129*
12, *117, 224*
12:1-2, *112*
12:2, *26, 93, 113, 152*
12:10, *117*
12:11, *117*
12:25-29, *224*

1 Peter
1:2, *179*
1:9, *160*
2:5, *123*
2:5-9, *173*
2:9, *124, 172*
3:21-22, *175*
4:11, *99, 195*
4:13, *210, 212*
4:14, *174, 179*
4:17, *210*
4:18, *210*
5:1, *211*
5:10, *212*

2 Peter
1, *179, 180*
1:1, *177*
1:1-9, *176*
1:2-3, *177*
1:3, *176, 177*
1:3-9, *177*
1:4, *177, 190*
1:5-7, *178*
1:5-9, *177*
1:8, *177, 179*
1:11, *180*
1:15, *180*
1:16, *76, 176*
1:17, *60, 76, 176*
1:18, *176*
3:3, *176*
3:4, *176*
3:13, *244*

1 John
1:8-10, *115*
1:9, *11*
3:1-3, *168*
3:2, *12, 30, 104, 184, 209, 248*
3:3, *185*
3:8, *123*
3:24, *185*
4:8, *240*
4:13, *185*

Revelation
1:6, *57, 172*
1:13-14, *57*
2:10, *243*

3:11, *243*
3:21, *188, 208*
4:3, *57*
4:4, *243*
4:9-11, *57*
4:10, *243*
4:11, *243*
5, *208, 245*
5:1-14, *82*
5:6, *106, 245*

5:9, *90*
5:10, *90, 208*
5:11-13, *58*
5:12, *212, 245*
6:2, *242*
11:15, *58*
13:8, *106*
14:14, *57, 243*
19:12, *57, 243*
20:4, *208*

21, *97, 208, 245, 247*
21:2, *13, 244*
21:3, *237*
21:9-11, *244*
21:11, *237*
21:21, *245*
21:22-23, *244*
21:25, *245*
22, *237*
22:3-5, *237*